HIDDEN CHILDREN

FORGOTTEN SURVIVORS OF THE HOLOCAUST

ANDRÉ STEIN

Penguin Books

PENGUIN BOOKS
Published by the Penguin Group
Penguin Books Canada Ltd, 10 Alcorn Avenue, Toronto, Ontario, Canada
M4V 3B2
Penguin Books Ltd, 27 Wrights Lane, London W8 5TZ, England
Penguin Books USA Inc., 375 Hudson Street, New York, New York 10014,
U.S.A.
Penguin Books Australia Ltd, Ringwood, Victoria, Australia
Penguin Books (NZ) Ltd, 182-190 Wairau Road, Auckland 10, New Zealand

Penguin Books Ltd, Registered Offices:
Harmondsworth, Middlesex, England

First published in Viking by Penguin Books Canada Limited, 1993

Published in Penguin Books, 1994

10 9 8 7 6 5 4 3 2 1

Copyright © André Stein, 1993

Used by permission:
The life story of Yaffa Eliach © Yaffa Eliach

All rights reserved

Manufactured in Canada

Canadian Cataloguing in Publication Data
Stein, André
    Hidden children

ISBN 0-14-017051-0

1. Jewish children - Europe - History - 20th century. 2. World War, 1939-
1945 - Jews - Rescue. 3. Righteous Gentiles in the Holocaust - Europe.
I. Title.

D810.C4S84 1994   940.53'18'083   C93-093513-5

To the memory of all those children
who were not touched by the goodness
of a rescuer and who died just because
they were Jewish at a time
when that was the biggest crime of all.

❖❖❖

To honour those who risked their lives
so that the children may live.

❖❖❖

To remember a child who survived the Nazi peril
thanks to the quiet heroism of a Jewish rescuer
but whose life was cut short
by the ravages of cancer —
Agi Stein-Carlton, my sister.

AS
❖❖❖

Acknowledgments

✧✧ From the moment I began working on this project I realized that the book I was about to write was not going to belong to me. At best, I would be one of many people who have worked to return the voices to those who, for one reason or another, remained in hiding long after the overt hostilities against them had stopped. Without the generosity, courage and dedication of each and every one of these people these ten stories of victory against the forces of the night would not have seen the light of day. Thus, I am grateful to all who shared my commitment to honour the silent survival of the hidden children and to pay tribute to their determination to do much more than "just" survive.

My warmest thanks to my agent, Denise Bukowski, who from the moment she read my proposal, embraced it and made sure that it found a publisher willing to risk a heart and not just money on this project.

And she found Cynthia Good, the publisher of Penguin Books Canada, who shared my enthusiasm for these stories from the very beginning. She and her associates made this often arduous journey safe and as painless as the writing of any book can be.

I feel indebted to my editor, Meg Masters who showed sustained support and respect for the hidden children as well as for the chronicler of their tales. Without Meg's expertise and professionalism, this book would be a different book, and its writer would feel like a different writer.

I am touched by the sensitivity and artistry of Tania Craan and Renée Cuthbertson whose work on the book's cover has succeeded in graphically expressing the drama in these ten stories.

I also owe gratitude to all my friends and supporters, near and distant, for their participation in this project. To Elie Wiesel and Harry James Cargas, I am indebted for their assistance in securing financial support for the project. I am grateful to Sarah Moscovitz and Robert Krell for introducing me to Ruth and Maya respectively and for inspiring them to trust their stories to me. Cybèle Stein Robinson, Jeff Johnstone, Deirdre Kwiatek and my wife Vicki Rosner Stein have all participated in the hard task of transcribing the interviews. Their contributions were invaluable.

For Vicki my involvement with this book has been both an enthusiastic and solitary experience. She has always felt the importance of the project in my professional and personal life. Thus, she stood by me even when it meant taking over my share of the tasks and burdens of daily life. It was she who became the bridge between our children and me when they became confused by my frequent "absent presence" in our home. In a very real sense, this book belongs to Vicki, too.

And to my children, too — Cybèle, Tristana, Adrian, Eliana and Sacha. Many times they had to "lend" me to the hidden children when they would have preferred to keep me home participating in their lives in my usual ways. But, in spite of their young years, they understood the importance of this work, and I like to believe that one day it will enrich their lives, too.

Finally, I wish to thank the Canada Council and The Secretary of State for Multiculturalism for their financial assistance.

Introduction

❖❖❖ A number of books have been written about the Holocaust, but very few have looked at the children who survived that terrible time. The reasons for the silence are complicated and painful. For many years after the trauma, child survivors found it almost impossible to speak about their experiences, and when they did, their stories were denied. "What could you know?" they were asked. "What could you possibly remember or understand?" Years of being hidden during the war were followed by more years of hiding after the war, hiding who they were and what they remembered. Since their memories were almost universally discredited by their adult counterparts, who were considered by many to be the "real" survivors, this population of hidden children has never — with few exceptions — spoken out loud to the world, not even to their own families.

Recently, with their children raised, homes purchased and professions well-grounded, and perhaps encouraged by the examples of contemporaries making peace and recovering the wholesomeness and worth of the abused and abandoned children they once were, a group of child survivors of the Holocaust decided to risk looking at their fragmented past.

On Memorial Day 1991, some 1,500 child survivors gathered in New York City. The moment I learned of this event, I felt a strange effervescence. I have attended dozens of conferences on Holocaust-related topics, but this one felt different. I prepared myself with a quiet respect appropriate for a painful commemoration, but I also counted the days: I felt I was about to embark on an extraordinary journey.

I attended the event as a child survivor and as a psychotherapist. The former was searching for some new connections to the past and, therefore, to the future. The latter was there to make better sense of how a child can live hidden.

A unique drama unfolded in dozens of intimate workshops, in plenary sessions addressed by the likes of Elie Wiesel, Nobel Prize laureate and the world's most illustrious survivor, and in impromptu encounters in the corridors, before, during and after sessions.

Two days after my return, I knew that I had indeed just taken a fabulous journey. I left as an orphan, but I returned with a glorious bounty —1,500 brothers and sisters; I left as a man still confused by a dogged darkness, and I returned with light in my heart. Its source: the stories of survival by the weakest of all — children abandoned to the night. I returned with promises from a fistful of new friends. Never again would I have to fear the darkness: the accounts of these people would keep me company.

During my research, I recorded many stories of survival, but for this volume I had to limit my choice to ten testimonies. In each of those I included, I found some special quality illustrating a different aspect of the hiding experience or its aftermath. Some of the people whose stories I tell here were those I had met in New York on that Memorial Day weekend; others emerged thanks to their courage and generosity or were signalled by a friend, a therapist or some other acquaintance. The interviews were both painful and elevating; they linked me to lives that demanded to be chronicled. Most of the ten people who graciously consented to make their accounts public did so out of a need to break the double wall of silence and invisibility. A few felt compelled to tell the world how, thanks to a sliver of goodness in a humanity that had incinerated its own heart, they survived and discovered new ways of being alive.

So once again, it's time to tell stories about a generation that survived in hiding thanks to the ground-level goodness of a small number of people and to the remarkable toughness of children. It is also time to tell our stories because we have a legacy — we are the last survivors. After us, there will be no one to stand and say, "I know what happened. I was there."

And we have to tell our stories for yet another reason. We are not only the unsung but also the forgotten heroes of the Holocaust. The victims have been offered monuments. The rescuers are honoured by the State of Israel. We have only silence. We do not want monuments: they testify to guilt. We want words. Now it is time to tell our stories to the worlds of today and tomorrow. It is time to show those worlds not only that we have survived but also that we are alive.

This book is an attempt to return their voice to the Jewish children — all under the age of sixteen at the time — who during the Holocaust were hidden by Christians and Jews or in forests, and many of whom have stayed hidden, invisible well into their adult years. It is also intended as an opportunity for them to be heard by a world that is finally ready to hear them.

Table of Contents

A Matter of Joy

The Story of
ROBERT KRELL

When Emmy and Eliasz (Leo) Krell of The Hague received their deportation notice, they did not ponder their choices long. If they were to report on August 19, 1942, as ordered in the official document, they would face an uncertain future. Several of their Jewish friends had already been deported, and nothing further had been heard from them. Leo Krell concluded that whatever happened to those who preceded him could not have been promising. Their decision was reached rapidly: the Krells, including their two-year-old son, Robbie, were not going to comply with the deportation order.

They had no time to waste. With Robbie in tow, Emmy Krell visited the Holls, an elderly Christian couple, to ask them to keep her little boy until she found him a more suitable long-term hiding place.

"The boy can stay with us for a couple of days," Mr Holl answered. "We, too, are being resettled to some unknown place in the country. It would appear they have no use for us old-timers in the city."

That same day, Violette Munnik, a friend of the Holls, dropped by for a chat as she did once a year or so.

"Who is this little fellow?" Violette Munnik asked.

"This is Robbie Krell."

"What's he doing here?"

"His parents are looking for a hiding place for him. He's Jewish."

"And for how long does he need to be hidden?"

"A couple of weeks probably."

"Oh, if that's all, Albert and I will keep him."

And so Violette Munnik took Robbie home to her husband, Albert, and their twelve-year-old daughter, Nora.

Leo Krell meanwhile found refuge in the attic of his partners, Mr and Mrs Oversloot; Emmy Krell, armed with false papers, moved. From then on, she lived on her own.

The Krells, unlike most other Jewish families during those extraordinary times, decided that to survive they had to sacrifice the harmony and security of the life they had known on Suez Street. They had to scatter in three different directions.

How did they muster the courage to trust their young child to total strangers? Many other parents found this decision beyond their emotional means. Some hid with their children, others sent them away, and still others vacillated between the two — hiding their children and then reclaiming them periodically. There was no wisdom to guide their decisions. They did what they could. The consequences of these choices still haunt many child survivors, as do the questions: How could parents abandon their children to strangers? How could they hold them rather than sending them away to a safe place? How was a parent to know what to do?

To this day, many people (including professionals) wonder if the parents did the best they could — whether they kept the children with the family, or sent them to hide with others. What most of us have learned is that without any previous stock of knowledge about how to save one's children everyone did the best they thought they could do. We also have learned to treat with suspicion statements by healers and philosophers who, from the safety of their offices in North America, put forth grandiloquent theories about decisions the parents had to forge out of despair.

Robbie was a happy and placid little fellow. His foster parents, the Munniks, showed him a great deal of affection, although they were not given to overt demonstrations. Their primary concern was with his safety. To this end, they had decided not to let him cross the threshold of their small apartment in the centre of The Hague. Trips to a playground, promenades in the streets — for that matter, outings of any kind — were out of the question. Robbie's appearance could have given rise to suspicion. Yet despite the restrictions, Robbie seemed at peace with the world. At his age he was too young to understand his situation.

He must, however, have sensed that he had been abandoned by his parents. Much of the time, without any obvious reason, he looked sad to his foster parents, and from time to time, he posed questions about the past that led them to believe something was simmering in his soul.

Most families hiding Jewish children had a cover story for the child's sudden appearance in the community: he was a young cousin evacuated from Rotterdam after that city's massive bombing; she was a young niece needing shelter because her parents were temporarily unable to take care of her. The Munniks, however, chose to tell their three immediate neighbours the truth.

At first, they told everyone that Robbie was staying only a few weeks while his family searched for a permanent place for him. It's not that the Munniks were reckless; they just hadn't realized the full extent of the risk they were running by not keeping secret the fact that they had offered shelter to a Jewish child. As a matter of fact, they had never even given much thought to Jews one way or another. Robbie was probably the first Jew with whom they had contact. They had no use for or inclination towards hatred and persecution. Their attention was focused on living a simple existence. They worked; they took care of their small home; they communed with the members of their very large family. That was all.

Moeder and Vader, as Robbie called his rescuers, were kind people, and it took very little time for him to learn to love them the way a small child loves his own mother and father. They were, indeed, fatherly and motherly in their solicitousness towards him. They even gave him their name. Thus he became Robbie Munnik. They also did their best to shelter the child from the harsh realities of the war. Moeder and Vader wanted him to have as normal a life as any child at that age. Yet, as much as Robbie loved Moeder and Vader, he never really forgot that they were not his real parents.

"All in all," recalls Dr Robert Krell, today a professor of child psychiatry at the University of British Columbia in Vancouver, "I guess I had a wonderful existence. I can't imagine anyone having a better hiding experience than I did, because the Munniks were wonderful people. And while many others were hidden in closets, barns and dingy cellars, I had a terrific room to call my own."

One day, as Robbie was watching Violette Munnik prepare supper, he asked her what she was peeling.

"These are tulip bulbs," she answered. "They are for us. For you I have potatoes." But the boy knew better. He could tell that what he ate were not potatoes. Yet with the spontaneous generosity of the small child, Robbie colluded with them.

"The potatoes were great," he complimented Moeder.

The Munniks' daughter, Nora, was delighted with her brand-new brother. She felt important when she took care of him, played with him and taught him new things. "Nora was a wonderful teacher," Robert Krell recalls. "If it hadn't been for her, I'd have been a very lonely and ignorant child." She spent hours playing games with Robbie. Among other things, she taught him to read and write. And all this with patience that was exemplary for an adolescent.

Albert Munnik, in his quiet way, also took care of many of the young boy's needs. He spent his days working for the city's Department of Water Works. At night, he would bring home wood and busy himself with making toys for his new "son," who had arrived at his new home without any toys. Robbie's favourite was a wooden dog that moved its legs and wagged its tail, which he has to this day. And when he was finished making toys, Albert would sit Robbie on his lap and read to him. Or he would sit at the piano and play simple melodies he had taught himself. Indeed, he was a man of many talents, and he put all of them to the task of cheering up the little boy who had been forced to live in captivity without the company of friends.

Despite the Munniks' best efforts and the deepest affection, Robbie had a clear sense that there was danger in the air. Because of all the whispering, he concluded quite early in life that something menacing was happening. No one told him that the world outside had declared war on Jews, even on the children. Besides, he did not know what it meant to be Jewish. He sensed rather than knew that he was at risk. Did he do anything to earn the anger of these unknown forces? He was told that he was at the Munniks' because it was no longer safe for him to stay with his parents.

In the beginning, Emmy Krell managed to steal a few moments with her son. Leo also came to visit from time to time. On one occasion, he put his little boy on his lap and he taught him to call him Oom Leo (Uncle Leo). No reason was given for this change, thus increasing Robbie's fears. When children, especially the little ones, don't have tangible facts to account for their experience, they often sense danger.

Robbie's anxiety was further enhanced by his realization that his father was carrying a gun in his left inside jacket pocket. What did he need it for? Was he at risk? Every time he leaned against his father's chest, the boy knew something dangerous was in the air. "Many years later," Robert recalls, "while my father and I were reminiscing, I reminded him of the gun he was carrying in those days. My father denied the validity of my memory. If parents only had more respect for their young children's memories, they could learn a great deal about what the little ones really endured. Indeed, on further reflection, he conceded the correctness of my recollection: he had slipped the gun into the inside pocket of his jacket to make sure it would not get into my hands, as it was his habit to fling his jacket over a chair. Children do not forget unpleasant events or feelings. That gun in my dad's pocket was a source of anxiety for me. Hence, the gun's hard contour could never fade from the memory of my chest wall muscles."

And then, one day, about two months into Robbie's hiding, Uncle Leo stopped coming to visit. Curfews and random raids made it impossible for Leo to negotiate the streets of The Hague. The authorities had made the curfews ever more restrictive: if found outside after six o'clock, a Jew was shot on the spot. In addition, the German and Dutch raiding parties swept the streets with dogged thoroughness. Anyone caught was shipped to the transit camp at Westerbork, in the north-eastern province of Drenthe, and from there to Auschwitz, Mauthausen and, later, as the Eastern Front was moving west, to Bergen Belsen in Germany.

As for Robbie, he silently watched and waited. Unable to join the other children at play in the park across the street and too young to understand the reasons, he just did as he was told. All he knew was that he could not go out into the street because some horrible harm would come to him. "So I stayed in," recalls Robert Krell. "Since I was too young to have been used to an active social life in the world at large, it was more a vague curiosity about what was not available to me than a pining to be one of the people in the street. I was indeed very complacent, playing it very safe on every level."

Like thousands of other hidden children, especially the very young ones, Robbie remained quiet. He didn't have the words to ask the all-important questions, nor the intellectual arsenal to give voice to his secret bewilderment, or, for that matter, the courage to speak out. After all, just as these people had taken him in, they could send him away.

Like most hidden children, Robbie knew with a precocious, unspoken wisdom that his task was to be agreeable and silent. The best and the safest thing he could do was to go along with everything, not give his foster parents any trouble, and obey without questioning. Robbie was indeed compliant and happy to be so. He quickly realized that complaints and demands were out of the question. Who knew what they could lead to? Most children do not worry that they will be put out on the dangerous streets if they harangue their parents. But even with foster parents as wonderful as the Munniks, Robbie could not risk giving them a hard time or expressing preferences that could have rubbed them the wrong way. Indeed, silence was wisest. Thus, like most hidden children, Robbie learned the necessity of taming and befriending silence. As we shall see later, for many, silence turned into a "second wound" keeping them company for most of their lives, if not forever.

Unlike many hidden children, however, Robbie Krell seemed quite comfortable with his quiet solitude. But shortly after his arrival at the Munniks, his complacency was tested. One day, Vader, a resourceful man, proposed that Robbie watch him kill a rabbit he had brought home. By then, meat was a scarce commodity in most of the country.

The young boy was terrified at the very mention of killing an animal. He ran into the other room and hid. Robbie heard the thud of the bicycle pump used to bludgeon the animal. For the well-intentioned Dutchman, all this was a benign joke. Robbie, on the other hand, was repulsed at the thought of witnessing a slaughter. Albert did not insist.

Eventually, Robbie rose above his squeamishness and even took his share of the rabbit stew, plucking the bones clean — hunger prevailed over his natural revulsion — but he continued to feel that it was wrong to kill rabbits. The worst of it, however, for the three-year-old was that he did not feel free to discuss his sadness and his indignation with anyone. Would he have felt freer with his real parents? Probably. But instead he opted for being gracious and complacent — qualities that are scarcely typical for children at that age.

Violette Munnik's friends visited frequently, and to all of them she told the truth about her new young house guest. A quiet conspiracy therefore followed to hide the boy's true identity from outsiders: what is amazing is that he was not betrayed. Robbie and the Munniks were most fortunate that the neighbourhood wove a net of secrecy around them, safeguarding them from the authorities.

Kitty corner across the street from the Munniks lived Mr de Vries, a well-known collaborator — one of some hundred thousand NSB-ers (members of the Dutch National Socialist Organization) who would have been only too happy to report to the authorities any suspicious individual. When in 1961, Robert Krell returned to his native city, he knocked on the door of the Munniks' flat. Mr de Vries opened his door first.

"Robbie?" the old man asked, not sure of his eyes. "Is that you?"

"Yes, Mr de Vries, it's me."

"You know what?" he asked. "You never thanked me for not denouncing you to the authorities. I could have made big trouble for all of you, you know."

"You mean it actually occurred to you to betray me?" Rob asked incredulously, even though he knew betrayals were commonplace during the war.

How does one thank a person for not betraying him? Robert was stunned. Was he supposed to go around the streets of The Hague and shake the hands of all those who, like Mr de Vries, didn't betray him and also cause the death of the Munnik family?

Although Robbie never went outside, everyone passing by the Munniks' place could see the child keeping a silent vigil by the window, a post he remained faithful to throughout nearly three years of hiding.

Nothing new ever happened outside, and yet it was worth watching — it was outside. Elsewhere Hitler waged war against Europe in general and against the Jews in particular. Battles were fought, bombs were dropped and Jews were deported to the killing fields in Germany and Eastern Europe. None of that was visible from the Munniks' window on Leonenschestraat in The Hague.

What the boy witnessed were the insignificant activities of everyday life in an occupied city street. He saw the same German soldiers in the park, horsing around like big boys, bullying one another and generally being rowdy. He had never seen anyone behave like them. He watched them urinate against the wall. In a more distant park, he saw misfired rockets land. Robbie observed the whole spectacle from his window.

In the fall of 1942, however, Violette and Albert noticed that the boy was becoming more and more downcast. They both knew that he suffered from being inside all the time. Although they received a lot of visitors, mostly members of their family, the boy was never allowed to pass beyond the threshold of their apartment. That, they decided, had to be the cause of his melancholy. He watched Nora go to school every day.

After carefully weighing the pros and cons, they decided it should be all right for Violette to take him with her shopping. What danger could they encounter? The next time Mrs Munnik went to get her food ration coupons, she took with her an ecstatic little boy. A few blocks from their house, a total stranger came up to her.

"Isn't this little Robbie Krell?" the woman asked incredulously. "What are you doing with him? I know his mother."

Violette was stunned. This surprise encounter robbed her of her ability to speak. As she frantically scanned her brain for a plausible answer, the stranger, realizing how bewildered she was, came to her rescue.

"Not to worry, I'm a friend of the family. Your secret is buried with me. Here, you are likely to need this." The stranger handed Violette a ration card, flashed a smile at Robbie and disappeared around the corner.

The incident frightened the Munniks. Never again would they allow the boy to go out. He would just have to cope. Violette promised herself to do her best to chase the dark clouds of sadness from her little boy's eyes.

Somehow, with the special intuition of children, Nora sensed that her little "brother" needed some help. Without a word to anyone, she put the boy in a buggy. Although he was close to his third birthday, Robbie was not too big to fit into the deep carriage. She covered him with a blanket and told him to be nice and quiet. Then she set out towards her destination.

Nora had been wheeling the buggy for quite a while when they reached a viaduct, where she was forced to stop because the passage was flooded. One of the German soldiers standing guard came up. Hearing German spoken, the little boy barely allowed himself to breathe, and he pulled the covers over his head. The German soldier then picked up the buggy and carried it over the flooded section.

Forty years later, Robert Krell asked Nora where they had been headed on that adventurous outing. Nora refused to believe that he could remember any of it. "You were not even three years old," she insisted. "You couldn't remember any of it."

"I remember everything, Nora," Robert answered. "You put me in the buggy. You covered me with the blanket. And we went along the streets until that flooded viaduct. I remember the German, and I remember how scared I was, expecting to be discovered by him. Where were we going? Why did you take me out in spite of all the risks, in spite of your parents' decision to keep me in all the time?"

"Well," she answered, "I was twelve years old. You were a little kid, scarcely bigger than a baby. I figured you needed to see your mother. So I wanted to take you to her."

"Did we make it. Nora?"

"No, we turned around and went right back after the German soldier helped us. When we got home, I received the first and only spanking of my life. I never took you out again."

Life continued along an uneventful path for the boy. Except for the great famine during the exceptionally cold winter of 1945, little disturbed his life. By then, more than two and a half years had passed since he had gone into hiding. He had not seen his mother or father for almost that long. For a while his elusive "uncle" would come and put him on his lap and tell him stories. But those memories evaporated into the thin air of youthful oblivion. Little by

little, all his memories of life before his arrival at the Munniks'
receded. As far as he was concerned, Albert and Violette were his
mother and father.

Then one day in May 1945, an extraordinary thing happened.
The adults around Robbie were all laughing and crying. Strangers
embraced and sang together. Perched at his look-out, Robbie saw
the street come alive. A most extraordinary spectacle, indeed. And
no one told him to step back lest someone might see him.

On the contrary, Violette and Albert, in spite of their habitual
reserve, hugged the confused little boy and told him over and over
that from now on he was going to be free.

The Munniks took Robbie on the flat roof of their building
where, together with other residents, they watched as the British
Air Force took possession of the sky. Everyone pointed at large
parcels that floated on parachutes towards the ground. The
British were dropping loads of white bread over Holland. That
finally convinced Robbie that, indeed, liberation had to be a
happy event.

A few days after liberation, a couple showed up at the Munniks'
door. Robbie did not know who they were, although they looked
vaguely familiar.

After a couple of minutes of whispering with the Munniks, the
strangers came over to Robbie. Moeder and Vader stood behind
them without a word. The woman reached out to hug Robbie, and
the man put a trembling hand on his shoulder. The boy recoiled
from them. At age five, he was no longer in the habit of being intimate with total strangers.

"Robbie darling," the woman said in a gentle but shaky voice,
"do you remember us? I am your mother, and this is your father."

The boy didn't believe his ears. What did this woman mean? His
parents were standing right behind the strangers. And how was it
that Moeder and Vader were willing to go along with this nonsense? Why didn't they ask these strangers to leave?

Robbie moved back a few more steps. With his eyes he
implored the Munniks to come to his aid. They both looked pale
and sad.

"You are not my parents!" he shouted at the couple. "Moeder,
Vader, tell them that you are my parents and to leave me alone."

Moeder silently nodded. For the first time, Robbie saw tears in her eyes. Then he noticed that the woman who claimed to be his mother was also weeping silently.

Robbie made a dash for Albert Munnik and threw himself against his vader.

"How can I convince you that you are our little boy?" Emmy asked through her tears. "We had to leave you with the Munniks. Believe me, we had to. And they took very good care of you and you love them and they love you. But now it is time to start living again as a family. Come, my darling. Come to your mother."

The boy held on to Albert's pants even tighter. None of this made any sense to him.

But what else could they have told him? That they were Jews and the Germans came and tried to kill them so they all had to go into hiding? That they gave him away, but now they wanted him back because somehow it all worked out? All that would have just further confused the bewildered child. How could they have explained what had pitted adult against adult, when the realities made no sense even to the parents? What are Jews? What is hiding? Is hiding living with the Munniks for as long as he could remember? Is it staying inside all the time? What's wrong with being inside when you don't know what is outside?

"Don't you remember me, Robbie?" Leo tried his luck. "I used to visit you a couple of years ago. I never said I was your father, though. I pretended to be your uncle Leo, just to make it easier for you. You would sit on my lap and I'd tell you stories."

Now that this man came forward and spoke to Robbie, a whisper of memory returned. Yes, he recalled Uncle Leo. Yes, he did like to sit on his lap and listen to his stories.

"So what if you're my uncle Leo?" Robbie asked defiantly. "That doesn't prove you're my parents. I want to stay with Moeder and Vader. Please let me be. This isn't fair."

The four adults looked at each other. They agreed with the boy; it was not fair to expect him to leave the only parents he knew. They had to take another approach.

The next day the Krells came back with an album full of photos of Robbie with Emmy and Leo in their home on Suez Street. At first the boy only glanced at the pictures. But after he saw a few of them, his heart sank. He recognized himself as a toddler surrounded by these people. There was not one picture of him and the Munniks.

"So what if I used to be your kid?" He continued to struggle for his cause. "You left me and now I'm Robbie Munnik. I'm not going with you. I'm not going with you anywhere."

He was screaming uncontrollably. Violette Munnik wanted to put her arms around her little boy, but she realized that now it was Emmy Krell's turn to mother "their" boy.

A little later, the Krells left the Munniks' apartment with their heavy-hearted son. Leo carried him down the stairs, while Albert gave a hand with his bagful of clothes and toys.

"You come and visit us, my boy, you hear?" Albert said as he waved goodbye. "Our door is always open to you. But for now have a good life with your wonderful parents."

Robbie whimpered all the way to his new home.

Little by little he learned to love the Krells again, who, in turn encouraged him to continue to love the Munniks, too. Although he was allowed to pay frequent visits to his moeder and vader, he missed his daily life with them. That sadness has never left Robbie. To this day, when he thinks of the Munniks, his eyes cloud over.

Liberation changed everything. No more whispers, no more worries about being seen by the wrong eyes, no more fear for one's life. But, together with all its gifts, liberation ushered in an era of upheaval for all survivors. For the little ones, like Robbie Krell, it meant blending two realities, neither of which made much sense. While in hiding, the children were occupied with daily concerns. In a very real way, Robbie was busy with the war, its rules and orders, while most of its disorders were beyond his comprehension. His world was tiny, as if it had been made to fit his years. In 1945, liberation forced him to expand his horizons. Gone was the quiet order of the Munniks' world.

Although he never felt torn between his two sets of parents, thanks to the spiritual generosity and the wisdom of the Krells and the Munniks, liberation for Robbie Krell-Munnik was far from liberating. It was only then that he began to learn how much he had lost during those years of quiet hiding. Like all hidden children, Robbie had been evicted from the natural flow of his childhood. He had lost the spontaneous joy of a free and unburdened child. The war against Jewish children had also robbed him of the simple security of having just one set of parents, the freedom to move about and to be at peace in a world that respected his right to be Jewish.

"You are the luckiest boy on earth," Leo Krell said one day. "Most kids lost at least one of their parents during the war. You gained an extra set."

Leo Krell was, of course, right. And Robbie never ceased to agree with him. But the years to come would prove to him that no one survived the Holocaust without bearing its curses.

After he moved back to his parents' home, the quiet order and predictability of Robbie's days gave way to an existence that changed from moment to moment. Indeed, as the gates of hell opened, the dishevelled survivors began to filter back to wherever they thought there would be a recognizable world waiting for them. Before the war, the Krells had been active in Zionist youth organizations. They had made it known to all that they would not comply with deportation orders. It was not surprising, therefore, that their apartment became the central meeting place for returning survivors. Soon, at all hours, their living-room was full of skeletal beings searching for relatives.

Thus, Robbie was thrust into yet another alien world. For the second time in his young life, he found himself living in the company of strangers. In addition, he found himself confronting what really had happened in the world while he was carefully protected and nurtured by Moeder and Vader.

The survivors told their ghoulish stories incessantly. And Robbie heard most of them. It would soon have turned into a nightmare for the boy if fate hadn't provided him with a world of his own. Among the survivors was his second cousin Millie, who had escaped to Switzerland and was three years older. In no time, the two of them were like brother and sister. A little later, they were joined by Robbie's first cousin, Nallie. He came over to the Krells' every fortnight. It was the tight bond that developed between the three children that allowed them to resist the whirlwind of the adults around them.

Together they listened to the survivors' stories, told primarily in Yiddish and German. Millie, who understood both languages, would translate conscientiously. Soon Robbie had learned enough Yiddish to understand them, but he made an effort not to acknowledge that he knew the language. Perhaps if he paid no attention, he could pretend that what he heard was not true.

Little by little, however, Robbie learned to accept the fact that no more members of their once populous family would return. Gone were his grandparents, his father's two sisters, his mother's two brothers and sister. His parents were orphaned, as was his cousin, Nallie. The more he heard about those who did not return, the more he became aware of the dimensions of the losses. A friend of his father would return to find that his whole family had perished. Another would respond to his family's demise by surrendering his sanity. There was grief all around. In spite of the levity the three cousins engendered, the world of Auschwitz expanded its grief and anguish right into their souls.

This duality was to accompany Robert Krell on his life's journey. With the natural penchant of young children to soak up all surrounding feelings, he developed not only a taste for fun and joy that linked him to the world around him, but also one for sadness, mourning and introspection within which he erected his own world of silence. Although many children whose childhood has been marked by similar journeys through the tragic world of adults abandon their natural lust for laughter, Robert retained his ability and thirst for happiness. Unbeknownst to him, however, he had also remained captive of the other, darker side of his childhood memories.

The fact that he has fuelled his life's journey with the urge to become whole again rather than allowing the pain of his losses to fragment his existence is largely the fruit of the love and nurturing lavished upon him by not one but two sets of devoted parents. Beyond saving his life, they had the moral and spiritual wisdom to put the child's needs and rights ahead of their own. The Krells, for their part, deprived themselves of the pleasure of having their boy next to them. The Munniks showed respect for the boy's heritage and never tried to make him a Christian. And when it was time for them to let him go, they wished him a good life with his birth parents, even though their hearts were breaking.

The Krells and the Munniks made sure that they would complement each other rather than compete for their "son's" affection. Through this commitment to Robbie's welfare, they minimized the harm done by the ravages of war and separation. To this day, Robert Krell feels equally loved by and loving towards the Krells and the Munniks.

And he is not alone in his double loyalty and devotion. Although many children abandoned to the care of strangers end up estranged

from their birth parents and their foster parents, others have
embraced all the people who nurtured them. Robbie Krell was one
of them. He and others like him emerged from childhood with
versions of love upon which they could build their own families.

By the time Robbie was seven, life in his parents' home began
to feel familiar, yet it was studded with paradoxes. For one thing,
the Krells put him in a Catholic school. They did so not to shelter
him from some malefic power but because it happened to be the
only school in their neighbourhood. And Robbie felt happy there.
He was the only dark, curly-haired boy in the school, yet he felt
right at home. And he was soon drawn to the lives of the saints,
the holy words of the Apostles and the peaceful and yet stirring
music. In short, he learned well, and he fit in perfectly. Soon he
became the nuns' favourite.

Not long after that Robbie's uncle Isaac took him to the little
shul (congregation) he had revived in Scheveningen, a resort area
near The Hague. Uncle Isaac, Millie's father, introduced the boy
to everyone and they all shook his hand.

"This is my nephew, Robbie Krell," he said. "Tell them, Robbie.
What are you?"

"I'm a Catholic," Robbie complied quietly.

They all laughed. Robbie went along with the levity, although
he thought that they were making fun of him. He felt out of place.
This was far from the world he shared with the nuns. Feeling confused about who he was and what he was doing there, he remained
silent.

Every hand I shook there, he thought later, was the hand of a
survivor. But what am I? Am I a survivor, too? The answer was not
within his seven-year-old means.

Children caught in Robbie's predicament had to walk a fine line.
Everything was happening too fast. From the time he was five and
a half he lived in the world of skeletal survivors lamenting their
ordeal and their subsequent awareness of everything they had lost.
And when he was away from Jewish suffering, he was submerged
in Catholicism. Could both these worlds be real? What was his
place in them? How was he to accommodate each one of them
without being disloyal to the other? If he betrayed one of these
worlds, he knew he would offend people he cared for and who
cared for him. Faced with this dilemma, Robbie had few options.

Without actually being aware of deciding to do so, he chose to adapt to everyone. Was there a price for this denial of his personal preference? What were the consequences of being the eternal "good boy"?

"I didn't know it then," explains Robert Krell, "but I have no doubt now that to a great extent my sense of well-being in the Catholic school was a natural continuation of my feeling of security while living with the Munniks. In other words, I felt more comfortable continuing the hiding — hiding from questions to which I couldn't afford to know the answer, hiding from a world permeated with losses."

Life began to be clearer and more congruent a year later, when Robbie entered public school. By then he was sufficiently grounded in the world of his parents to know that he was a Jew. In fact, he requested to learn Hebrew. But his best efforts were not crowned with success: Mr Krakauer, his Hebrew teacher and a survivor, was too preoccupied with contemplating his losses to facilitate the boy's learning. Instead of learning Hebrew during his sessions with Mr Krakauer, Robbie learned the necessity and the impossibility of being Jewish. Planet Auschwitz, rather than receding, began to loom larger for the boy. He no longer just tolerated the survivors' laments, he embarked on a quest to unearth the secrets of the Nazi killing fields. "You can't really know it as a kid," Robert reflects, "but trying to come to grips with my Judaism at a time when all around me was death was a piece of insanity. In fact, I refused to try to speak Yiddish thinking that it was German and I had a learning block for Hebrew."

Robbie had greater success at school. Thanks to the devotion of Nora and Albert Munnik, and to his thirst for knowledge, he became an avid reader by the time he was in Grade 1. Soon Robbie didn't just read books, he devoured them. Confused by the harrowing facts of his life, he attempted to find in books the knowledge that would give him mastery over the chaos that had reigned around him.

Like so many other Dutch people, the Krells began to contemplate leaving the Old World behind them. The city was saturated with bad memories, countless losses and bitter accounts that could never be settled. Besides, the country had suffered too much destruction to recover soon enough for the survivors who were eager to put their lives back on track. The New World loomed mysteriously and full of promise.

Shortly after the birth of Israel in 1948, Leo and Emmy visited the new Jewish state. They returned, resolved to look elsewhere for a new home. It was clear that bloodshed was on Israel's horizon and they were not ready to live through more wars.

In spite of his sorrow at the thought of leaving the Munniks behind, Robbie was eager to get out of the Netherlands. With the visceral urgency of a ten-year-old, he wanted to start afresh. He knew that a new life was possible only somewhere else.

On February 24, 1951, the Krells boarded the freighter *De Diemerdijk*. After a five-week journey, they arrived in Vancouver, where Emmy had an uncle. After a month-long house hunt, Robbie moved into his first home in the New World.

Life was hard for a few years for these new Canadians. Leo's work in the fur business allowed him barely to sustain his family. Eventually, he took out a real estate licence and began selling houses. The career shift paid off. After many years, the Krells ended up enjoying financial security and comfort.

Vancouver opened up slowly for Robbie. At first, he spent a lot of time at the movies, walking around in the streets and getting acquainted with the city and its language. When he began school, his fledgling English kept him back a year.

A month later, Robbie met Connie Michas, a Greek boy who lived across the street. Connie took Robbie under his wing and introduced him to the neighbourhood and to other kids his age who were happy to make him one of their own.

For Robbie, life began to feel comfortable. By the end of the summer, he spoke English like a native. When classes began in the fall, his teacher quickly realized that a mistake had been made, and after six weeks, Robbie was helping mark math assignments. The school administrators were not so quick to acknowledge their mistake, but Robbie Krell had been toughened by his early experiences. He studied extra hard and earned back his year. Thanks to his general popularity, already in Grade 8, Robbie was elected president of his class.

The past gradually released its hold on Robbie. If it hadn't been for the letters to Moeder and Vader, and to his cousins Millie and Nallie, Robbie would not have given a second thought to his native land.

As for Judaism, it, too, receded. Robbie was bar mitzvahed at the traditional age of thirteen, but by then he had let go of most religious activities. Then in his late adolescence he discovered Zionism. He joined a youth group. Once again, he found wonderful friends within the organization he joined. But above all, it was Israel that attracted him. From his Zionist connections emerged a fundamentally tolerant attitude towards any version of Judaism. "I don't care what you do specifically," he says, "as long as you do something that links you to Judaism. I want Jews to be Jewish. There are many ways of being Jewish. There is something for everyone."

His awareness of loss has kept Robert Krell linked to his childhood and made him sensitive to the losses of others, especially children. Whether as a senior child psychiatrist, or as the vice-president of the Canadian Jewish Congress, he is never far from attending to human suffering. Some child survivors go through life with their intolerable memories safely tucked away in a protective unconscious. Others, like Robert, remember everything. For them, every event is a link to an inescapable past.

A daily diet of unsavoury memories can be troublesome fare. And Robert knows that. He is never far from a tear as he contemplates all that was lost. He is never far from his own pain when he reaches out to other child survivors and their families. Drawing on personal experience as well as on the countless testimonies he has heard from others, he refuses to look at the survivor's troubles with life and its shadows as examples of pathology. Instead, he prefers to help himself and others by leaving the therapeutic milieu and joining the world of Holocaust education. He has audiovisually taped over one hundred survivor accounts, knowing that it was healing to bear witness. As an antidote to their pain, survivors often become teachers of children.

"Some people wonder," says Robert Krell, "if being so intimately linked to the world of the Holocaust is not an impoverishing experience, if it doesn't rob me of my peace of mind. And my answer is to the contrary. When I attend a Holocaust education symposium, I learn as much or more than when I go to psychiatric conferences. I formulate new themes, form clinical impressions, get fresh ideas. Then I make them work in psychiatry. No, it's definitely not an impoverishing experience for me to be involved with Holocaust-related learning. It's enriching. It is most enriching to be in contact with Elie Wiesel, Yaffa Eliach and Martin Gilbert and to write to one another as friends and acquaintances. Mine is a circle of privilege. My work brings me together with the most generous people imaginable.

"I hear the sceptics ask, 'What is there to teach? Hasn't everything been said already?' What is there to teach? You never know. Tell a story and something will come up and you learn from it. That's why I started the Vancouver Holocaust Society for Remembrance and Education. We remember, we erect monuments and we tell stories. What can be more healing? How better to combat racism? We have problems in Vancouver that go far beyond Jews. I want an education centre where the Holocaust is the example of the extremes of what can happen. And I want it to serve any people to whom it could potentially happen."

This commitment to the welfare of all animates the life and activities of many hidden children. Their lives have been touched by instances of human goodness. They feel inspired by it. Indeed, a very large number of hidden children work in the "other-centred" professions — education, health care, counselling, community service. Although there is no statistical evidence available for North America, a French study sets the number of child survivors in "prosocial" occupations at three times as high as the non-Jewish French population in similar professions and twice as high as for the rest of the Jewish population of France. It would seem, then, that children who experience the gifts of altruism are prone to use their experiences as inspiration in their adult lives — a thought that deserves the attention of all those who live and work with children.

"I credit, in part, my Dutch moeder with helping me make it into medical school," Robert says. "Violette Munnik inspired me and built up my confidence by insisting on the virtues of service to those in need. I owe her more than just my life. Without her guidance, I would have been a different person. She insisted that as a child who was spared, I should help other children."

"So I spend a lot of time shuttling between education and therapy. There is no better healing for a survivor than education. That, of course, includes me, too. It is wonderful work, time-consuming work. My wife, Marilyn, worries for me at times, because there are too many demands. But, as I explain to her, nothing comes easy. So I shoulder these demands as they come. And by the force of experience they become easy. And because she and my children are so solid and loving.

"Besides, I feel comfortable with my survivors. Lots of people don't like survivors. I love them. I understand them. I can work with them as patients or as colleagues in education. When I went to the 1981 World Gathering for Holocaust Survivors in Jerusalem, my friends asked me if that was not too depressing. They cannot understand (and I don't blame them) that to be with survivors is a celebration. Just because we cry real tears for real losses does not mean we have become depressed.

"I don't find tears depressing. They are appropriate. I am a great crier and I am a great laugher, too. I love the stronger emotions of life although I am capable of hiding it all. Indeed, that is what I do best. To this day, there are moments when I still struggle with my urge to hide."

2

The Woman Who
Could Not Trust

The Story of
ANIKO BERGER

With the obliviousness of a five-year-old, Aniko had not noticed that her parents, Ella and Làszlò Berger, violinists with the Budapest Opera Orchestra, had been spending more time at home than before. In the spring of 1944, Aniko still enjoyed every moment spent at home, in the local park or on the island of St Margaret near her home. She was unaware of the increasing menace to Hungarian Jews that had permeated every aspect of their lives since the Wehrmacht took possession of the city on March 19. The young musicians had long been banned from their seats in the orchestra pit. Now the steady flow of new laws tightened the circle around their daily movements, as did the rumours of deportation to camps in Poland. Although they came to accept their fate, night after night the Bergers plotted to rescue their young child. But each plan was more impractical than the last, and they knew it.

Then, one evening in the middle of July, their housekeeper, Hilda Bognàr, approached them with a solution. She would take

Aniko to her parents' farm near the ancient town of Tihany, about eighty kilometres west of the capital. The child could stay there for as long as was necessary.

None of the Bergers' wild ideas had ever included letting the child go, alone, to strangers. They both shook their heads resolutely.

"What alternatives do you have?" insisted Hilda, more a family member than a domestic. Registered as a lodger with the Bergers (a law prohibited Jews from employing Christian domestics), she too had heard the rumours about the camps in Poland. It was easier to find food on a farm than in the city. Besides, having lost several children, her parents would welcome the presence of a young girl.

It was largely her persistence that moved the bewildered parents along the path towards a rational decision: this plan had the best chance of keeping Aniko out of harm's way. When they told Hilda they wanted to visit her parents just to make sure, they were stunned to hear her categorically reject the idea. The child was to arrive discreetly, in her company, and the Bergers were never to get in touch. They need not worry about their child's fate. Her parents were simple peasants, but they would provide Aniko with food and shelter. Hilda would execute the plan without delay.

Other Jewish parents across Europe shared Ella and Làszlò's bewilderment. How could they abandon their young child to strangers? How could they risk untold harm to the child at the hands of people with possible hidden purposes? How could they sever the basic bond and explain to their dumbfounded children that they were not betraying them, that, on the contrary, they were leaving them behind to save their lives? Many parents opted for what seemed the lesser evil and kept their children with them. Others, like the Krells and the Bergers, discovered that their emotional boundaries were more elastic than they would ever have thought.

Prior to the war, none of them would have consented to leaving their offspring in the hands of strangers. And yet with the arrival of the Nazi terror, they did just that. A lot has been said about the altruism of the rescuers who sheltered the endangered Jewish children. We sometimes forget that the parents, by defying the instinct to shelter their own little ones and not surrender them to an unknown fate, put the welfare of others ahead of their own happiness. But it is important that, while we pay tribute to these parents, we do not cast a stone at those who had defined their reality in such a way that separating from their children fell beyond the frontiers of that reality. To them, other solutions were superior to separation and the risk of trusting a stranger with the life of their child.

No matter what their decision, all parents tormented themselves with self-doubt: what if they made the wrong choice? This cruel taskmaster was to keep them company throughout their ordeal. With that pain hovering in their eyes and on their lips, how were they to inspire confidence in their young children about the wisdom and safety of the journey that awaited the young ones? They certainly could not afford to communicate to them their own doubts about the possibly dark adventure awaiting. The process was a heart-wrenching one.

For days the Bergers did not speak about their impending separation from their five-year-old. But finally they had to prepare their child for the journey. When the Bergers finally told Aniko of their decision, she was outraged and indignant. She had never gone farther than the island without her parents; now she was to live without them, with strangers in a strange place.

Yet in spite of her desperate protests and endless bargains, Aniko ultimately resigned herself to the inevitable. Her friend Hilda was going to accompany her; that made the prospect less threatening. Aniko asked an endless stream of questions: Will I have my own room? Who will help me with my ABCs? Who will come to me if I hear scary sounds in the night? How often will you come to visit me? She sensed more than understood that this trip was more than a vacation. She had to co-operate. But how could her parents wish to live far away from her? With the bitterness of betrayal and fear, Aniko accepted her responsibility to obey. In short, with the legendary resilience of children, once Aniko accepted the inevitability of the separation; she attended to taming the monster. Just as terminally ill children, once they get tangible answers to all their questions, can visualize what is waiting for them rather than being bogged down by dark fantasies, so Aniko, by asking questions about the everyday life waiting for her, began to shape her new world. By doing so, she embarked on the process of mastering her future before she even left home.

The Bergers pretended to go about their lives normally. But the laughter grew quieter, the music a little more mournful and the games a little less exuberant. Inwardly, the three of them were grieving for a way of life that was about to come to an end, perhaps forever.

Then, suddenly, the dreaded day was upon them. "Everything's ready," Hilda informed them quietly. "My parents are expecting us."

While Aniko behaved like a "fine young lady" (as her father had called her since her fifth birthday), inside there shivered a terrified little girl who thought only of how her parents were about to abandon her. Had she done something wrong to deserve this? Wasn't she always an obedient and loving daughter? Their reassurances simply isolated her further because they sounded like lies. She "knew" they were never going to come for her.

Hilda prepared a sumptuous meal, including all the child's favourites. But to no one's surprise, the delicacies went largely untouched.

"I just won't go." Aniko's proclamation shattered the glum atmosphere of the farewell supper.

Làszlò looked at her with a silent smile and slowly caressed his daughter's black mane. His touch was a light as air, as if he feared hurting her. Ella just sat there.

Suddenly, the doorbell lacerated the silence. Ella and Làszlò stole a glance at each other. They knew that this could not be a friendly visit. They heard crisp male voices intermingled with Hilda's assertive words.

"Mr Berger, two gentlemen insist on speaking to you and Mrs Berger at once. I told them that you'd join them in the vestibule. I'll stay with Ani."

Husband and wife walked mechanically towards the door. Mentally, they had practised this scene a thousand times.

"I'm going, too," Aniko announced with the resolute voice of an adult.

Her parents didn't object. Perhaps they didn't even hear her.

In the small vestibule were two men wearing black suits and black hats.

"We'll be back in half an hour, at most, darling," Aniko's father told her woodenly. "On the way back, we'll bring you a treat."

With that he and Ella disappeared down the staircase. Neither cast a last glance at their dumbfounded five-year-old.

Aniko sensed it would be wrong to make a fuss. She held Hilda's hand, squeezing it with all her strength, as if to fuse her whole being to the maid's body. Holding that hand allowed her to remain at least outwardly calm, like a "young lady."

"My mommy didn't say a word, not one word," Aniko said. "She didn't even turn around to say goodbye. I hate her."

What the young child could not know at the time, of course, was that if Ella had turned around, her resolve would have drowned in the teary sadness of Aniko's eyes; perhaps she would not have been able to part with her.

A life of hiding began for Aniko. Her hosts were not only strangers to her, they also seemed strange. Uncle Miklòs, a vintner, was always grumpy; Aunt Irén, his wife, was not much more cheerful. She was always busy. She never opened her lips for a song or for a word, unless she needed something. No one ever smiled, not even their sons, fifteen-year-old Pista and fourteen-year-old Imre. Most of the time, they didn't seem to notice their distraught young guest's presence. After being the centre of attention in her own family, the journey to this taciturn abode was a shock.

After two days, Hilda returned to the city. Before she left, she took Aniko by the hand and led her to the room where everyone except the parents had a bed, one in each corner. The stark white room was decorated only with a small black crucifix.

"Now, Ani, you'll be a smart little girl. My folks are good people. They don't say a lot of fancy words, but that doesn't mean they don't care for you. After all, one wrong word and you can bring harm upon their heads."

"What harm can I do?" The child was confused. "I'm just a little girl."

At that moment, Hilda realized that the child didn't know anything about being Jewish. Not all that clear herself about why the Jews had become the enemy, she explained to the child that these were crazy times and the only thing to do was to hide. Aniko was bewildered. Wasn't she Hungarian like Hilda? She had heard the word *Jewish* before without knowing what it meant. It sounded dangerous to be Jewish. She now understood: her parents had been led away for being Jewish.

Since she had no idea what it meant to be Jewish, she didn't know what it was about being Jewish that had to be hidden. Like so many other Jews, the Bergers had been assimilated into the mainstream of Hungarian life. Jewishness was not a topic Aniko had heard discussed.

It must be very bad to be Jewish, she decided. I want all of us to become Christian. It's like a big punishment to be Jewish. I hate my parents for making me Jewish.

Aniko spent much of the first two weeks at the Bognàrs' alone. Her solitude forced her to think a lot more than is usual for a five-year-old. She daydreamed about how sweet life used to be. Invariably she would burst into tears, burying her face in her pillow to make sure no one heard her sobs. It seemed that every time they noticed her, it was to make her cry. The boys kept touching her face to check "how soft Jewish skin was," or they reached under her dress to check "how silky Jewish panties were." Aniko made up her mind never to let them see her cry. She was going to show them that being Jewish meant being proud and brave. Her resolution comforted her.

Every day for those two weeks, Uncle Miklòs showed her the ropes of her new life. He drilled into her that they were hiding her *because* she was Jewish. And that it was because she was Jewish that she had to become Annamária Bognàr, his niece. And it was because she was Jewish that she had to evict her family from her memories, lest someone ask her who her father or mother were, where they lived and why she was living with the Bognàrs. She was to stay out of sight. "If people don't see you," said Uncle Miklòs, "they won't ask stupid questions. If they ask stupid questions, I can't give them smart answers because there's nothing smart about hiding a Jew."

And it was because she was Jewish that she had to learn to behave like a perfect Catholic, to cross herself, to pray and even to confess.

"Confess everything," Uncle Miklòs ordered her on her first Sunday on the way to church, and from then on every Sunday, "except that you're Jewish."

No one paid much attention to the little girl during the day. They all went about their chores. Ani was given her breakfast — warm milk in a big enamel mug with black chips that made her think the mug was dirty and a hunk of dark, peasant bread. Lunch was a bowl of greasy soup, most of the time bean or lentil with bones in it. Dinner was again some milk and bread and perhaps a big yellow apple.

Between meals she just wandered around the dirt yard in front of the house, watching the animals. Having never seen animals outside the zoo, she was curious about them, but she kept her distance. They're like me, she thought. They just roam from feeding to feeding, and then they're locked up for the night. No one cares for them any more than they do for me. They're lucky, though; they don't have to be Jewish.

Many a hidden child sheltered by reserved, preoccupied or just uncaring rescuers came to Aniko's conclusion: their life was of little value since it was no longer rewarded with attention and affection. For hidden children, coming from assimilated families where Judaism was at best a rare visitor, being Jewish meant only that it alone was responsible for their predicament. Once they reached that conclusion, the shame of being Jewish began to grow like an indomitable weed.

Shame is a cruel taskmaster; when it becomes a sustained, toxic presence, it may even crush the child's soul. To mask the psychic blight it leaves behind, without realizing it the child hides behind a false self. For those hidden children who, like Aniko, were old enough to recall happier days and who were physically or emotionally abandoned and betrayed by their rescuers, shame became a relentless companion.

"Why would I have to hide if my very being was not unsightly, ugly?" Aniko Berger remembers asking herself time and again. "I didn't understand the reasons that it was an embarrassment to be Jewish, but I had no doubt that something about me was repulsive only because I was Jewish. Since I didn't know what it was, it was best to hide my whole being. But it was bigger than what I could comprehend at my age. If at least they had said that I did this or that, I could have felt guilty. But it wasn't something I did: it was my way of being. How do you live with something like that? How do you go beyond it at age eight, or even later? Well, I didn't. I just went deeper into hiding. Darkness became my best friend."

Years before, Aniko had learned to trust her parents. They were predictable; they spent a lot of time with her; they nurtured her in ways that had become familiar to her; they touched her with tenderness. Together, they had formed an emotional bond. And this bond gave her the strength and courage to confront the separation from her parents. It was with the knowledge that such a bond can be developed with adults that she approached the Bognàrs. Robbie Krell had approached the Munniks with a similar expectation, but he was lucky and found people with whom he could duplicate the bonding process. A continuity was achieved. Aniko did not have the opportunity to create such a continuous link with the Bognàrs. They did not afford her either time or attention; above all, they did not set clear boundaries for their ward within which she would have felt safe. Without such boundaries, Aniko felt exposed and disoriented. And since it seemed to her that the Bognàrs were wicked, and since she had no clear boundaries to delineate where they ended and she began, Aniko concluded that she, too, was wicked.

"On the one hand," she explains, "I felt ashamed of being Jewish — that is, different from them. On the other hand, every time I looked at them, I felt ashamed for feeling that I was just like them — bad. Shame got me coming and going. All my life I have been struggling against this dual oppression of my self. That false self behind which I learned to hide, if I wanted to survive, kept sticking to me with remarkable stubbornness."

Not all hidden children are as eloquent and as insightful as Aniko Berger, but many of them attest to the grip of shame. Fearing exposure, many endeavoured to create private worlds away from the public eye, rather than joining existing communities. Hence, relationships have caused problems for many of them. Having been truly abandoned on several levels, many hidden children, among them Aniko, never again found a being who would mirror for them their true selves. Without this opportunity to mirror one's inner being, relationships are very tenuous, even impossible to develop and sustain. Ultimately, that version of solitude leads to an inner alienation and isolation — a psychic prison in which one's self becomes an alien.

"There have been times in my life," Aniko Berger recalls, "when I couldn't stop wondering who I really was. Was I the unsightly Jewish kid who had to be hidden from the public eye, or was I someone who could have been a valuable and beautiful person if

I hadn't been Jewish? It took me many years to conclude that perhaps I never really allowed myself to reflect my real persona when I looked into the mirror because the only mirror in which I had learned to see myself was held to me by the Bognàrs."

At first, hiding from unwelcome eyes left Aniko continually uneasy. She was always scared of doing the wrong thing. But with time, she became an expert in matters of truth and falsehood. She learned to distinguish between the wrong truth and the right lie. At times, when that proved to be too much for her, Aniko relied on her other well-honed skill: hiding.

Once when Borbála, the local notary's maid, called on Aunt Irén, Aniko had to hide in a cupboard between the kitchen and the bedroom. She was told not to come out until someone opened the door for her. "Not a peep out of you, no matter what. If you're discovered, you know what'll happen."

Borbála stayed in the kitchen gabbing endlessly, as if she planned to stay forever. To make the time pass faster, Aniko counted as high as she could. Then she counted down to zero. Then she made a mental picture of her room. Then another picture of all the things she had ever eaten. She was running out of tricks when suddenly she heard the noise of scurrying feet — a mouse or a rat!

Aniko was terror-struck. "Not a peep out of me!" But something had to give. Tears bathed her face as she realized that urine was trickling down her legs. But by then vigilance had been drilled into every cell of her body. "The difference between life and death is alertness," Uncle Miklòs had said.

The youngster didn't know how long she was in the cupboard with the rodent circling her feet. She felt she had disappeared into a bottomless darkness. All she thought of was the shame of being discovered. Finally the cupboard door opened, but Aniko refused to budge. They quickly lost patience with her "bratty tantrum." Uncle Miklòs was about to drag her out when the rodent made a dash towards the light.

"A mouse, for goodness' sake, a tiny little mouse!" Uncle Miklòs let out a boisterous belly laugh. They all thought it was hilarious.

Finally, Aunt Irén took pity on Aniko. She reached into the cupboard and gently pulled out the humiliated child.

"You've peed all over yourself," she exclaimed. "A big girl like you!"

"I was scared of the mouse," Aniko whispered. "I'm sorry."

Her announcement occasioned another bout of laughter in the kitchen.

The Bognàrs were not alone in their harsh and, at times, inhumane treatment of the Jewish child under their roof. Until recently, only those rescued Jews who had been privileged and lucky to find a benevolent and caring home came forth with their rescue stories. This led to the idealization of all Christian rescuers of Jews. In the last couple of years, however, hidden children have told stories of abandonment, cruelty, selfishness and even abuse. Many are still unresolved about their experience. Some still carry the burden of anger towards the people who hid them. Others, while acknowledging the harm this second wound created in their already shaken existence, are willing to articulate a modicum of gratitude towards their unkind rescuers who, after all, did save their lives.

There was little Aniko could be grateful to the Bognàrs for. To Uncle Miklòs, she was only a step above the barnyard animals. His crude anti-Semitism, common to many Hungarian peasants, made things worse. Aunt Irén was also ungenerous towards Aniko. Although she was happy to have a little girl in her house, she never embraced Aniko emotionally. It is hard not to suspect that she resented the very existence of this worthless Jewish child after she had buried her own daughters. Aniko had no alternative but to distance herself from these people, who were only one step away from her enemies.

Ani soon learned to think of her hosts as her tormentors. She knew that a sneeze or scream could cost her her life. She felt overwhelmed. "How much longer?" she asked the darkness that night. She swore that she would never sneeze or cough again. Like most hidden children, Aniko Berger realized that one way or another she had to rise above human susceptibility to illness — it would just attract unwelcome attention, attention her world preferred not to afford to her. The same held true for sadness and fear — tears were the privilege of the free. During their hiding, these children learned that, to a great extent, whatever misfortune fell upon them was of their own doing. It paved the road to lives of excessive self-reliance and to an unwillingness to show their feelings. Since, as did Robert Krell, many hidden children embarked on "other-centred" professions, one wonders if one of their motivations was not to extend help to others, thereby deflecting the attention from themselves — their own needs and their own pain.

Some weeks after her arrival in Tihany, Uncle Miklòs put Aniko to the test. He quizzed her on her "past" and on all the prayers a five-year-old would be expected to know. He was so pleased with her answers that he gave her permission to leave the property. She could go with Aunt Irén to the market and to church. And he would take her to the forest to pick berries and mushrooms.

But first Uncle Miklòs cut her black hair to just below the nape of her neck. Then Aunt Irén bleached what was left with peroxide. The terrified girl could not fathom why.

"Because you look too Jewish with that thick black hair," Aunt Irén said.

"But my mommy has short blond hair, and she is Jewish," Aniko replied. "If you really don't like Jews, why do you keep me here?"

"Because you're a runt," Uncle Miklòs answered. "Besides, it was Hilda's idea. No one should harm kids."

Then Aunt Irén gave her some worn but decent-looking clothes. They had belonged to one of her children who had died.

"You're a Jewish runt," Uncle Miklòs said with a hint of sadness in his voice, "but not for long. We'll make a Bognàr out of you yet." And he interrogated her one more time on her name, where she came from and why and if her parents had any Jewish friends. "No, sir, a friend of the Jew is the enemy of the God of the Magyars!"

That night Aniko was no longer sure if she had ever been anyone other than Annamária Bognàr. And yet she felt as if she should apologize to all Jews for betraying them. In bed, she said a Hail Mary for every Jew and, in particular, for her family.

Such paradoxical emotional gambits often confused and afflicted hidden children. They were in the grip of conflicting truths that coerced them into a trance-like silence, which in turn reinforced their sense of abandonment and alienation. Their lives were not based on a network of collaborative efforts. Instead they experienced everyday existence as a solitary struggle against enemies who sometimes were manageable but at other times loomed larger than life. Such silence was Aniko's daily companion on the Bognàr farm.

The trips beyond the Bognàr property were fraught with terror. How can one hide in public? she wondered (yet another paradox challenging hidden children).

"What if I slip? What if someone tricks me into saying the wrong truth?" she asked.

"One word out of place, one shifty glance, one wrong gesture, and you're done for," Uncle Miklòs kept reminding her.

One Sunday, about two months after her arrival, as they filed out of church, Aniko noticed a girl making faces at her. The girl then bumped into her on purpose. Ani sensed that the bully was bent on getting her into trouble. The girl whispered names at her: "Ninny, stupid, retard." Aniko remained calm, so the girl escalated her assault.

"No, you're not a ninny. You're a Jewish ninny, a stinking Yid," she said.

Aniko felt her knees were about to cave in. "That's not true," she pleaded as bravely as she could. "I'm not a stinking Jew, I'm not."

That weekend, Hilda came home for a visit. The girl clung to her like a lizard to a rock. She had been starving for kind words and a tender embrace. "Finally someone from my world, someone who knew me as Aniko."

Hilda had disheartening news about the Bergers. The police had interrogated them about some absurd Jewish conspiracy. Then, when they were about to transfer them into the hands of German authorities, the young couple, aided by a mysterious party, made a run for it. Laszlo was captured, and there was no word about Ella's whereabouts.

"Where are my parents, Hilda?" The child cut to the quick of the matter as soon as the two of them sat in a corner of Aniko's bed.

"I don't have the answer you need to hear, little one," Hilda said with genuine sadness. "I wish I had something to tell you, Ani, but I don't."

"When, Hilda, when will I see my parents?" asked Aniko.

Hilda told her all she knew about the Bergers in a way understandable to the five-year-old. Hilda knew nothing about Làszlò, but her mother was probably still free. Aniko could thrive on the hope that her mother would come to get her.

Whenever she went into town, Aniko straightened her back and thrust her chin forward. She assumed the gait of a princess. When anyone spoke to her, she remembered the promise she had made to herself about being strong and invisible. No barbs ever again pierced her protective shell. She successfully split her being into two fundamentally different creatures. The world around her saw only the self-assured young girl with two feet firmly planted on the ground. But inside she was a confused, numbed, frightened five-year-old. She would laugh with others when they made fun of Jews but inside she felt the pangs of shame and betrayal.

The night after Hilda left, Aniko felt glum and furious. Once more she had been left behind. She had done her best to sweet-talk Hilda into taking her back to the city, but Hilda had refused. Although she had resolved to remain composed in the face of adversity in public, in the privacy of the dark night Aniko allowed herself to drop the mask. She felt the full thrust of her abandonment.

Aniko spent her days waiting for her mother. Every day she went to sleep a little more discouraged, a little more lonely. Soon she stopped eating and no longer wanted to go to market with Aunt Irén. She gave up everything except the stubborn vigil for her mother.

The next Sunday, Uncle Miklòs sent her to pick mushrooms in the forest. The girl obeyed without energy.

Aniko reached the forest, and within minutes she had filled her basket with huge mushrooms. She could have been back at the house within half an hour, but she enjoyed the peaceful solitude of the forest. This was one place that she could be who she was — the trees didn't care if she was Jewish.

"If it isn't the runt! Well, I'll be!"

Aniko jumped to her feet, stunned. The two Bognàr brothers had followed her to the forest. She picked up her basket and started to run away.

"Not so fast, runt," Imre said. "Let me see first if you picked the right kind of mushrooms. There are lots of toadstools around here. Just one of those and we could all croak."

The little girl was willing to show him the contents of the basket, if for no other reason than to prove what a good job she had one.

"These seem to be in perfect order," Imre said, still holding the basket by the handle. "Now let's see if you are all in perfect order," he said, laughing as he winked at his brother.

When Aniko came to her senses again, she opened her eyes and she saw that the sky was solid red like blood, without the shred of a cloud. It hurt her to look so she closed her eyes. It was only then that she realized that the pain didn't come from looking at the sky above; it came from within. Her entire body ached as if it had been ripped into many pieces. She wanted to stand but her legs wouldn't obey. When she rose to her knees, an involuntary howl escaped from her lungs. There were blood stains all over her lower body, and she was stark naked. She fainted again.

"Get going, lazy bones" were the first words she heard. It was Pista's voice. "Time to go. The parents will be wondering."

"What happened to my clothes?" Aniko asked. "And why am I hurting so much? Why am I covered in blood? What happened to me?"

They made her swear on the head of her "Jewish whore mother" that she would not say how she got hurt. If she did, they would kill her. She swore. Aniko was beginning to remember, through the fog of pain and nausea, that one of the boys had pinned her down while the other had removed her panties.

She rose to her feet, but she couldn't walk. One of the boys picked her up like a sack of potatoes and tossed her on his shoulder. The other carried her basket of mushrooms. When they reached the house, he dropped her on the ground of the barnyard. Aniko wished the earth would open and swallow her.

That night she vomited until she lost consciousness. When she regained her wits, she continued to vomit greenish yellow bile. Aunt Irén touched her forehead: it was burning hot. Her teeth were chattering, and her whole body was shaking. Aunt Irén sent one of her sons to fetch the doctor. She couldn't cope with the anguish of another dead girl-child in that bed.

Amid whispers, Aniko protested. She had sworn on the head of her "Jewish whore mother." Uncle Miklòs raised his eyebrows as he looked at his wife. They understood that something terribly wrong had happened to this child.

Aniko teetered on the edge of life for several days. She had lost a lot of blood. Everyone believed her injuries were a result of falling from a rock in the forest that she had climbed. They had found blood marks on the rock. That explained why her body was covered with bruises and why her clothes, including her undergarments, were torn to shreds. Luckily, the boys happened to be nearby when they heard her scream and came to her rescue. Aniko owed them her gratitude for saving her life.

The young girl acquiesced without a word. She was Jewish, so she had to obey.

Ten days passed before she regained her strength. Her body no longer hurt so much, but her nights began to torment her. She dreamed of cannibals tearing at her flesh. She forced herself to stay awake, but the sleeplessness only made her weaker by day. Even the gypsy healer's tonic had no effect on her.

Then a miracle occurred. About a week after Aniko began to walk again, Uncle Miklòs heard the dogs barking ferociously. Thinking it was a fox, he got out his hunting rifle. It was Ella, Aniko's mother.

The weak child and her exhausted mother barely recognized each other. But something drove them into each other's arms. They embraced for over an hour. They wept, laughed, and they wept again. Then they fell asleep hugging on Aniko's bed.

It was nearly midday by the time the child awakened from her first night's normal sleep since the forest incident. Ella brought a cup of warm milk and a hunk of bread to her child and sat next to her on the edge of her bed. They sat in a tight embrace, immobile, like a statue of two people. The child wanted to spill out all the bilious contents of her heart, but one look at her mother's exhausted, tormented face made her change her mind. She sensed that it was not the right time.

"So how is my big beautiful peasant daughter?" the mother asked with a smile in her voice. Since by then the child had become an expert in matters of right lies, she reassured her mother that her life was just perfect. At night she slept like a bear. Ella seemed relieved. She, too, had been sleeping the sleep of innocents. She had never slept as deeply as the night of her arrest. Once again, Aniko felt burdened with betrayal — yet another thorny barb in her soul. How could she sleep so well after she left me behind? she asked herself.

Ella's visit had to be very short. For one thing, it was not safe for her to be so close to town. After all, the authorities — German and Hungarian — were looking for her. It was also too risky for her to be under the same roof as her daughter. If she were caught, the child would be caught with her, and so would her hosts. Besides, she was expected by her friends in the underground. But, most of all, Uncle Miklòs had given her only forty-eight hours to stay in his house. Sheltering the child was fine, but not her Jewish Commie enemy mother.

The night Ella left, Aniko once again concluded that her mother didn't love her. Her hatred for her mother kept growing. And yet she craved her voice, her touch, her presence.

Ella's visit was a rare treat. Most hidden children did not benefit from such a luxury. Very often, the parents had no idea of their offspring's whereabouts. Most rescuers preferred it that way for reasons of safety. They feared that over-eager parents might not take the necessary precautions or that the authorities would be after them in hot pursuit. Other children had to be moved so many times that, even if the parents wanted to remain in touch, they could not. Lastly, most parents had been deported, or they, too, were in hiding. But, of course, Aniko had no way to know how lucky she was to have her mother drop in, especially at a time when she felt emotionally depleted by the hardships of her life on the Bognàr farm. In spite of her ambivalent feelings towards her mother, she experienced the visit as a lifeline. Although she was angry with Ella, she craved tender sustenance. Aniko still did not forgive her mother for having abandoned her to these cruel people without as much as a backward glance. This feeling formed the foundation of a lifelong resentment towards all those who had abandoned her and of all the relationships she would avoid for fear of being, once again, abandoned.

The child didn't have much time to lament her fate. Within minutes of her mother's departure, death began to rain out of the starless sky. From that night on, Allied bombing raids became a predictable nightly event. Although Tihany was not on any pilot's itinerary, residents could hear the rapid bursts of destruction visited on nearby urban centres. In spite of their apparent safety, the Bognàrs insisted on hiding in the wine cellar every time they heard the ominous humming of bomber squadrons making their way towards the capital.

Soon Aniko developed a keen ear; she could hear the planes before anyone else, so they made her "air alert responsible." At first, she was proud of her importance. It made her feel like a grown-up. But as the planes came closer, she became terrified. It occurred to no one to comfort her.

The bombings grew more and more intense. Aniko wondered how all those planes could fit in the sky, and how it was that the bombs didn't hit each other before hitting a target on the ground. More and more, the child gave herself to daydreaming about matters like these, leaving less time for musing over her own particular abandonment.

As they approached Christmas, Aunt Irén noticed that the child had lost all vitality; she went through her days with a mechanical detachment, saying little. Aunt Irén gave her a foul-smelling tonic to drink with every meal. Its odour convinced Aniko that it was some kind of a poison. Terror took hold of her: they were slowly killing her!

The next time she went to confession, Aniko's secret gushed out of her mouth without her even realizing it. Only when she was outside the church did she realize the enormity of the danger she had placed her hosts in by revealing their well-sheltered secret. She feared not for her hosts' safety — they could all have died a thousand deaths for all she cared. What terrified her was the prospect of what might happen to her if Uncle Miklòs found out that she had divulged the secret to the priest.

Aniko decided to run away that night. She would go to the forest and wait to die. It had to be less painful than what was in store for her at the farm. This grizzly prospect somehow comforted the child. But, that evening, before she had a chance to execute her plan, she had to face her hosts. The priest must have spoken to them.

The whole family was in the kitchen, looking severe and forbidding. Uncle Miklòs told Aniko to sit and listen carefully. The child was so insulated by her panic that she understood nothing he said until his final sentence: because of her ungratefulness and lack of respect for their safety — instances of typical Jewish selfishness — they were going to get rid of her.

Instead of remorse or fear, Aniko received the news with joy. This was the first piece of good news in a long time! No place could be worse than this. Aunt Irén looked at her with sadness and anger in her wrinkled face. In spite of her tender age, the child recognized in the woman's eyes the shadow of betrayal.

The next night, a young peasant woman came to fetch her. To her great surprise, Aniko felt terror. Although she detested the Bognàrs, she didn't want to leave. They were evil in ways familiar to her. Who was this woman? Where was she going to take her? How would she treat her?

The adults whispered words that Aniko could not decipher. Finally, the stranger tossed her head back in anger as she reached for Aniko's hand and pulled her towards the front door.

A horse and buggy were waiting for them outside. They rode through the countryside in silence. For the first time, Aniko experienced the inevitable bombings outside. To her great surprise, she was less scared of the menace in the open than she had been in the wine cellar.

After a couple of hours, they stopped in front of a hut. Aniko's eyes scanned the horizon. There was no sign of life.

Inside the hut, her hostess lit a petroleum lamp. The flickering flame disclosed a tiny room with a bed, a rickety table, a chair and a wash-stand. There was a bench around the stove in the far corner.

The young woman put a clay mug of milk in front of her and motioned to Aniko to sit on the bench by the stove. Her name was Jolàn, she explained; she was a doctor's maid in Siòfok, a nearby tourist town. She had agreed to keep Aniko until the end of the war. But since even the body of Christ wasn't guarded for nothing, she had expected to be paid for feeding and sheltering her. However, when she went to the Bognàrs, they told her she would not get a penny. Instead, they were going to just abandon Aniko in the forest. Jolàn feared for her soul, so she took the child in anyway. She was a good Christian, she went on, and if Aniko wanted to be on good terms with her, she had to become a good Christian, too. Jolàn worked for the doctor's family from dawn to dusk seven days a week, so Aniko would spend all her days alone. She was never to leave the hut. They were on the edge of town, but it made no difference. At night, she had gentlemen callers, who provided her with a few extra *pengös*. During those visits, Aniko was to hide under the bed.

Jolàn uttered every word in a calm voice that signalled to Aniko that she was not a mean person. And yet the child could not divest herself of her fear. How was she to survive on her own all day long? How was she to sleep at night on the packed dirt floor under the bed without the slightest sound? How was she to survive without a word to anyone for who knew how long? But Aniko knew the rules: obey without a question.

As silence settled into her soul, shame emerged with an ever-increasing clarity. There must be something very ugly about her, since it was so important to everyone to keep her out of sight. Many hidden children who, like Aniko, fell into abusive or neglectful hands learned the bitter taste of shame. Their parents had abandoned and betrayed them. It made no difference that they had good reasons to do so. All that mattered was that they had been evicted from the comfort and security of an affection-ate home. Children like Robbie Krell were doubly fortunate: they were too young to recall the circumstances of their separation from their parents, and they were received by loving surrogate parents. Shame was not often on the emotional map of those who were well-treated and who were too young to assess in words what was happening to them. Those who, like Aniko Berger, were old enough to interpret their daily vicissitudes often felt devalued and flawed. They concluded that it was their basic infe-riority that was responsible for the treatment meted out to them. After all, how could people show so much scorn to an ordinary child? For many, those days laden with shame were the source of long-term difficulties in life, and they led to one version of social or emotional hiding. For those whose principal source of shame was their Judaism, it also led to a fear of being uncovered even once they no longer needed to cover up their Jewish origins. But, then again, for those hidden children, that day often never came — to be Jewish remained forever a source of shame. They changed their names, they married Christians, they even uttered anti-Semitic slurs to establish credentials in a world that often did not concern itself with their ethnic or religious heritage. For Jean-Paul Sartre, hell was others; for the hidden children who remained in the grip of shame, hell was the memory of their tainted childhood. That childhood was tainted by the blemishes a perverted world projected upon helpless and vulnerable Jewish children.

Aniko's life hovered between two solitudes. By day she was alone, and at night she remained invisible to Jolàn's gentlemen callers. During the day, she listened to the quiet sounds of nearby farm animals. At times, Aniko spoke out loud to herself, just to make sure she still knew how to speak. She had long ago abandoned the practice of counting and making lists to keep her mind busy.

She made a pact with silence. She surrendered to its might, and in exchange she promised to concentrate all her powers on bringing back her father. It kept her spirit afloat to conjure up memories of the two of them in the park, on the island, playing the violin, reading bedtime stories. Father was the safer parent for her to concentrate on. She had more faith in his return than in her mother's. At times, she remembered, when the three of them had been together, she had to fight for his attention because Mother wanted it, too. At times, she thought her mother was angry with her because it was she who sat on her father's lap when Mother would have preferred to be there. Yes, definitely, she put more faith in Làszlò to come for her than her mother. In a very real sense, it was this shadow father who saved Aniko from sinking into a hole from which no one knew the way back.

The empty days limped on, one after another. The ground was still covered with snow when Aniko heard an unusual metallic rumble stirring the countryside. It grew louder and louder. She heard shreds of human voices. She did not dare to open the door, and the hut had no windows. When she could no longer contain her curiosity, Ani opened the door a sliver. A line of tanks and trucks full of strange-looking soldiers was slowly advancing. She slammed the door immediately. Were they going to come to her door? She scurried under the bed, held her breath and waited for the worst.

Several hours later, Aniko learned that the soldiers she had seen were Russian. She had just been liberated.

But liberation made no difference in Jolàn's daily routine. Now that it was not a matter of survival for Aniko to be hidden, the little girl ached to bathe herself in light, to see the outside world. What kind of people lived around her? Were there also children? What about Jews?

Just because the Russians had taken over did not mean that the world had dropped its grudges against Jews. If Aniko wanted to be safe, she was to remain hidden. Jolàn also had to figure out what she was going to do with her. There was no room in her life for a child.

Once more, Aniko was about to be moved. But by now she had learned to accept her world as ever-changing, never permanent.

It took her three days of indignation and frustration to work up the courage to disobey her host's stern warning to remain hidden or else. The bright sunshine bounced off the snowy countryside when Aniko opened the door. Her legs shook with fear and excitement. Her first gesture as a free person filled her with courage.

Aniko was fascinated by an undulating ribbon of armoured vehicles. As ominous as the spectacle appeared to her, she was not afraid. So she ventured outside. Soldiers perched on their vehicles waved at her.

She felt a chill of panic in her throat when she saw a soldier signalling her to come closer. All she could see was his big gun. What could he want from her? The soldier kept waving at her. As slowly as she could, Aniko moved towards him. When she was close enough, he began to call to her in his language.

Finally, he climbed down from his vehicle, picked her up and hugged her tightly to his chest. Aniko felt his tears against her cheeks. He reached into his jacket pocket and pulled out a crumpled picture of a little girl. Then he carried Aniko to the cab of his truck and gave her a hunk of black bread and a slab of bacon. This was the first affectionate gesture shown to her in months. She was no longer scared of the rough-looking stranger. He showed her the picture again. "Natasha, Natasha," he said. "Natasha." This time he pointed at Aniko. His name was Sergey.

A man in civilian clothes walked up to Aniko and her new friend. He was Hungarian but spoke Russian. He asked Aniko all sorts of questions about who she was, where she came from and who was responsible for her. As she broke into tears, Sergey knelt in front of her and sang a sweet song. Its mysterious words and lovely melody soothed her. She told the Hungarian her story, and he translated her words to Sergey. The Russian gave him an agitated answer. The Hungarian informed Aniko that Sergey thought she must be an orphan. He would take her to Budapest; if no one wanted her, he would take her back home with him as his own.

Aniko had never thought of herself as an orphan. But she liked the idea of riding back to Budapest with Sergey. She felt safe with him. He sat behind the wheel and stretched out his huge hand.

"Natasha?" he said.

Aniko understood. From here on, she was going to be Natasha. It felt better than Annamária. But it was still not Aniko.

Once in the capital, Aniko could not believe her eyes. The buildings spilled their insides into the street; charred automobile carcasses littered the pavement; streetcars lay on their sides as if they were dead.

After a great deal of difficulty, they found her house. Aniko thought she was in a dream. The last time she had seen the building, a great solitude had settled into her heart. Now she looked at the house, then she looked at Sergey's smiling face, and once again, she felt connected to the world around her. She was no longer a solitary child.

Sergey carried her upstairs. Aniko enjoyed being treated as a little girl once again. It masked her anxiety about who would open her apartment door.

When Hilda opened it, they both screamed in surprise. Aniko leaped out of Sergey's arms and embraced Hilda. Sergey flashed a generous smile at Aniko. Using his whole body, he made her understand that he was going to leave and come back soon. But Aniko never saw him again.

After the initial joy of the reunion, Aniko felt the need to talk. She wanted to tell Hilda all about her life in hiding. And she wanted to know what to expect. She needed lots of answers. Although the horrible ordeal she had sustained on the Bognàrs' farm was still vivid in her memory, it never occurred to her to make her beloved Hilda accountable for any of it. She made no connection between her friend and her friend's family. Hilda belonged to the happy world she shared with the Bergers; the Bognàrs were the embodiment of all the miseries that had been dumped on Aniko since she had been separated from her parents. Thus, hidden children were often able to compartmentalize good and evil. It allowed them to return to a version of normal life. By bracketing off bad memories they were able to invest their trust in a possible future, surrounded by people who felt more or less safe. For Aniko, Hilda was safe; the other Bognàrs belonged to the nightmare.

Although her heart was in the right place, Hilda was not insightful enough to realize that her young ward had endured extraordinary times, far from her own world, in the middle of a war that was waged as much against Jewish children as their elders. According to the young maid, Aniko could not have suffered from the hardships of the war. She had been in hiding, Hilda reminded her. What did *she* know about the bombings or about hunger? Besides, nothing could be gained from conjuring up old phantoms: it was time to move on. As for the future, she didn't have a crystal ball. Hilda promised the child, however, that she would stay with her until one of her parents returned. In the meantime, she had to find food in a world in which everyone was hungry. Aniko was not a baby any more. She would understand that the days of luxury and games were gone, at least for a while. As for her other questions, Aniko was to wait for her parents' return for answers.

So Aniko had to resign herself to freedom as a new version of silence. Once again, she had to settle into a world animated by only her own solitary voice. Hilda was gone all day, working and hunting for food in a chaotic, grieving city nearly paralyzed by a violent siege. For her own safety Aniko had to stay at home; besides, somebody had to be there to open the door when her parents came back. Aniko did as she was told. She stayed in her old room. Nothing much had changed, except that the windows had been shattered by explosions. Hilda boarded up the broken panes; after all, it was still winter. Thus, a world of darkness reminded Aniko that the hiding was not yet over.

One day in March, Aniko decided to venture outside, just to take stock. To her surprise, it was a warm spring day. She walked tentatively, as if stealing every step. Every time she passed someone, she wondered if the person knew she was Jewish. Aniko didn't raise her eyes from the sidewalk. Periodically, she glanced back just to see if anyone was following her.

Without intending to do so, she ended up at the park by the river. A bunch of kids were playing blind-man's buff. She wanted to join, but a much bigger child shoved her aside and she fell on her back. Her back hurt, but the children's foul oaths about her Jewishness hurt her even more. If only she could conjure up Sergey! He would teach these bullies a lesson.

Night terrors began to haunt Aniko. She would bolt out of deep sleep and scream at the night: "Don't kill my mommy! Don't hurt my daddy! Don't touch him, leave him be." Night after night, Hilda was yanked out of her sleep by the child's bone-chilling howls.

One night, however, long after both Hilda and Aniko had retired, they were jarred out of their sleep by the doorbell. They both got out of bed to see who the late-night visitor could be. They opened the door, and there stood an old woman dressed in a tattered black and white striped dress, her coarse dark hair cropped close to the scalp, her feet wrapped in rags inside heavy military boots much too big for her fine bones. She looked familiar to Aniko but she couldn't place her.

It was Ella Berger, her mother.

An uncomfortable shame settled into Aniko's heart. She could not accept this shell of a woman as her mother. Her mother was vital, young, loving. Her eyes had sparkled, her words had sung like a violin! How was this sorrowful creature to help her?

Hopes for a jubilant reunion were dashed. There was no hero's welcome for the survivors. Ella seemed to have left her spirit behind. And Aniko was angry with her for having left her in the first place and for having come back to her broken. Silence settled between them like a wall. The child was stuck with her unwelcome words, and the mother had sunk into a story for which she lacked the words or the means to forget. They lived side by side in worlds that intersected only during their daily rituals.

Aniko's experience with her returning mother was significantly different from Robbie Krell's. It did not take long for the Krells to earn back their son's trust and affection. They had been lucky in avoiding the vicissitudes of deportation. Thus their emotional journey back was shorter than Ella's. They both returned, whereas Ella returned from the killing fields a widow. Robbie was disoriented and afflicted by his losses, but his mother and father came back as active and vibrant people. Indeed, their home became a centre for returning survivors. As much as the shattered beings deepened his sense of loss, they also fascinated and challenged him. Aniko's lot was uncomplicated: there were only losses and griefs. Life was never going to be the same for her, not only because the "event" had happened but also because her beloved father did not return. With him went the idyllic experiences of her childhood. In less than a year, her wonderful world was replaced by one made up of betrayals, ruins, laments, terrifying-looking survivors, grisly tales and shame.

Along with the shame, she discovered another emotion, one that was also familiar to Robbie Krell — guilt. This guilt was not a result of having done something wrong; it was simply for being, for having had a relatively easy time of survival. The two children — together with thousands of others — concluded that they had enjoyed luck beyond their merits. When she listened to the litany of fleshless survivors, Aniko went to the extreme of even denying her right to remember what happened to her in the forest. She looked at her mother, and next to the anger, Aniko found an increasingly loud presence. "Look at your mother, look at how wretched she is," she would admonish herself. "What right do you have to complain, to demand, to even hurt?" The voice of guilt grew increasingly louder. She approached the threshold of agreeing with the Nazis about her right to exist. What a diabolical accomplishment: to cause children to doubt their right to breathe!

Shortly after Ella's return, Hilda went off to build her own life. At first, it was painfully hard for the child to stay alone with a mother who needed to be cared for like a child. But Aniko proved to be a good parent. She pampered her mother, catered to her needs, comforted her when she dozed off in the middle of the day and began to whimper. At other times, however, she wanted to scream at her mother, to shake her out of her shadowy existence. Ella could carry on animated conversations with visitors; why wouldn't she make the effort with Aniko? All they talked about was who didn't come back and who did, who survived and how. Nobody ever asked her how *she* had survived. Or, for that matter, how she was doing now.

She kept pleading with her mother to share those distant memories. And each time Ella would stare into the emptiness and quietly refuse. What had her mother come back for, anyway? Aniko asked herself. It would have been better if her father had come back.

The first time the thought came to her, she ordered herself to shut up. But one evening her mother said the same thing. Hearing her mother say it, Aniko felt a bit liberated. Indeed, Aniko began to idealize her absent father because he hadn't come back. And she hated her mother for returning the way she did. She didn't have the chance to spit her anger at Làszlò Berger for abandoning her, but she could let her mother know how angry she was with her.

About a month after Ella's return, Aniko went on an errand to a neighbour. When asked how her mother was doing, Aniko blurted out without hesitation that she had died. The neighbour was stunned; she had seen Mrs Berger the day before in the street. But Aniko insisted that her mother was dead, that she hadn't woken up in the morning.

The following day when Ella returned from the Opera House, she took out the old suitcase and began to pack without a word. She was leaving. Panic gripped the child. What about her? How could she think of leaving her again? "I learned later," Aniko explains, "that to my mother it was clear that I had no need for her since I had already told people that she was dead. If she had known how wrong she was!"

When Ella was about to leave the apartment, Aniko threw herself on her mother and begged her forgiveness for the wicked lie, for being an evil child. How was she to survive without her? Her mother still walked towards the front door. Aniko grabbed her mother's ankles, howling in panic. Her desperate humiliation moved the mother to violent tears. She collapsed next to Aniko, held her against her chest and asked her forgiveness for coming back instead of her father.

Once again, Aniko concluded that she deserved to be abandoned, and that abandoning their children is something all parents do. Children reaching such poisoned wisdom are likely to hold on to it throughout life. Very often they have serious misgivings about becoming parents themselves: What if they duplicated their parents' tendency to leave? How could they care for their little ones if they had never learned to do so? Only those fortunate enough to find at least one person who showed them a sustained generosity had an alternative to the model of abandonment and betrayal. Aniko was not among those lucky children.

From that day on, Ella made an effort to return to the world of the living. She even sang now and then. But her songs spoke of dead mothers. Each time she sang, Aniko hugged her mother. Hugging was the only language in which Ella could allow herself and her daughter to express love. And Aniko kept hugging her. To keep her.

One day, Ella told Aniko that the child's unforgettable last look when they separated at the Bognàrs' had saved her life. It said to her that, in spite of all, there was love in the world. Wherever she went, she remembered it.

Another time, Ella explained to Aniko that she did not look back as she was departing with the police because a backward glance would have anchored her in grief and love and that would have been disastrous. Not looking back afforded her a painful numbness that saved her life. Aniko was too young to understand her mother's explanation. That day her love and grief had been rejected and she was abandoned — that was all she knew.

Once Aniko entered school, she threw herself into learning. She greedily soaked up stories about how people lived in other lands, stories without separations and hiding, without wars and victims. On the other hand, she was underdeveloped and pale. Her dark hair grew back. Aniko was jealous of the blonde and blue-eyed youngsters who seemed to be happier than she. She was not nice to look at; it was bad to look Jewish.

So the girl sneaked off to a nearby church. It was peaceful inside and she felt safe. There she began to toy with the idea of becoming a nun. How protected they must feel, she thought. But then she remembered the anti-Jewish posters around the church in Tihany, and the times she had heard people refer to the Jews as Christ killers. These memories sobered her, and her sense of safety vanished.

Whereas the world of the nuns was a source of solace for Robbie Krell, anchoring him to a Christian world in which he felt safe and serene, that same world was no more than a mirage for Aniko Berger. She was convinced that nothing in the world could make her feel safe because she had been born Jewish. While Robbie discovered a possible life in both cultures, Aniko found peace in neither. Both these hidden children's confusion about their Jewish identities and their Christian affiliations have been duplicated by other hidden children. For some, the confusion extended into their fifties and sixties and is likely to keep them company for the rest of their lives. For others, various significant events brought them back to the community of their origin. For still others, a minority, the Christian façade remains their hiding place. For Aniko, hiding her Jewish birth seemed to be an elusive solution. Somehow people always knew that she was a Jew. It bothered her immensely; she felt defeated by it. The only thing she did well was to hide, and yet there seemed to be no place to hide from who she was. The knowledge threatened to immerse her deeper and deeper in her shame.

Then, one evening in May, a stranger came and asked for Mr or Mrs Berger. A young boy in an orphanage claimed to be related to them. It had to be Tomi, Ella's sister Ilona's seven-year-old son! Aniko first begged, then demanded, to be taken to meet Tomi, her favourite cousin.

Life took on a new hue when Tomi moved in with them. Aniko was no longer alone. Tomi was not afraid of anything or anybody; he had seen everything in his young life. He had hidden in the forest with a gang of adolescents, fending for themselves, surviving even though a local gendarme patrolled the forest. Tomi was proud to be tough and Jewish. He told story after story to his cousin, and every one of them had a Jew for hero. Aniko had never heard such wonderful stories about Jews; in no time, she grew less vulnerable to bouts of despair and shame. She no longer felt the need to run away from bullies. One of the bigger kids tried to wrestle her to the ground, but she swore to herself that no matter what, she would neither give in nor shed tears. The bully could not pin her down, and finally they were separated by the gym teacher, who expressed admiration for Aniko's raw strength and courage. From that day on Aniko was proud, and no one beat her up again.

One night, after lights out, Tomi asked his cousin to tell him how she had weathered the war. She finally told her story. For the first time, Aniko knew that she was someone, and she emerged from behind the protective cloak of silence and shame.

She also relied more and more on friends — Jewish children without functioning parents, orphans of one sort or another. Thanks to Tomi, who had assumed full responsibility for his life, Aniko became street-wise. Gone were the days of cowering and hiding. She continued to excel in school, relying more on her sharpness than on diligence. She loved school, not only for the sake of learning but also because it has provided her with a family.

Aniko had barely settled into her high-school graduation year in October 1956, when the streets of Budapest erupted again, this time with rebellion against the Soviet empire. For the first time, looking out the window, silently watching the massacre below, she started to weep for the dead, for her father, for her stolen childhood, for the hidden child she was, for the lost years. With Tomi's help, she learned to honour those precious wounds; they were the bridge between lost love and future love. Aniko learned to appreciate her wounds as evidence of human vulnerability and precarious innocence.

Like so many other Hungarians, the Bergers left their country after the October insurrection of 1956. The New Year found Aniko in San Francisco. Her first steps in the New World were awkward and hesitant, until she was taken to the Pacific shore. As she stood there, she felt compelled to drop to her knees and kiss the sand. How could anyone not feel free on the edge of that endless ocean? She swore to herself that she would never again live without the boundless spectacle of the ocean.

Aniko threw herself into her university studies at San Francisco State College. Surrounded by a flood of students and without a past, however, it didn't take long before Aniko felt that she had no alternative but to hide again. No one asked about the war, her primary reference point, the organizing theme of her life. She was also profoundly embarrassed by her faltering English. Since all she got was tuition-free education, she was forced to wear the clothes she had brought out of Hungary, which had "alien" written all over them. She was intimidated by all the tall blondes sporting deep tans. She wanted to be like the others — normal. So, just as in Tihany, she had to pretend that she was somebody else. She stayed aloof from other immigrants. To Aniko's dismay, the double life continued but in a different way.

The two cousins never let each other out of sight. Although Tomi was two years ahead in his studies, Aniko proved to be an equal study partner. They decided to become pediatricians; to take care of the children, Ella played in the back of the violin section of the San Francisco Symphony. She gave private violin lessons, and, on her off nights, she and another Jewish musician played in a little Hungarian restaurant pretending to be gypsies.

On rare occasions, they would take the bus across the Bay Bridge to Berkeley to participate in the student rebellions. but no one was interested in the wisdom they had gleaned from their war. All the students cared about was the fire in their own backyard. Undone by the futility of it all, Tomi and Aniko beat a hasty retreat. What was the use of having survived, of having a story to tell, when there were no ears to hear? Aniko began to slide down the spiral of shame.

"Our childhood is not our shame, Ani," Tomi said to the silently weeping young woman.

"We must keep telling our stories," Aniko replied. "If we do not tell all, we collude with the torturer. We must expose all, not only the good. We must hide nothing. But to whom?"

"To the children," Tomi reminded her.

Tomi finished his pediatric residency in 1968, Aniko hers in 1969. They both joined a medical collective for the poor. Today Aniko's love for children still attracts youngsters from everywhere. She can heal with a smile, with a touch of the hand, just as she can silence the most recalcitrant youngster with a long look from her quiet eyes. Tomi, on the other hand, has become the hero of the young rebels. The fire of his zeal — or perhaps his continuing anger as an abandoned child — sets ablaze the dispensary and the street below.

Aniko's private life is a lot quieter than her professional world. She still has difficulty getting close to people or trusting them. At times, she feels a deep melancholy about her solitude and her inability to let her guard down enough to fall in love.

"I fear ending up as a loner," Dr Berger concedes. "The thought of always living by myself is not an easily tolerated one. It sends me back to those horrible days with the Bognàrs and then with Jolàn when I was convinced I was entirely alone and resourceless in a hostile world. The fear of being abandoned and rejected by someone in whom I had invested my trust has been my loyal companion since those horrible days in 1944 and 1945. Being alone has the advantage of never having to worry about being rejected or abandoned. To stave off the ugly spectre of solitude, I throw myself into my work until there is nothing else left in me to give."

Dr Berger has built herself more than just a career — she has achieved the reputation of a local Schweitzer. She insists that she likes to be self-sufficient, but not solitary. But Tomi, with his philosophical bent, has taught her that her self-sufficiency is a mirage. "You can't work with people if you wish to remain a loner," she finally admits. "Nor do you choose to become a professional helper if you want to end up alone."

Today, Aniko Berger operates two free clinics in California for children. Tomi Berger works in Israel as a child psychiatrist, helping the children of war, Jews and Arabs alike. Aniko has never married, but that hasn't stopped her from raising two adoptive sons, Leslie and Sergey.

It is impossible to know the shape Aniko Berger's life would have taken had her childhood not been intruded upon. It is, however, safe to say that her self-confidence was severely undermined, if not shattered, by the abuse and abandonment she sustained during the war. In spite of her professional and humanitarian achievements, Dr Berger remains a fragile, vulnerable and mostly solitary person.

Although some children sustain blows but later give themselves and the world another chance, others do not. The difference appears to be the presence of a "benevolent witness." Those children who find someone to honour their testimony of horror and shame are often able to bounce back. The only such person in Aniko's life turned out to be her cousin, Tomi, another child survivor. While he had inspired her to rise above the pain and the rage, he was only a child. Without an adult benevolent witness, Aniko had no one to emulate. No such adult emerged on young Aniko's horizon. Therefore, although she did have a model for helping children in distress, she had none for helping herself. To a great extent, Aniko Berger is still in hiding. Alone.

3

❖❖❖

Child of Shadow,
Child of Light

The Story of
YAFFA ELIACH

Everyone in the eight-hundred-year-old Lithuanian *shtetl* of Ejszyszok knew Yaffa Sonenson even though she was only five years old when the hostilities against the Jews began. One of Yaffa's ancestors was an original founder of the village, and one way or another she was related to 236 members of the small community, which counted around thirty-five hundred Jews among its inhabitants. One of Yaffa's grandmothers, Chaya Sonenson, was a business woman, active in several charitable organizations, and the other, Alte Katz, was a pharmacist and an accomplished photographer.

Yaffa's first years were idyllic. Her father, Moshe Sonenson, was a solid businessman; her mother, Zipporah, was a professional photographer. They owned a wax factory, a tannery, a wholesale fur business and a large forest. The family spent the entire season in a pleasant summer home on the edge of the woods. Yaffa and Yitzhak, her brother, four years her senior, spent much of their time playing and swimming when they were not picking berries or mushrooms under the old trees. At other times, they would delight in watching the adults play tennis. "We were a very close-knit family," Yaffa comments. "And our summers were truly picture perfect."

But during the summer of 1941, they heard something that cast dark clouds over their carefree horizon. The Sonensons were among the first in Ejszyszok to have purchased a radio. They were fond of putting chairs out in the garden around it, as if they were in an open-air theatre. Usually they enjoyed the musical programs, but on this occasion they heard a shrieking male voice making a speech in German. To Yaffa, he sounded very funny. She couldn't understand why the adults looked more and more gloomy as the speech wore on.

"This is Adolf Hitler." Somebody pronounced the speaker's name with awe. But to the five-year-old, the name meant nothing.

That summer, the number of refugees who had been passing through Ejszyszok since 1939 swelled to a constant flow. They knocked on every door, including the Sonensons', terrifying everyone with their bone-chilling stories. With the fever of terror in their voices, they recounted how the Germans had taken over their homes and locked them up in ghettos.

"Don't pay attention to these stories. Nothing like this is ever going to happen here," Grandmother Sonenson reassured Yaffa. She remembered the Germans from World War I — they were wonderful. They brought culture and civilization to that otherwise primitive region. Those miserable refugees must have done something to deserve such hard treatment. But Yaffa's father, Moshe, was worried enough to want to leave and find peace somewhere else, the farther away, the better.

But it was too late. The Wehrmacht was already rapidly advancing towards Ejszyszok.

On June 23, 1941, the day the Germans occupied the *shtetl,* Alte Katz took out her camera to snap some pictures of her granddaughter feeding the chickens.

"Let's remember this summer, shall we?" she said to Yaffa.

"That was the last photograph she would ever take," says Yaffa. "And it was my last picture as a free person."

Zipporah Sonenson was pregnant and did not feel like staying at the summer-house any longer. So the family returned to the *shtetl.*

That day the *shtetl* looked like a ghost town. There was no one in the street. All the shutters were closed. Yaffa saw through the cracks of the shutter the procession of soldiers dressed in black uniforms on motorcycles and atop tanks. She also saw a Christian couple climb on a tank and kiss the German soldiers on it.

Within days, the ordeal began for the Jews of Ejszyszok. Yaffa was stunned to see the Germans force her uncle to climb on a roof. Her father, a member of the volunteer fire department, was ordered to hose down his brother or they would shoot him. So for two long hours, Moshe soaked his brother with the fire hose before the Germans found some other amusement. The young girl did not understand how they could do such a terrible thing. Or why they would make the Jews clean the cobble-stones with their toothbrushes.

Shortly after that, Zipporah gave birth to a baby boy. The ritual circumcision had to take place behind closed doors.

And then Yaffa, along with all other Jews, was ordered to watch as they tortured the members of the Jewish council, among them her father. They herded them down to the river and released their attack dogs on them. The bloodthirsty animals tore at the men's clothes and at their flesh.

Yaffa was more and more confused. Why was this necessary? What did all this mean? Why did two hundred bearded Jews tear each other's beards out? And why did she have to watch all this?

Within days, Jewish life became more and more restricted. All radios, fur coats, linen and light bulbs were confiscated. Every day there was something new the Jews had to surrender. By the end of August, they were dispossessed of most of their belongings.

Just before the High Holidays, the Germans announced that the Jews of Ejszyszok could worship during Rosh Hashanah and Yom Kippur in the local synagogue.

Moshe was suspicious of this act of generosity. He repeated his desire to leave the *shtetl* and go somewhere beyond the reach of the Germans. Once again Yaffa's grandmother Alte Katz opposed this idea. Since Moshe would not leave without his mother-in-law, he was forced to remain. He did, however, insist that the children should be sent somewhere safe, just in case.

Zipporah put a nice powder-blue dress with a white lace collar on Yaffa, and a pair of white patent leather shoes with white socks on her feet. Moshe sat down with Yaffa and calmly explained to her that she was to go to the house of Zosza, a woman who used to work for them as a nanny and whose family had worked for the Sonensons. If asked, Yaffa was to say that she was going to her aunt Zosza's house. Then, it was Yitzhak's turn. He was to be received by a member of Zosza's family. They had to go to separate hiding places. That way, should one be betrayed, the other still would be safe.

A bit shaky but brave, Yaffa set out for Zosza's house. On the way, she was stopped by a Lithuanian sporting a gun.

"Where are you going, girl?" he asked her in Polish.

"To my aunt Zosza's house," she answered without hesitation.

He slapped her across the face.

"You little liar," the man said. "I know you're a Jew. You're Alte Katz's granddaughter. But I will let you go this time."

Zosza was a robust peasant woman with an endless appetite. Although she was in her forties, she gave the impression of being much younger, because she was always laughing and singing.

At Zosza's house, Yaffa saw through the back window that there were gun-toting men in the garden. Yaffa had never seen them before. They were barefoot Lithuanian volunteer militia. Looking out the window facing the street, Yaffa saw droves of Jews being dragged towards one of the three synagogues of the *shtetl*. She was relieved not to see her parents among them. Now and then, she heard gunshots.

After a couple of days of watching this gruesome spectacle, Yaffa could no longer contain her tears. First she whimpered just for her mother. But when she saw a wagon loaded with all kinds of goods, on top of which were perched her own dolls, she began to weep uncontrollably. She also recognized their candlesticks.

"Why are they taking our things, Zosza?" she asked amid tears.

"Don't worry, little one. You'll get everything back," Zosza answered.

But Yaffa was not consoled. Finally, Zosza, moved by her pain, agreed to take Yaffa to her mother. When they were near the synagogue, they were told that the Jews had already been taken to the horse market. At the market, they were sent to the cemetery. The main road was littered with all kinds of household items, clothing and bodies, but Yaffa didn't realize that they were dead. On market days, she had seen a lot of drunks sleep on the cobble-stones.

Near the cemetery a Lithuanian guard stopped them.

"They're shooting everyone," he said to Zosza. "And they throw them into the pits. If you go near them with your little girl, they'll think you're Jewish, too, and by mistake they'll kill the two of you."

Zosza bundled Yaffa in her big peasant shawl and hurried home. That night, Yaffa noticed a man running through the garden. People were shooting at him. He kept on stumbling and rising to his feet until he finally disappeared from sight. "I didn't know it then," Yaffa explains, "but that was my father trying to get inside Zosza's house. But he couldn't because of the shooting."

A few days later, a shepherd boy showed up on Zosza's threshold. He took one look at Yaffa and shook his head.

"The way she's dressed, anyone can see she's Jewish," he said.

Zosza wrapped the child in some old clothes.

The boy explained that he had been sent by Moshe to bring Yaffa and Yitzhak to his hiding place. Yaffa headed off with the boy to pick up her brother.

Yaffa was thrilled to see her brother. After a long walk, they got to the village where Moshe was hiding.

"We must leave here at once, or they'll catch up with us," he said after they rejoiced at being reunited.

He then took his two exhausted children on an even longer walk. When they came to a river, Yaffa saw two sisters she used to know from Ejszyszok lying on the river bank. They were covered in blood, and their heads were resting on pillows.

"Why isn't Blumka getting up?" Yaffa asked her father.

"Because she's dead," he replied. "And the dead don't get up."

Yaffa didn't understand. She went up to Blumka. "Blumka, get up," she said, and she shook the dead girl's inert arm.

"Did I understand that she was dead and that she would never get up again?" Yaffa asks herself today. "Could I afford understanding such a horrible reality about a friend who could have just as well been me? I don't know."

To Yaffa it seemed that the walk would never end. "Where's *Ima*," she kept asking her father, "and where's Grandmother and everyone else from our family?"

"They are all dead," he replied, with his usual matter-of-fact sincerity.

When they finally arrived in a small town called Vassiliosk, Moshe spoke to the local Jews; with the exception of his wife and baby and his two young children, everyone had been killed. He had jumped out of the synagogue window and had rushed to make arrangements to rescue his wife and baby. In all likelihood, he warned, the Jews of Vassiliosk would be next. As usual, no one believed the messenger of ill tidings. They were not even willing to give shelter to Moshe and his children.

On the eve of Yom Kippur, a former business acquaintance finally opened his door to them. Late that night, there was a knock on the door. Two policemen entered and took Moshe away. The next day they came back and told Yaffa and Yitzhak to bring some food for their father. Their host gave the children a loaf of egg bread and a bottle of milk.

At the police station, the two children were taken to a room. Soon a broken old man, bleeding from several wounds, was brought in. "It was our father, who had turned completely grey overnight," explains Yaffa in a quiet voice.

"Do you recognize this man?" a policeman asked the children. They shook their heads, truly not recognizing him.

"You don't want to feed strangers, do you?" the policeman asked mockingly. He then spilled the milk and trampled the bread in front of Moshe.

The two children were sent back to the home of the businessman. That night, a knock on the window woke Yaffa and Yitzhak. It was Moshe. He had managed to escape despite his wounds.

"Come, children, as you are. We must leave at once," he whispered. "When they notice I'm gone they'll look for me all over." And the three of them, once again, ran into the night.

They spent the night in a freshly dug grave in the Polish cemetery. The next day, they continued their quest for a hiding place. After two days of walking, they came to Radun, a Jewish town known for its rabbinical school and for being the resting place of the famous spiritual master, Hafez Hayyim.

There, at a friend's house, to the children's boundless joy, they were reunited with their mother and baby brother. They scarcely had time to recover from their respective ordeals when it was announced that a ghetto would soon be established. The Sonensons shared a house in the ghetto with the Rogovski family

— business associates of Moshe's. In the middle of October, they relocated to a house that sheltered sixteen people in a small bedroom.

"It was quite terrible," Yaffa recalls, "but it was bearable because it was not yet winter."

When the weather became more inclement, they burned the furniture piece by piece, then the inside doors.

Yaffa learned to tell time in the ghetto from the corpses swinging from the gallows. "I learned," she says, "that in the middle of the day the shadows are very short and that they grow longer as the day grows longer."

But life went on, and attempts were made to create some kind of normal life. One such attempt was the establishment of a school in an attic. In fact, there were four schools, one in each corner. One was Hebrew speaking, another Yiddish speaking, yet another was for children of socialists, and the last one was for Zionist-oriented Jews. Yaffa went to the illegal Hebrew speaking kindergarten whereas her brother and father reported for work every morning outside the ghetto. Yitzhak joined the others in smuggling in food for the family.

Moshe and the other men worked in a mill outside the ghetto. Thanks to the flour and potatoes they smuggled into the ghetto, they did not starve, but more and more people suffered from the sharp teeth of starvation. Yaffa's baby brother was on the edge of malnutrition. But somehow the family survived its first winter in captivity.

On May 10, 1942, they learned of a plan to evacuate the ghetto. "Liquidation, not evacuation," Moshe said. "We've got to hide." But it was already too late. Moshe looked out the window and saw a German soldier pacing back and forth. After observing him for a while, however, Moshe had an idea how they could escape. The next time the soldier turned his back and began his forty steps, Moshe told his family, one of them would jump to the ground and hide behind the house. Yaffa was to go first, then Zipporah with the baby, then Yitzhak and, at the end, Moshe.

On his signal, they dropped one by one to the ground. When they were all assembled in the garden, Moshe revealed the rest of the plan.

"See that carriage house?" He pointed towards the house on the corner. "The ground floor was used for horses, and the attic was used to store fodder for the animals. That's where we're headed."

In the same order as before, they made a run for it, one at a time, each time the German turned his back. A ladder led to the attic. When they gathered at its base, they looked up and saw a row of eyes. All of a sudden two hands reached down for the ladder.

An ugly scene followed. Moshe tried to climb the ladder. When he reached the top, desperate men began to gnaw at his knuckles.

"Go away," they hissed. "We don't want any children. They'd be the death of us. Sixteen lives are at stake. Go away!"

But Moshe would not think of leaving. He held the baby and Yaffa against his chest and he climbed up again.

"You'd better let us come in, or I'll let the Germans know that there are sixteen Jews up there."

Finally, they made a deal. The sixteen people would let the family come up but the children would be their hostages. If any of them made a noise, they would be silenced.

An hour later, as Germans passed the carriage house on their motorcycles, the baby, sedated, just turned his head towards the noise. Fearing he might cry loudly enough to be heard from the outside, the people who held him, smothered him.

In late afternoon, the Sonensons came down, carrying their dead baby. In the setting sun, the corpses cast long shadows on the ground wherever they looked. It was the harvest of cadavers left in the wake of the massacre. Yaffa recognized the bodies of their next-door neighbour and his wife.

All the Jews of the ghetto had been killed. Sixty people had been left alive to clean up the town, to collect the valuables to be shipped to Germany, and to cover up the mass graves. The backs of the survivors had been marked with an X.

Moshe told his wife and children to lie flat on their stomachs. With two lashes of his belt, he marked each of them on their bare backs. Then he gave the belt to his wife and told her to mark him. When she refused to inflict pain on him, he called out: "Jews, have pity on me! Beat me up! Save my life!" A young man came forth and marked Moshe with his belt.

All the remaining Jews were to register with the authorities. The Sonensons left their dead baby in his cradle and went to the market-place to register. Before they could register, they all had to lie flat on their stomachs so the Germans could see the Xs on their backs. The regional commander decided that it might be amusing to walk with his jackboots on the backs of the Jews as if they were a carpet. "I'll never forget the sound of bones cracking in our backs," Yaffa says. If anyone so much as raised a head, the commander put his revolver to the person's temples and pulled the trigger. Moshe pushed the faces of his children into the stone. "To this day," she continues, "I remember chewing the grass that grew between the stones. I'll never forget the taste of that grass."

At the end of three days, when they were finally allowed to get up, there were more dead bodies than living Jews.

It was time to bury the dead. Zipporah and her two children followed Moshe. When they reached their house, they gathered up the baby who by that time had turned yellow. When the wagon full of dead bodies passed, Zipporah was to put the tiny body on the heap of corpses. Instead, she carried him in her arms. When they reached a huge grave, she placed her child's body in a corner so that he would face the tomb of Hafez Hayyim. Then they covered the grave.

After that, the ghetto became very small — three houses, no more. On May 28, convinced that their turn to be killed was near, Moshe took his family out of the ghetto. Once again, it was time to find a place to hide. Yaffa's birthday was three days away. Moshe gave his daughter his word: "We will be alive on your birthday and we will be somewhere safe on your birthday." That promise was Yaffa's birthday gift.

Eventually they reached a river studded with large chunks of ice. On the far side was a forest. It was to be their next shelter. To cross the river, they jumped from one ice chunk to the next. When Moshe noticed that his children looked terrified, he picked them up, one by one, and carried them across the water.

Once on the other side, while they were looking for shelter, they ran into other Jews hiding in the forest. They told Moshe that the forest was big enough for all of them, but they worried about the children making noise.

Moshe and Zipporah gave a lot of thought to their next destination. Finally, Moshe thought of an old family acquaintance, a Polish Catholic aristocrat, named Kazimirz Korcucz. He was unlikely to turn them away. Korcucz was not only a friend, he was also in the Sonensons' debt: Yaffa's grandparents, Alte and Uri Katz, saved his life during World War I when the Russians were hunting for Poles. So the Sonensons set out for Korcuczan, the village named after the Pole's family.

"Kazimirz, give us shelter. We're living in the forest, like animals," Moshe pleaded with the Polish aristocrat.

"My mother would die of fear if she heard I let more Jews in," he answered. "Besides I'm already hiding a family in the stable. And where would I find that much extra food?"

But Moshe did not give up. Finally, the Pole agreed to find them a place and for eighty gold roubles per person he said he would find food for them.

He led the Sonensons to a cave outside his house. A nearly invisible entrance led from the house to the space under the pigsty. A hole allowed air and light to enter. The ceiling was so low that an adult could not stand up. The damp and filthy cave was to be home for the Sonensons.

Yaffa learned to read and write in that unlit cave. Her mother drew the letters on the wall with her finger. Whatever her parents knew by heart, they taught to their children — prayers, biblical passages, poetry. They taught them phrases in Hebrew, Yiddish, Polish, Russian, even in German.

Occasionally, they would go up to wash themselves and boil their clothes, which were infested with lice. "We looked like people from another planet," Yaffa says. "We covered ourselves with animal skins while our clothing was being washed and dried."

On one of those occasions, Yaffa was inside the house with old Mrs Korcucz, Kazimirz's mother. Jews were a mystery to her, and she was ill at ease with them. She would look at Yaffa, shake her head in disbelief and say, "Such a little girl, and already Jewish."

Unexpectedly, there was a knock on the door. It was a neighbour making an unannounced visit. Since there was no time for Yaffa to run back to the shelter, she hid under the bed. The woman came inside. Unaware that a Jewish child was hiding underneath, she sat down. Mrs Korcucz and her visitor chatted about many things, including the fact that so many innocent Jewish children were being murdered during those horrible times.

"It's a real problem," the woman said. "If so many innocent

Jewish children come to the Garden of Eden, there won't be any place for us Christians."

Soon after, rumours began to circulate in the village that Korcucz was hiding Jews. Kazimirz told his guests that these stories frightened his mother so much that he had no choice but to ask them to leave.

It was the dead of winter. Moshe pleaded with his friend to let them stay until a stormy night when the snowfall would cover their tracks. Kazimirz consented. The Sonensons prayed for good weather. But eventually there was a storm and they were asked to leave.

Moshe was determined to get to the estate of another Polish friend. On the way there, a pack of hungry wolves attacked them, but Moshe fought them off with his bare hands.

The Polish friend did not want to take a chance on being denounced. There were too many people around who hated the Jews. But while in his house, Moshe became very sick. His body was covered with huge boils. It frightened everyone because no one knew what it was. "Today we know that it was due to severe lack of vitamins," explains Yaffa. One boil was so enormous it was actually choking him. He begged his family to cut it open but no one dared. Finally he gave Yaffa the knife.

"Here, you will do it," he ordered the petrified little girl.

She had scarcely touched it when it exploded, and fluid, gushing forth, splattered into her face. Zipporah made a bandage out of Moshe's shirt.

Moshe's illness allowed the family to stay in the Pole's house for several months. But then the savage murder of thirteen Jews, including Yaffa's uncle, Avraham Sonenson, and the Polish woman who was hiding him terrified their host's wife.

"I don't want the White Poles [Polish Home Army] to come and burn me alive as they did our neighbour. I want our Jews to get out of here. I'm not going to die because of them."

Once again, the Sonensons were homeless and Zipporah was pregnant again. For lack of any alternative, they returned to Kazimirz Korcucz and implored him to let them stay.

"I really can't let you in," he said. "But I know I can't let you go." He let them return to their old hiding place, their "grave," as Moshe called it.

When it was time for Zipporah to give birth, they went up into the stable. There, surrounded with cows, sheep and horses, Zipporah gave birth to a little boy. She put him in a basket with a note: "This boy was born out of wedlock to a prominent Polish family. Baptize him and name him after the patron saint of the town." To prove that he was from a good Catholic family, they put a handsome sum of money next to him in the basket. Moshe took the basket to another village and tied it to the roof of the priest's barn to be sure it would be noticed.

And on the saint's day, Korcucz came back from church to report that the baby was indeed baptized and that he looked healthy.

Finally, the front came so close that they could hear and feel the rumbling of the earth. The Sonensons were delighted, but they feared they might be massacred before the Russians could reach them. They whiled away the time by playing games and creating fantasies.

"What will we do when we are liberated?" they asked each other. Zipporah was convinced that everybody was going to love everybody. It just couldn't be any other way. "I'll settle for a nice warm bath," Moshe said cautiously. Yitzhak wanted a bicycle. Yaffa was itching to go to a real school.

On July 13, 1944, they were finally liberated. Kazimirz Korcucz came down to announce the good news: Ejszyszok was free; they could go home. But he asked them to leave at night. He did not want his neighbours to know that he had hidden Jews.

The next morning the Sonensons walked into Ejszyszok. They were full of anticipation. Perhaps the rumours had been exaggerated, perhaps other members of their family had survived.

"How is it that you're alive?" was the first question the local Christians asked them. "How is it that they didn't kill you? You're like cockroaches creeping out from all the cracks."

"There were three thousand five hundred Jews in the town before the war," Yaffa states. "Twenty-nine of us survived. And we were told that Hitler did not do a good job."

They found their home destroyed. Strangers wearing Jewish clothes, eating Jewish food and spending Jewish money had occupied Moshe's mother's house. The most upset to see the Sonensons return was the son of the Polish pharmacist. He and his father thought Zipporah was going to open her mother's store.

A constant flow of German prisoners was brought into town by Russian soldiers. They were beaten, dirty and unshaven. As they passed, they begged for mercy and flashed pictures of their wives and children, but the Russians kept no prisoners. Whomever they captured, they shot. One soldier invited Yaffa and her family to spit and throw stones at the Germans' corpses. Zipporah wouldn't hear of doing such a thing. "If we went, we'd be no better than they were," she insisted.

Moshe was allowed to return to his mother's house and was able to find and bring home their baby. The church was not happy to lose this budding Catholic, but Moshe agreed to supply the priest with a large quantity of wax for church.

On October 20, there was a great party at the Sonensons' house to honour the baby's return from his Catholic home. They named him Chaïm for "long life" and for his grandmother, Chaya. Yaffa and Yitzhak were allowed to stay up late for the special occasion. There was a great deal of eating, drinking, singing, dancing. Everybody was there, even some Russian soldiers. Then they all went to bed, the parents upstairs, and the children downstairs in their room.

In the middle of the night, Yaffa was awakened by a noise that could have been a knock on the window next to her bed. She and Yitzhak leaped up and ran out of the room. The moment they crossed the threshold, a grenade crashed through the window and exploded.

By the time the two children made it upstairs, Moshe and Zipporah and their guests were up, screaming and running around. Everyone else jumped out of the second-storey windows, but Yaffa's parents could not jump: they had the baby.

Once again, the family had to hide. Moshe, faithful to his basic principle of never splitting up the family, looked for a place big enough to shelter all of them. There was a closet in the master bedroom. Moshe opened the door and found it suitable for all of them. The sloping ceiling allowed only for Zipporah to sit on the floor with her baby in her arms. Yaffa sat behind her. For Yitzhak and Moshe there was room only if they lay flat on the floor behind them. After having dragged a piece of furniture in front of the closet door, Moshe squeezed past it and hid with his family.

For Yaffa, Yitzhak and their mother, who was holding Chaïm in her arms, there was nothing to do but wait. They could hear loud voices coming closer to the stairs. Yaffa recognized the voice of the pharmacist's son, accompanied by white Partisans. "He came accompanied by some of his comrades who still wanted Poland free of Russians and Jews," Yaffa explains.

Then she heard another voice: "There's no point looking for Sonenson and his wife. They must have escaped with the others."

And another one said, "Let's just check upstairs."

Upstairs they touched nothing. They were not interested in money or things. They wanted to kill Russians and Jews.

"Look at the floor here!" Yaffa heard from inside the closet. "There's a fresh scratch on the floor from dragging a piece of furniture. Let's just see where it leads."

They followed the scratch to the closet, moved the piece of furniture and opened the closet door.

Inside they found Zipporah sitting on the floor with her head touching the ceiling. In her arms, she was holding her baby. She rose to her feet immediately and stepped into the room. The pharmacist's son had a gun.

"Kill me first, not my baby!" she said calmly. She knew why he had come.

But they shot the baby first. They put nine bullets into his tiny body. And then fifteen into the mother. "What made me count the bullets?" Yaffa asks herself in a scarcely audible voice. "To this day I don't understand."

Zipporah's body fell back into the closet, on top of Yaffa. The child stumbled back under her mother's weight. She felt numb and heavy. She thought that the bullets had killed her. She felt that insects were already eating her flesh. So that's what it feels like being dead, she thought. Then she felt something warm and sticky on her skin. It was her mother's blood.

Yitzhak and Yaffa survived the carnage without being hit. Their mother and baby brother's bodies took most of the bullets. One that got past them, grazed Moshe's ear but it was without consequence. He lifted his dead wife's body, then pulled out, one by one, his petrified children.

Downstairs, the friends who had come to celebrate the birth of Chaïm and to wish him a long life gathered again, this time to say Kaddish for the victims. And perhaps also for themselves.

Moshe brought down the bodies and laid them on the floor, surrounding them with shrouds and burning candles. He placed the baby in his mother's arms.

"I want them to be buried like this," he said.

For the first time since the other baby had been killed, Yaffa saw a faint expression of peace on her mother's lips. That was the last image that Yaffa's eyes captured of her mother

"We buried her in the Jewish cemetery," Yaffa says. "As we walked through the streets, they were lined with townsfolk. They were saying, 'See what's going to happen to you?' "

Since the town was clearly not safe for Jews, Moshe sent his children away to Aran, a town even smaller than Ejszyszok but with its own railroad station and a strong Russian presence. He stayed behind to find the assassins. Since they were all local people, he had an easy task. But as soon as they were arrested, they were released again, since all were related to the chief of police.

Soon after that Moshe himself was arrested by the NKVD, Stalin's infamous secret police. He was charged with all kinds of crimes against the state. In December 1944, Moshe was sent to prison to await his fate. There seemed to be a vague possibility of striking a deal with the authorities to set him free. It took the government nearly six months to come up with a guilty verdict. In the summer of 1945, Moshe was sentenced to forced labour in Kazakhstan for life.

"Later we found out that his accusers were from among the twenty-nine Jewish survivors of our *shtetl*," Yaffa recounts. "It was a banal case of settling accounts, animated by competition and business jealousy. Before the war, they were my father's competitors in the leather business, so they had him deported and made us into orphans. Those were not sentimental times. My mother's dream of universal love after liberation remained a dream."

Thus liberation brought more hardship for Yaffa. Like Aniko, she had new kinds of hardships to overcome.

From Aran, Yitzhak and Yaffa joined some former Jewish partisans. After two weeks in their company, Yaffa left to join her uncle, Shalom, her father's brother. He had lost his wife and a child during the blood-baths. Afterwards he married a friend of Yaffa's mother, also a survivor. He and his new wife planned to leave the theatre of bad memories for Palestine and to take Yaffa with them. Before they left, Shalom took Yaffa to say goodbye to her father.

"All I could see through the prison gate," she recalls, "was his sad Jewish eyes burning a hole in my heart. And he gave me his blessing. 'Never forget that you're Jewish, never stop learning. No one can take from you what you have in your head.'"

Shalom had lived in Palestine for years before the war and had a British passport, which said that he was married with children, so Yaffa assumed the identity of one of his children.

But they had to overcome many hardships before they reached Palestine. Because Moshe was a political prisoner, his family had to hide their names from the Eastern European authorities. They therefore travelled with false identities, crossing several borders under Soviet control.

In Prague, while waiting in line for free food distributed to the homeless, Yaffa was asked to state her name. "Shennele Yaffa Sonenson," she said. As soon as she pronounced her real name, she knew that she had made a terrible blunder. She whispered to her uncle what she had just done. Without wasting a moment, he, his wife (who was nine months pregnant) and Yaffa jumped from the second-storey window into the street. They ran to the train station and jumped on the first train leaving Prague. They ended up in Carlsbad, where Yaffa's aunt gave birth to a little girl. But that could not slow them down. They wanted to get out of Soviet control as soon as possible.

When they arrived in the American sector in Germany, Yaffa came down with the mumps. Fearing that she would pass the contagious illness to them, Shalom sent her in an American ambulance to the nearest hospital. By mistake, she ended up in a nunnery instead. "Nobody knew where I was," Yaffa comments, "and nobody cared."

But one of the nuns took pity on the sick child and she found Shalom and his wife.

"When you get to the Holy Land," Sister Henrietta told her patient, "send me a branch from the grave of Our Lord. Then I will know that I have been forgiven for letting a sick child out of my sight."

The journey was long and tedious. But finally at the end of March 1946, they received their permit to enter Palestine via Egypt. The train ride through Egypt was harrowing. They had to share the space with chickens, sheep and other barn animals. The stench was overwhelming.

A woman next to them engaged Yaffa in conversation. "What's your name, little girl? Where do you come from?"

"I am coming from the land of the pharaohs," Yaffa said. Then she told the woman her tragic story. The woman wanted to know her parents' name.

"My father is Moshe and my mother was Zipporah." At that moment Yaffa realized the significance of her parents' names and of the fact that she was her way to Jerusalem, coming from Egypt. What's more, it was the eve of Passover.

"What chutzpah [nerve]! Such a little girl and already a liar," the woman said.

"My dear lady," Shalom replied, "she's told you nothing but the truth."

When finally they arrived in Palestine on April 5, an apartment was waiting for them in Jerusalem thanks to the efforts of some acquaintances of Yaffa's parents. Yaffa kept her promise to the nun. With help from a Franciscan monk, she got a branch from an olive tree against which Christ had leaned on his last station to Golgotha and sent it to Germany.

Shortly after they settled in Jerusalem, Yaffa and her uncle saw a funeral procession — one coffin followed by a long line of mourners.

"Who killed them?" she asked.

"Him, not them," said a passer-by.

"That's wonderful," she answered happily. "Only one dead Jew and so many living Jews walking behind the casket!"

"You'd better teach her the meaning of death," the passer-by said to Shalom.

From such incidents, Yaffa quickly concluded that people did not want to know what had happened to her in Poland. She therefore decided to act as though she were a Sabra, born in Palestine. She already spoke Hebrew fluently. Because of her new name — ben Shemesh — she was often taken for Sephardic. In fact, when the first American ambassador, James McDonald, came to Israel, officials looked for a child who hadn't grown up in the ghettos and who had not endured the hardship of hiding. They picked Yaffa to present him with flowers. Little did the ambassador, or for that matter most anyone, know that Yaffa ben Shemesh was a child of the shadow. "And I wanted to be a child of the light," Yaffa states.

Yaffa wanted to be a scholar more than anything else. But first, it had to be decided what school she would attend. Was she going to have a secular or a religious education? To determine her fate, she was asked questions about her family's level of religious observance.

"Answer yes or no to the following questions," she was told by the examiner, Dr. Hans Bait, the Head of Youth Aliyah [Israeli youth immigration service]. "In the past two years, did your father attend services in a synagogue?"

"No."

"In the last two years, did your mother light candles on the Sabbath?"

"No."

"Have you been eating kosher for the last two years?"

"No."

He wrote "non-religious" on a piece of paper and sent her to a kibbutz with a special program for secular children.

Just before leaving Jerusalem, Yaffa went to say goodbye to the rabbi, a most devout Orthodox man.

"Goodbye? Where are you going?" he asked.

She showed him the sheet of paper.

The rabbi looked at it and jumped up from his chair.

"The granddaughter of Yitzhak Uri Cohen Tzedek [Hebrew for Katz] will not go to a secular school. I want them to ask you those questions again!"

And they did:

"Before the war, did your father go to synagogue?"

"Of course he did."

"Before the war, did your mother light candles on the Sabbath?"

"Every week."

"Before the war did you eat kosher?"

"All the time."

And this is how Yaffa ended up in a religious school for sixty children, located in a beautiful building in the middle of an orange grove, near Tel Aviv. But even there Yaffa continued to hide her story. Except for her closest friends, nobody knew it.

When the time for secondary school came, she was sent to an agricultural school. But Yaffa had other dreams.

"Children without parents can't choose," the counsellor told Yaffa.

But she was a determined youngster. She sought out Betty Gottsfeld, the head of the American Mizrahi Women in Tel Aviv, for help. The American woman was sympathetic to Yaffa's concern: "My dear girl, I've a perfect school for you at Kfar Batia, a village that bears my name. They have a terrific young principal, full of creative ideas on education. The two of you will get along just fine."

They got along so well that, in 1953, at the end of high school, Yaffa and the principal, David Eliach, a seventh-generation Sabra, were married.

"I wouldn't even have considered any man who wasn't seventh-generation Sabra," quips Yaffa.

Shortly after, Yaffa and David Eliach moved to Brooklyn, New York. They gave the world two children, Yotav and Smadar. Yaffa became a poet, a playwright, a storyteller and a historian at Brooklyn City College.

While most people, including the survivors, were still busy trying to rebuild the world rather than bear testimony to the industrial-scale atrocity perpetrated against European Jews, young Yaffa Eliach confronted her demons with courage. She began telling her story privately and publicly in the late fifties. She was among the first to realize that healing herself and those who listened to her account could come about only by mastering her story rather than by burying it.

In 1969, when she was preparing to teach a course — among the first in North America — on the Holocaust, she realized that what documentation existed was mostly from the perpetrator's perspective. To the survivor and to the historian, it was untenable that future generations should find no material on the victims' and the survivors' version of the calamity.

Yaffa's attention was drawn to individual experiences. While other researchers' eyes were riveted on the losses, Yaffa was fascinated by and committed to finding out more about the power of survival. While others were showing the world images of the horrible losses, of Jews caught up in the gearworks of the Nazi killing machine, Yaffa kept cautioning people not to lose sight of the sweetness of Jewish life before the Nazi deluge. To this end, in 1970, she began to conceptualize a unique travelling photo exhibit that would document the lives of Jewish children before they were forced into hiding. This commitment launched a twenty-year project that was a source of both love and grief. The exhibit, We Were Children Like You, began its journey throughout North America in 1990.

Leaning over her own memories and listening to countless accounts, Yaffa concluded that what distinguishes the Holocaust from all other mass catastrophes was the lack of options: no expulsion, conversion, collaboration, bribery or treachery could extricate Jews from the final predicament — it was illegal for them to stay alive. And yet in this world without option, thousands of Jews spent each breath searching for and creating options. It was that struggle that Yaffa wanted to put before all generations, current and future. The Nazis turned Jews into ashes, the scholars reduced them into tales of horror, all kinds of institutions limited them to body counts. Yaffa decided to resuscitate their humanity.

Yaffa faced the challenge of her life on several fronts. When she began to teach a course on the Holocaust, among her students were not only children of survivors, some born in DP camps, but also the offspring of liberators. They needed answers fast to make sense of their parents' experiences. The response from the students was overwhelming.

Teaching her course highlighted the urgent need for ground-level documentation of the Holocaust. She realized that hers was an impossible task: there were no books in the library that would document the Holocaust from the Jewish perspective.

The issue of creating options where there were none was constantly on her mind. She kept coming back to her own family's experience with creating options by hiding, running, struggling with all adversities. There was always yet another place to try, another window to jump from, another tree's bark to eat. It was teaching a child to read and write on a clay wall in the darkness of a cave to maintain a semblance of dignity. It was focusing on what they could do to save themselves, adults and children, rather than on what their enemies did to them. It is largely out of those reflections on her memories as a hidden child that her oral history program grew, the first of its kind at an American university.

So, creating an option, in 1973, Yaffa Eliach decided to open the Center for Holocaust Research dedicated exclusively to exploring the history of the Holocaust based on the victims' experiences. She was also keen to document the ground-level heroism of Christian rescuers, a much neglected topic at the time.

By the time she formally opened her Center for Holocaust Research, another historical first on the continent, Yaffa Eliach was fully aware that her training in intellectual history would be of little help to her in the work ahead. So the same year, she went to study oral history at Columbia University. "So I didn't know anything about oral history," Professor Eliach confesses. "I went to Columbia University and learned how to do it from the experts. And I began to interview everybody — children, Chassidim, camp survivors and liberators.

"The first thing I learned was that if I wanted to establish oral history as a respectable discipline of Holocaust studies, I had to start with my childhood experiences. To do so, in spite of all the scepticism of my historian colleagues, I trusted my childhood memories. You don't forget when your mother's dead body falls on you. It was not a matter of what I did on Labor Day. Those were matters of life and death. To recall them I just had to choose to do so."

Soon after the centre had achieved a respectable status, Holocaust research institutions started to appear like mushrooms after the rain. But none achieved the high level of methodological integrity and sophistication of Yaffa's. In 1976, President Ford's visit officially put the Center for Holocaust Studies on the map.

Professor Yaffa Eliach's commitment to every Jew's history as well as her erudition were honoured by President Carter when, in 1978, he appointed her to his Holocaust Memorial Commission. As a member of this group of prominent thinkers and community leaders, led by Elie Wiesel, Yaffa visited ghetto and camp sites. It was her first return to Eastern Europe. When they flew above Vilna and Ejszyszok, she looked down from the airplane over that land, and she knew that somewhere there lay the invisible *shtetl* of her interrupted childhood. She wanted to get to know it as a historian. But inside she was driven by her indelible memories. She was going to shine a light in that dark cave under Korcucz's pigsty.

What she saw in Eastern Europe shook her profoundly. "They

totally distorted Jewish life," she explains. "They either destroyed or tampered with the documents. I had no time to waste."

Yaffa wanted to show the faces, as well. She remembered her multiple layers of hiding and the faces of all the hidden Jews she had met on her journey towards survival and beyond. They would first lose their details, then their contours before completely disappearing unless they were recorded forever. She decided to collect all the photographs she could put her hands on to illustrate daily life and the people of the *shtetl*. She wanted to show the world one Jewish village.

"Every Jew is a story," she reminded researchers and survivors. "We must listen to the survivors before it is too late."

Yaffa remained the director of the centre until 1991 when she decided that it was time to close it. By that time she had a staff of seventeen. Holocaust research centres, including hers, had turned into a movement, and she decided that just as she was the first person to open such a centre, she would be first one to close one. It was time for her to continue doing the same work but somewhere else. There was no need to duplicate the work and material of other places, especially the ones in New York. She donated most of the holdings to a future Museum of Jewish Heritage.

Yaffa deflects most of the credit for her extraordinary journey to her husband and their two children. More than anything else, in different ways, they chose to see in her the empowered Israeli rather than the pathetic child of the shadow. "I never hid the truth from them," Yaffa declares. "I also didn't dwell on my tragedies. They had to know what happened to me, my parents, their entire family, and the community where we lived, loved and were killed. And I wanted them to know also how fortunate I was, a lot more fortunate than most children of the Holocaust, though hidden, though in terrible conditions. I witnessed the death of so many people I loved. But at least we were all together."

In the late fifties, Moshe Sonenson was allowed to leave the Soviet Union. He settled in Israel and became a farmer. He died in Yaffa's house during his granddaughter's wedding. For the first time in her life, Yaffa felt the burden of mortality. As long as she could remember, even during the worst of her ordeals as a hidden child on the run, and even during the years of silence while he languished in forced labour camps, she felt that nothing bad could happen to her — he was there to protect her. Didn't he do just that in the forest, under the pigsty and in the closet where her mother and brother were killed? For Yaffa, her father was indeed the guarantor of her life. To a great extent, his basic principle of the family's inviolability, especially during moments of threat, instilled in Yaffa an unshakable confidence in her father's power to stave off everything. "Didn't he save all of us by keeping us all together, Bruno Bettelheim not withstanding," she asks rhetorically. (Bruno Bettelheim, a tragically misguided psychologist, himself a former inmate at Dachau while it was still a camp for political prisoners, imputed highly incendiary responsibility to those parents, among them Otto Frank, Anne's father, for not scattering their family, thereby condemning one and all to the same fate most often — destination.)

"For me, he was superman. He stood between me and the Angel of Death. With him gone, I was next on the front line. I had lost my protector." Moshe was more than just her protector; he was also the prime motivator in Yaffa's life. It was he who inspired all her work, including her history-making achievement on the *shtetl*.

Had Yaffa not had her parents' protection as a little girl, she would most likely have turned into a much more vulnerable adult. Many children who survived thanks to the presence and efforts of a functioning parent found themselves better off later in life than those whose principal experience in hiding was one of abandonment, neglect or abuse. Children who hid with a parent or even an older sibling tended to fare better as adults. And those extremely few children who hid with both their parents report feeling empowered by what seemed like an extraordinary triumph over a whole world hostile to their tiny family. To a large extent, Yaffa derived much of her power, and her decision to study Jewish life rather than Jewish death, from her mother and father's devotion to their children, and from their unwavering commitment to the family as a unit.

Outrageous as it may seem, it can still be said that even witnessing the brutal murders of her mother and two brothers was preferable to the endless anxiety of those children whose family members were swallowed up by the night and fog. They can never put to rest either their vanished loved ones, or their hope that one insane day they will show up alive and well. Yaffa, on the other hand, was there to bury her mother and her baby brothers. Eventually, her wound lost its sharp edges, if not its depth.

Hiding with her parents under Christian roofs also helped Yaffa to preserve her Jewish identity. Moshe and Zipporah did everything to prevent the erosion of their children's pride in their Judaic birth and the great tradition to which it linked them. They did not allow their children to blame themselves for the evil in the murderers' heart. Nonetheless, although Yaffa remained Jewish when that was beyond the emotional means of many, she was not necessarily a Jew like those she was to meet in Israel. Her parents made sure that she would always know who she was, but who she was was the composite of many faces and many tongues. Yaffa has lived with this multiplicity. It has constantly forced her to remember who she was in what company. She could not afford to express the wrong words, the wrong name in the wrong company. The price of a slip of the tongue, like the one on the food line in Prague, could have been a bullet in the chest or a noose around the neck for her and her family. She was afforded no spontaneity, no innocence, no childhood. "From playing in fields of buttercups, we were taken to the killing fields. We aged overnight, we became old people.

"My grandmothers were murdered in German, my aunts and cousins were killed in Lithuanian, my mother and brother were shot in Polish. I live in English, love in Hebrew and teach in Humanism," she told a crowd of 1,500 whom she addressed during the First International Gathering of Hidden Children in New York. But Yaffa does not stop at this macabre inventory worthy of a diabolical Babel. She has found the way to throw a bridge between the language of the executioner and that of the survivor. The result is her version of humanism. "Polish, German, Dutch and all the other languages of the murderer were also the language of life, our guarantee of a possible survival." Can we fail to see the link between this keen awareness of the commonality among all tongues and Zipporah and Moshe's teaching their child in the darkness beneath the pigsty the rudiments of Polish, Yiddish, Hebrew and even German?

In spite of Moshe and Zipporah's best efforts to preserve personal pride and self-worth in their children, how could Yaffa and all children in her situation fail to conclude that a child was not only a worthless thing, but also a terrible burden? She saw, time and again, that they were rejected by fellow Jews and by her parents' Christian friends only because children were feared as the enemies of survival. She saw Jewish teeth gnawing on her father's fingers. She saw Jewish hands smother the life out of her baby brother's chest only because they saw in children the involuntary allies of the murderer. She was yanked from a home full of protection and love and thrown into a world where children meant more need for scarce food, where parents had to sacrifice everything, including their lives, to protect their children, where she knew that children were, by law, forbidden to live; later, the presence of children meant a greater hardship in the process of reconstructing their lives and gaining admission into the New World. With all that evidence, Yaffa and the other hidden children had to conclude that there was something evil about children. Once in hiding, Yaffa learned that she was not allowed to talk for fear of attracting unwanted attention and she quickly realized that it was no use to complain. Instead, silence became her private companion as she trained herself to avoid all the actions that are natural to free children — expressing their feelings and acting on the experience of those feelings. Instead, she learned to be reasonable before reaching the age of reason. "We were old before we were young" is perhaps the most frequent statement made by hidden children. And many a hidden child never again discovered that lost youthfulness. But once again, Yaffa was at least not abandoned by her parents, and she had the occasion to witness some generous acts of Christian hearts. Those experiences prepared her to look for beauty, even in the worst of life.

Indeed, when she decided to write *Hassidic Tales of the Holocaust*, her enterprise was fuelled by the unwritten rule that every Hassidic tale must end on a positive note. No authentic Hassidic tale can end with a tragedy or without the conflict in the story being resolved. That model made sense to Yaffa. It also reminded her of Zipporah's fantasy about life after liberation — universal love as the only consequence of the blood-bath. Though her mother's dream most certainly did not come true, Yaffa retained her spirit; even after what they had endured during their years of exile, she could imagine only a happy ending to their ordeal.

Hassidic Tales of the Holocaust was embraced by readers in sixteen languages around the world. Was it because Hassidim had been largely forgotten by all, except the Nazis? Was it because in these times of metallic hardness the world was longing for stories born in fervent spirituality? Or was it just because people around the world are attracted to a superb storyteller? Indeed, it was for all these reasons; in addition, Yaffa's stories have encountered universal enthusiasm because they were bathed in the authenticity of a hidden child nurtured rather than abandoned during a time when humanity had incinerated its own heart.

"Already as a hidden child," Yaffa says, "without knowing it, I was practising spiritual resistance. And I wanted my readers to feel that in every story. I also wanted to offer them a chance to examine Jewish values in the context of the Holocaust. In addition to all the life-preserving and life-enhancing gifts my parents had lavished upon me throughout the entire hiding experience, they had shown me the primacy of those values."

For hidden children, like Yaffa, who survived the calamity with parents who never gave up looking for options, the Holocaust became a yardstick. Some measure everything against it, and that becomes a constant source of friction and frustration. They demand that their children trivialize all their ordinary trials and tribulations: "You'll survive it. I had to face hunger, torture and all kinds of deprivations, and, see, I survived it all. And you complain about a nasty teacher . . . a fight with your boyfriend . . . having to walk to school. . . ."

Yaffa, like others, treats her Holocaust memories as private tests of endurance. It helps her to keep things in perspective. It also inspires her to connect her survival to the commitment she feels towards society. She is alive today because Zosza and other good people risked their lives for her. She converts this gift into an opportunity to reach out to the world in which she lives, to teach teachers how to teach the Holocaust, and to be involved in civic and community affairs. Just as Zosza made a difference in her life, she knows that she, too, can make a difference.

"I am a great optimist," Yaffa says with a gentle smile that underscores the meaning of her words. "I know that the world can be a better place because of the Holocaust. It was an event that constantly put on the line the issue of life and death. If I go to a demonstration, I feel I am doing my share, because if others had come to demonstrations, so many more of us would be still alive. If one group of people needs help, be they Ethiopians, Russians or the boat people, how could I expect others to stand up for me if I am not ready to stand up for them? I credit my experiences in the Holocaust, especially what my parents and others did so that I could survive, with having very clear priorities. That means that my people come first, but I am there for everyone in need."

Being a great optimist and having her perspectives and priorities straight and clearly in place at all times does not mean, however, that Yaffa Eliach has not experienced the same intense pain as all hidden children do. Some have been overwhelmed by their all-consuming rage towards what was taken away from them. Some carry around a more focused anger at specific perpetrators and even at their parents and rescuers. For others, including Yaffa, rage or anger turns no wheels. All these years, to a greater or lesser extent, she has been in the grip of a lot of pain. "Terrible pain," she states. "At times I feel it in every muscle, every bone in my body. When I went back to my *shtetl,* to the cemetery, to the graves, just strolling through those streets, I had the feeling that I was standing or walking on a whole town."

She remembered her grandmothers, whom she loved dearly, and she felt afflicted by the crushing pain of knowing that they, too, were down there, with all the others. "I can never forget it. Not that it is constantly with me, but when I see an injustice done or I see a Jew suffering, immediately I become aware of the pain of the Holocaust."

While she was in Ejszyszok, looking for some evidence of all that she lost, she found Zosza. They hugged, kissed and shed tears together. The old peasant woman who had saved her life took Yaffa around the town to show her every Jewish house, every Jewish place. Then they stopped in front of Yaffa's grandmother's house, the house where they settled after the war.

Standing between her husband and her rescuer, Yaffa Eliach could not order her legs to go inside. She thought, What will I see in there that I haven't seen millions of times? I remember the shots that will echo in my mind forever. I will always see the peaceful face of my mother after losing her second child, lying on the floor and hugging my baby brother. There is nothing in there that I can learn. And without going in, she left, taking with her the pain that is never too far from her chest.

But for Yaffa, each bout of pain is always followed by a decision. "All right now, what am I going to do with this pain?"

While in Ejszyszok, Yaffa felt compelled to visit the cemetery where the entire Jewish population of her *shtetl* was buried. "Standing on the silent ground of that cemetery, I felt suddenly surrounded by the spirits of all the martyred Jews of the *shtetl*. Until then, I knew them only from their birth certificates, private letters, family portraits. But at that moment they were all tugging at me, imploring me, demanding that I tell their stories. So I gave them my word that I would do so."

Finally the face of one of her grandchildren appeared to her and his sweet voice said, "Ejszyszok." That gave her the strength to leave. During the next ten days of the visit, she was devoured by her pain. But when she returned to Brooklyn, her first thought was, "What can I do with this pain?"

For fifteen years, Yaffa collected whatever she could about her *shtetl*, Ejszyszok. Out of her promise and countless sacrifices — private and professional — grew her Tower of Life at the U.S. Holocaust Museum in Washington, D.C. On April 22, 1993, Yaffa Eliach opened her Tower. It is animated by the photos of all the Jews of Ejszyszok. Yaffa gave back their *shtetl* to the dead souls.

"The Tower returns their face to them," explains Yaffa. "It shows Jewish life on their terms, as they sat or stood in front of the local photographers, trusting their privacy to them."

A few days after the Tower's opening, the museum began to receive requests for permission to hold bar mitzvah or wedding ceremonies in the Tower by descendants of the Jews of Ejszyszok. One day, in a rare moment of quiet anonymity, Yaffa stood in a corner of the Tower. Next to her, a woman said that the Tower reminded her of her own town in Wisconsin.

"But it's my town in Lithuania," Yaffa told her. The strange woman threw her arms around her sobbing.

"I was very pleased that my Tower became everyone's town." In a very real sense, Yaffa, instead of erecting a monument, inspired life through her vanquished *shtetl*.

"I'm also pleased as a historian," she adds, "that I could allow the material to speak for itself, to let it be its own testimony, its own meaning."

During these days of universal accolades, Yaffa is longing for a few moments to herself to be alone with the villagers, to feel that she has kept her promise and in return, to learn that she has pleased them.

"I believe they approve of what we did," she concludes.

Yaffa's Tower will serve as a model of the Jewish life that was destroyed and as a symbol of the pain of that destruction.

"I don't sweep pain away," Yaffa explains. "I confront it. The more painful it is, the harder I search for something positive I can do. I have never been good at living like a victim."

Yaffa is definitely not a victim, and she is a lot more than a survivor — she is ALIVE.

4
❖❖❖

A Struggle Against Guilt

The Story of
ADA WYNSTON

One night in the spring of 1942 there was a loud banging on the front door of the Moscoviters' comfortable home at Slingerbeek 15, in suburban Amsterdam. Sara and Maurits, six-year-old Ada, four-year-old Betty, two-and-half-year-old Sidney and Bertha, their German nanny, were fast asleep.

Maurits Moscoviter, a popular piano teacher in the predominantly affluent Jewish neighbourhood, went downstairs to find out what the ruckus was all about.

"Open up at once. Police!"

By then the whole family was in the hallway. Maurits opened the door and found three men outside.

"We've come for the German Jewess living at this address," a plainclothesman stated crisply. "Where is she?"

"Asleep. Where else, at this hour?" Sara quipped. She was an impetuous, powerful young woman, owner of the famous Cune Hair Salon on Noorder Amstel-laan (today Churchill-laan), across the street. She was not used to being pushed around.

"We need to see her at once. Take us to her room," the man demanded.

Maurits was more diplomatic than his wife. He motioned for the three policemen to come with him. The rest of the family followed silently in their wake.

The men yanked Bertha out of bed and took her away without any explanation. The three Moscoviter children were stunned to see their nanny treated like the worst of criminals, but Ada alone was old enough to sense that there was something profoundly wrong happening to them all, not just to the much feared, very strict nanny. She drew closer to her mother and reached for her hand. Later she learned that Bertha had left her country in 1939 to escape the Nazi authorities. Now they had caught up with her.

A couple of months later, Amsterdam witnessed massive raids on its Jewish population. There were public demonstrations, even a strike by dock workers, but to no avail. The Germans, and the Dutch authorities who emulated them, especially the NSB, the Dutch National Socialist Organization, carried out their anti-Jewish measures relentlessly. These measures filtered into every aspect of the Jewish population's daily life, including the lives of schoolchildren. Ada had just started Grade 1 in the public school next door to her mother's hair salon. On the first day of classes, a stern-looking man announced to her class that the school had been declared an exclusively Jewish school. There was nothing to fear, he said. It was all part of the government's effort to regulate the activities and movements of the many foreign Jews who had run away from Germany and Poland. The children had nothing to fear, the man reassured them in a not too reassuring voice, as long as they followed orders and reported suspicious alien elements. The police would keep a close eye on the school.

Ada didn't have a chance to settle into school. Almost every day after that, a new law further restricted the freedom of movement of the city's Jews. The law that disturbed her most declared that she had to wear a yellow star on her chest every time she left home. It had to be sewn on securely. One day, on her way to school, a policeman stopped her to check if her star was properly fastened to her jacket. One branch was a little looser than the rest, so he ripped it off, cautioning her to make sure it didn't happen again. He was going to keep an eye on her. "I believe that is how I learned

to sew," muses Ada, now a trustee in bankruptcy and a radio broad-
caster with her own daily show serving the Dutch population of
southern Ontario.

Soon after the incident, Maurits and Sara decided to keep their
daughter home. It had become too risky for Jews to be in the street.
They learned every day of acquaintances who had been picked up
in raids and taken to Westerbork, the transit camp in the north-
eastern province of Drenthe. From there, they were shipped to
ominous destinations east of Holland. By that time, Sara had been
forced to close down the hair salon. Since most of her clientele
were Jewish women, her business had been withering away with
each new anti-Jewish law.

But Sara Cune Moscoviter was not a woman to sit still. She was
accustomed to making her own decisions. She had always earned
her living and couldn't imagine taking orders from anyone. She
came and went as she pleased. She had gone on holidays by herself
to Switzerland and had let Bertha take care of the children. Maurits
had always respected his wife's free spirit. It was hard on her to stay
cooped up at home. Indeed, she would often venture out, secure
in her ability to avoid getting trapped in a raid.

One day, Sara had an errand in another part of the city and took
Ada with her, travelling by streetcar. At the end of the three-kilo-
metre journey, they stepped into the street, right into the hands of
German and Dutch authorities looking for Jews. Ada's star happened to be covered by her coat, but her mother was not so fortunate. A uniformed German grabbed her by the arm and took
her away.

Without saying a word, Ada walked away calmly. She boarded
the streetcar going in the opposite direction and went home.

"The Germans took Mommy," she informed her family. Her
body was shaking, and a veil of tears hid the terrible pain of guilt.
How could she just turn her back on her mother? What kind of
child could be so cruel, so unloving? Why hadn't her mother asked
Ada to go with her?

That night, Ada lost forever the natural innocence of children
— and with it, her right to a peaceful sleep.

"I let my mother go." Ada incriminates herself even today, as if
she really could have stopped her mother from going. "I turned
my back on the woman who gave me life. If I had done something,

oh God! But I let her go. I could have turned around. I would have gladly gone in her place. I was only six. At six you are worth nothing. I've been living with that worthlessness until recently; I have been prone to apologize for everything, for being. Then one day I realized how absurdly unhealthy it was to keep effacing myself. So I ordered myself to stop. But the guilt of that day in 1942 will be with me for as long as I live. There are times when I don't feel it. At others, it comes back to haunt me. When I think about it, I know there is nothing I could have done to save her. But when I think how I lost my mother, I feel the same old guilt."

While the authorities were concentrating massive numbers of adult Jews in the Stads-Schouwburg, a famous theatre, to be dispatched to Westerbork en route to the infamous camps of Germany and Poland, they didn't forget the children. They kept them under strict surveillance in various locations. The three Moscoviter children were taken daily to attend the crèche (day-care centre) next door. Germany soldiers stood guard in front of the building to make sure that no Jewish child would go unaccounted for.

The Dutch resistance, however, was not idle. Various groups sprang up to rescue children of all ages, including babies. One day a gentleman arrived at the crèche and offered to make life more pleasant for the children by taking a group of them on a walk to a nearby park to let them run off some pent-up energy. Each day, the man left on his promenade at the head of a line of twenty children. As they were leaving the building, the German guard counted them to make sure that none would disappear.

When the group reached the streetcar tracks, a woman from the resistance would be waiting for them and would snatch two children from the back of the line and hop on the streetcar with them. But when the guard counted the children on their return, he was satisfied: all twenty were present. Two children from inside the crèche had been smuggled down through the back door and were waiting for the other children to return from their outing. They then joined the back of the line without anyone noticing the subterfuge.

The NV Groep, a Dutch resistance group, managed to whisk away thirty-two children from the crèche. Most of them ended up in Brunsum in the province of Zuid Limburg, in the south of

Holland with one family until other homes were found. Ada was one of the children. Before boarding the train, she was reminded to remain quiet. That way she was going to be quite safe. But the warning made her wonder just how safe she was if they had to send her away from Amsterdam to total strangers.

Ada was delighted to find out that her brother and sister had made it to the same holding place. The brave couple who sheltered them welcomed thirty-four children in their cellar. They already had ten children of their own.

"We all learned to peel potatoes real fast," Ada recalls. "Those fine people had forty-four hungry children to feed."

After about three weeks, however, the couple was warned that they and their wards might be in danger. The underground decided to scatter the children around the region. A man from the NV Groep — the underground cell that took care of placing these children in foster homes — came for Ada. His name was Ted Meines, but Ada did not know it at the time. He took Ada to his house and spent three weeks in the cellar with her. When it was finally safe, in January 1943, on a very dark evening, he accompanied the child to Leerdam to the home of Ali and Jerrit van Breugel.

Dini, the van Breugels' twenty-one-year-old daughter — the eldest of four sisters and a brother — was waiting for Ada on the threshold. She greeted the child with gentle warmth and youthful friendliness. From that day on, the young woman was to spend a great deal of time with the seven-year-old Jewish child. Since Ada could not go to school, Dini took charge of the education of her new "cousin" from Amsterdam.

Surrounded by a loving family, Ada's life was quite pleasant. To be sure, she was never alone, not even in the dark of the night when sleep was avoiding her — her guilt for leaving her mother kept her constant company. And she missed her family. The NV Groep tried to find the three siblings one foster home, but that was too much to expect. The successful outcome of the rescue mission demanded total secrecy about the whereabouts of every hidden child. Thus Ada had no idea where her brother and sister were, and they knew nothing about her hiding place. And although everyone was wonderfully warm to her, it was expected that she should never speak about her Jewish life to anyone. The family had to be totally ignorant about everything concerning their foster

child; should they be caught, who knew what seemingly insignificant detail would cause the death of others. Ada therefore cast a
veil of silence over everything that preceded her arrival in Leerdam.
It was as if she had never existed before. She learned to take up less
and less space in her own skin. Every day was a new experience in
increasing invisibility. The van Breugels saw only the persona she
became. They had no idea what she was really like.

At times, when she allowed herself to think of it, Ada felt
doubly hidden. Her body was hidden from the enemies of the
Jews, and her soul was kept invisible from the enemies of
children. Hidden children often regret and resent this second
layer of hiding more than the first. It is one thing to have the
world as an enemy; it is another kind of abandonment to be
condemned to solitude and have no one with whom to speak
about the loneliness. Ada was old enough to recognize her anger,
but there was nothing else she could do at the time except go on
with the business of a child's life.

Later, that rage would find a voice. But in the meantime, Ada
was grateful to be in the home of a caring family at a safe distance
from the theatres of destruction. Her foster mother tucked her in
every night and sat with her for a prayer. She bought her new
clothes.

"My foster mom and her daughters were hugging me all the
time," Ada recalls. "Jerrit van Breugel was more aloof, but not any
more than to his own kids."

Then, one day, it all came to an abrupt end. The NV Groep had
made a mistake: they had placed another girl named Ada under
the same roof. It was unlikely that both would be children of the
same family. When the van Breugels were warned that they had
been betrayed by an opportunistic friend, there was no doubt in
their minds: the older of the two girls, Ada Moscoviter, had to be
removed from sight. In fact, it was recommended that Jerrit van
Breugel disappear for a while as well.

"When I tell you," Dini briefed the frightened but attentive girl,
"you go upstairs and hide between the springs and the wood board
that is under the mattress. Don't come out until I come for you.
And I'll send little Ada to her bed to sleep."

Ada nodded without a word. They could count on her. By then
she was a wizard at disappearing.

Soon they received a visit from a German search party. Ada hurried upstairs and hid as she had been told to. She scarcely breathed underneath the wooden plank, even though it and the mattress with all the bedding on top weighed heavily on her small body.

"We are not equipped for black-out," Dini said to the unwelcome visitors. "And you know the law, you made it; it is forbidden to turn on the light in a room not prepared for total black-out."

The search party did not turn on the light, but the soldiers came into the room and poked their bayonets into the mattress. They then left shrugging their shoulders; they had received a bad tip about a Jewish girl hiding in the house. Thus, the van Breugels' rebellious gesture of sitting in the dark every evening rather than covering all windows with black-out material saved Ada's life. But although Ada could not feel the points of the bayonets, she felt that her soul had been lacerated forever. "I remember this as a very traumatic experience," she asserts today.

The next day, Ali van Breugel put in a call to a member of their family in Nieuwendyk, a tiny town thirty-five kilometres from Leerdam, in the province of Noord Brabant. They came to the point: we have been betrayed; it is no longer safe here for the older Ada; come pick her up and take her back with you.

That night, Ellie Rombout, one of the van Breugels' four nieces, set out for Leerdam on her bicycle. On the return trip Ada sat behind her, not knowing whether to feel excited by the adventure or to be terrified of the horrors that might await her if they were stopped.

They made it back to the farmhouse of Ellie's parents, Peter and Anna Rombout. Mrs Ali van Breugel and Peter Rombout were brother and sister. Both families belonged to the Christian Reform Church and they attended to their faith with zealous devotion.

"They took the risk of hiding me," explains Ada, "because their religion required them to safeguard an innocent life."

The Rombouts were well-to-do farmers and owned a furniture store. They had a spacious house that was comfortable for their five children — four girls and one boy. But they didn't have access to their second floor: there were several Germans billeted upstairs.

As luck would have it, the occupants did not bother them at all. Once one of the Germans looked at a family picture on the wall.

Thinking that all the children in the house were Rombout off-spring, he asked Anna why Ada wasn't in the picture. She responded hastily that the child was not feeling well the day the photo was taken.

"You don't go to have pictures taken when one of your children is sick," he admonished the dumbfounded woman. But he let the matter drop without a further word.

Life was a bit freer for Ada in Nieuwendyk. She was allowed to go freely in public as the Rombouts' niece from Amsterdam where the citizens were beginning to experience food shortages. She also started to go to school again. But with her new freedom also came new concerns. The town, which was near the strategically important river Meuse, was heavily occupied by Germans. It was also on the path of the infamous V1 and V2 rockets. Death rained from the sky without warning.

One day, Ada and a foster sister were taking a bath in a large tub in the back garden. Suddenly they heard Anna yell: "Girls, come in at once. Rockets are coming! Hurry up and run down to the cellar!"

The two naked girls jumped out of the tub and did as they had just been told.

The foster sister ran down to the cellar with Ada in tow. In her rush Ada didn't see a tub of half-churned butter. She slipped and fell, bottom first, into the butter. Half crying, half laughing and dripping with near-butter, she made it down to the cellar.

"Don't let anyone tell you that hidden children never laughed," Ada warns. "We were hidden all right, but we were still children. Those occasional funny moments were as important as bread and butter."

With her physical freedom came another concern. "If you see a stranger come towards you," her foster mother warned Ada, "run to the kitchen and hide under the table." At all times, a long cloth covered the kitchen table. It fell almost to the floor. "Don't come out until you're told that the coast is clear."

With all these precautions, the time came when the Rombouts thought that it was too dangerous for Ada to stay with them, so they sent her back to Leerdam. The van Breugels were happy to have her back. This shuttle was repeated one more time before liberation. Each time, she made the thirty-five-kilometre journey on bicycle. On one of those occasions, her dark hair and dark eyes aroused the suspicion of a German soldier. He made her get off her bike.

"Are you Jewish?" he asked.

"What's Jewish?" Ada replied.

Dumbfounded, the German let her go and continued on his way. Had he looked back, he would have seen Ada, shaken by the incident, fall into the ditch, which was full of water.

Although she loved both families, Ada didn't like being tossed back and forth between them. She knew it was necessary for her own good, but children, even hidden ones, don't always like to do what's best for them. But she had acquired enough adult wisdom not to blame her two sets of foster parents. In fact, she grew accustomed to thinking of their welfare before allowing herself to rebel against the fact she had no say over what was to happen to her. She knew that her survival depended not only on not being betrayed but also on her behaving like a model child. Like most children who experience abandonment, Ada learned to put others' needs ahead of her own. "I had no choice but to be a perfect little girl," Ada explains. "But later in life, when I no longer had to put everyone ahead of me, I was still doing it. And at other times, I did more than my share of trouble-making. I had the full gamut of faces, from angel to devil."

This is, indeed, another version of the duplicity to which legions of hidden children refer. They were barred from the simple, straight path that is the life journey of children who are not burdened with betrayal. For the Adas of the world, everyday existence is always about something else — it's about self-denial for the sake of survival. The spontaneity of innocence is replaced with bargains — my freedom, my *joie de vivre*, my omnipotence for a chance, just a chance, no guarantees, to live. When children are under the wings of quiet heroes like the van Breugels and the Rombouts, much of their life retains a spurious freedom which, to the child, with her natural commitment to the moment at hand, feels like the real thing. Thus, Ada recalls tender moments of intimacy with Dini and her cousin Ellie. But the shadow was never too far away. It crawled into bed with her every night. "To this day," Ada admits, "I'm not at peace with darkness."

But Ada never felt the self-hatred other Jewish children learned.

Indeed, she felt confused: why were the Jews being hunted and killed? What did they do, what did she do to deserve persecution? One fact she discovered very quickly: it was dangerous to be Jewish.

Once when she was lost in thought, Dini asked what she was thinking about.

"Should I feel ashamed of being Jewish, Dini?"

"Definitely not," the young woman replied emphatically. "Jews are just as good people as anyone. They are God's people. And that makes Jews special."

When this same issue came up at the Rombouts', Uncle Peter said the same thing: the Jews were God's chosen people, and she must be proud to be Jewish. It was their enemies who must be covered with shame.

"Then why are we being killed, Uncle Peter?"

"I don't know, child," Rombout answered honestly. "We humans are good and wicked. Some are more wicked than others."

Nieuwendyk was liberated in May 1945. When Anna Rombout heard the news, her first thought was, "Where is my Ada? She must know this wonderful news at once." She called for her and looked around the house, but the child was not to be found. A wave of worry came over her: Had something happened to the child now that she was no long at risk?

While Mrs Rombout was worrying about Ada, the whole town, including Ada, had heard the news. A group of angry townsfolk gathered to flush out a woman who was a well-known traitor, an NSB-er. They were going to settle their accounts with her. Ada wanted to see how justice was going to be carried out, so she joined the crowd. Indeed, the crowd found the traitor. They dragged her to the public square where they confronted her with her cowardly betrayal of her country and her neighbours. Then they condemned her to be publicly shamed: they cut off her long hair.

Ada had all the proof she needed that liberation was not just another adult word. The wicked were getting their just deserts. Perhaps life would take on its free face once again. Without intending to conjure her up, suddenly, she saw her mother's face. A wave of hope swept through her young body: perhaps soon she would see her again. It was at that moment that her foster mother showed up on the square. Relieved, and moved by their brand-new freedom, she didn't scold the child. Instead she hugged her very close and said a prayer of gratitude.

From then on, Ada was allowed to come and go like any other child in town. She could go out and play whenever it was appropriate. She was no longer a hidden child. In the fall, she returned to school.

Liberation ushered in a third stage in Ada's young life. Before she went into hiding, she had been a headstrong child, mindless of others, spoiled. While she lived with foster families, she understood that her survival depended on behaving well. Once her life was no longer in danger, it took her only a short time to regain her spunk. She became belligerent, asserting her will each time she felt her rights were trespassed on. Those who knew and loved her were first taken aback when confronted with Ada's new face. But they made allowances for her, never forgetting what she had just undergone and that she had had no news whatsoever of her family.

Three months later, early in September, a stranger showed up on the Rombouts' threshold. Ada saw him through the glass pane of the kitchen door. Without a moment's hesitation, she ran to hide under the table, forgetting that the war against the Jews had been over since May.

The stranger identified himself to Anna as Maurits Moscoviter, Ada's father. He had come to see his daughter. Anna went into the kitchen to tell Ada the good news, but the child refused to come out. This man was an impostor. Her father was a young man with reddish blonde hair. This beaten old man had a dirty grey mop on his head.

Mrs Rombout understood that the ordeals Maurits had just survived had aged him to the point that his own daughter couldn't recognize him. She suggested that he come back another time with some object that the child would identify as evidence of who he was.

With a heavy heart, Maurits got on his bicycle for the two-hundred kilometre trip back to Amsterdam without having even laid eyes on his daughter.

A month later, Maurits returned to Nieuwendyk. This time, he came with an old doll of Ada's. The child peered through the kitchen door, recognized it and came to meet her father. She did not want to see him; she wanted her doll. She had no desire to be with this man. As much as she longed to see her mother and two siblings, nothing about this stranger aroused any memories. In fact, although he tried to hug her, she would not go to him, in spite of her foster mother's insistence. But she got her doll back.

Anna invited Ada's father for lunch. Seeing her father wolf down his food as if he hadn't eaten in days embarrassed his daughter. "He cut himself a thick slice of bread," Ada recalls, "and he spread on it an inch-thick layer of butter and as much jam. All I could think was 'What a pig!'"

Once again, Maurits left without his child. His wife hadn't come back, and his comfortable home on Slingerbeek Straat had been occupied by another family. He didn't dare ask the authorities to return his house for fear of losing his children; they might deem him incapable of taking care of them without a wife.

He did, however, want his three children to live under the same roof. Mrs Rombout therefore packed up her foster daughter's belongings and with a teary kiss put her on a train to her brother's foster parents in Schaesberg, an hour's ride from Nieuwendyk. It was a tiny town with a devout Catholic population. By the time Ada was reunited with her six-year-old brother, Sidney, he was a fervent Catholic.

In Schaesberg, Ada remained an outsider. Without any friends, she was restricted to Sidney's company. Sometimes they got along well and played in the garden. At other times, the boy treated his older sister as if she were evil.

"You're a Jew. You'll go straight to hell," he would yell at Ada.

"If I will, so will you because you're as much a Jew as I am," she'd reply.

"No, I'm a good Roman Catholic."

At times, Ada would shrug off her brother's bigotry, but at others she felt particularly vulnerable. She'd wonder if she was indeed still a Jew. After all the comings and goings, after all the pretences and charades, she didn't know who she was and what she should do.

Her new foster mother didn't make things easier for Ada. She was hard and tough. So tough that Ada began to feel more and more like escaping.

For Ada three months passed at a snail's pace. She endured those months more than she lived them. One Friday morning, Ada went to church. Her brother was there with his class, and when she saw her brother take communion, without giving it any further thought, she took communion, too. The nun who taught her the mass knew that Ada was Jewish, and she was outraged. Her anger made no sense to the young girl. It was all right for Sidney to take communion because they had thought that he was a Catholic. But why was it such a crime for her to do the same? Why was he seen as a fine little convert, and she the villain?

Grabbing the young girl by her hair, the nun dragged Ada to see the priest.

"What did you do, my child?" the priest asked Ada. "You've just eaten the body of Our Lord Jesus Christ."

The image was so strong that together with the humiliation of being dragged by the hair, Ada made herself vomit.

"Well, if I ate the body of Jesus Christ," she replied with insolence, "you can have him back." And with the tip of her chin, she pointed towards the puddle of vomit on the floor.

"But don't let my bravado fool you," Ada interjects. "It was such a horrendous experience that I have never ever allowed myself to vomit again. In fact, I immediately sent a message to my father that I wouldn't stay in that wretched town if my life depended on it."

Maurits Moscoviter took his first-born's plight to heart and arranged another transfer for her. This time she was to join her sister in a village only fifteen minutes from Schaesberg. Neither Sidney nor Betty had been told they lived within walking distance of each other.

The Hamstras, Betty's foster parents, a childless couple, had welcomed Betty under their roof and were thrilled to receive Ada, as well. They had learned to love Betty as if she had been their own. So when her father asked if they would offer shelter to Betty's older sister, they naturally agreed, even though they knew that her father would want her back one day, and that would cause them pain and grief.

As soon as Ada settled into her new home in the tiny town of Nuth, she began to go to school like any other child. Except she was not any other child. Her experiences had made her fearful. Every time she saw a stranger or heard an unexpected sound, she began to fret. She had a hard time falling asleep at night. Sharing a bed with Betty made it a little easier, yet she wet the bed every night because she was scared to confront the darkness if she were to get out of bed. Ashamed of wetting her bed at her age, she blamed it on her younger sister. But Mrs Hamstra knew the truth. Without a comment, she would put the sleeping child on the potty.

In spite of her fear, Ada enjoyed her stay at the Hamstras' modest home. Not only were they kind and affectionate people, they cared about the values with which these children would grow up. They taught them to care for others, to be humane and responsible. They gave each sister a lamb. The animals' well-being, in fact their lives, depended on the girls. Ada and Betty rose to the occasion; they felt very important to have a living creature's fate in their hands. Looking after the lambs occasioned much laughter and cama-raderie between the two sisters who had been separated so long. They got to know each other and learned to enjoy playing together. Not having playmates of their own age, neither had learned to play with other children. That was definitely one of the casualties of the hidden years.

As it was for many other hidden children of their age, their favourite game was hide-and-seek. It afforded hidden children the opportunity to master the experience of dreading to be found. But it also allowed them to learn that, this time around, when they were found, nothing bad would happen to them. It also helped them to realize that if someone friendly was looking specifically for them, they were not completely abandoned. Thus, the hiding portion of the game was a mixed experience — wanting to be found and wanting not to be found. The seeking portion of the game, however, was often harder because it emphasized that for so long no one had been looking for them, a fact that reinforced their sense of abandonment. Some hidden children would act out their anger by on purpose not finding their playmates for a long time.

Another thing Ada enjoyed while staying with the Hamstras was laughter. As loving and caring as her foster families had been during the war and after, they were serious people and their hard lives did not inspire laughter. But with the Hamstras she learned to laugh at anything and everything. The years of silence erupted into an endless stream of giggles and chuckles. Ada felt as if a stone statue had been living inside her, and now she was chiselling it away bit by bit. With each laugh she felt lighter and breathed more freely.

"Ever since then," Ada comments, "I've thought of laughter as the most important tonic for whatever ails me. I wish I had had more of it when I was younger. To this day, I mourn the loss of levity. I believe it perished with the disappearance of my family. When I get together with people who had survived together or who regrouped after liberation, I feel warmed by the joking and merry-making that marks these gatherings. Every year I am invited to celebrate a friend's birthday. The whole family gets together, they tell funny stories, they tease each other, they banter, they make good-hearted fun of everything and everyone. 'It's a good thing you've only one birthday a year,' I tell my friend. 'It would be too painful if I was reminded more often that I, too, could have a family like yours, if only —'"

Ada spent the happiest eighteen months of her life in Nuth. "I had a real family life there," she explains.

In addition to playing, the two sisters spent a lot of time visiting friends of the Hamstras. The girls felt important and included, as if they really belonged to their foster parents' world.

Neither Betty nor Ada ever mentioned their mother, or for that matter anything or anyone else from their Jewish life. It was as if they had been born at the time of going into hiding. Ada now lived the life of a Christian girl. At times she had the vague sensation that she was living someone else's life, and at those moments, she hid in a corner and felt sad.

Most hidden children, even those who lived through the war under the best possible circumstances, recall similar feelings of being exiled from the world into which they were born, but few had the good fortune of hiding with a brother or sister close to them in age.

When finally Maurits was ready to have his children back and begin some kind of family life with them, none of his children were eager to leave their foster parents. As for the Hamstras, they were devastated. They had been dreading this moment. How were they to go back to a life without the laughter that now animated their home? How were they to continue living without the daily purpose of making a home for their two "daughters"? They let Maurits know that they would be happy to have Sidney with them also if it would make him feel better to have all his children under the same roof. But Maurits wanted his children back.

Mrs Hamstra could not stop crying for days. The children dragged their feet, as well. The last thing Ada wanted was another disruption, another departure. Even though she was returning to her father, there was nothing familiar for her to go back to. She had no affinity with this shadow of a man. He was a stranger to her. Her new home was not the house she had known before her hiding began. What's more, her father was going to remarry. His future bride was a Christian woman who had hidden a distant relative of Maurits's. Ada was not looking forward to having a step-mother. But most importantly, she could not imagine being happier anywhere other than where she was. Once again, Ada had to do what adults told her without anyone caring what she wanted. "My father wanted us, so we had to go," she recollects. "And we had to be there with him, like furniture."

Indeed, in spite of his immense desire to live with his children again, Maurits Moscoviter had never been able to free himself from his grief over the loss of his wife and the destruction of his happy home. He never spoke about his own experiences during the period that the children were hidden, but his silence was eloquent. Like most Jews, he must have discovered his own personal version of hell. To save his children the agony and to spare himself the ordeal of reliving some dark torment, he chose silence. To Ada, that decision felt like another abandonment. He chose to live, she concluded, in a world where there was no room for her. She stored away her sorrow, right next to her rage.

With heavy hearts, the Hamstras took the girls to Amsterdam. Mrs Hamstra wept quietly. The moment of separation was yet another torment, but the Hamstras managed to resist the temptation to get it over with and disappear so they could nurse their pain in private. "You didn't get a chance to say goodbye to your parents," she said to the girl. "We don't want you to leave us without properly saying farewell. God bless you, and we will always love you. Try to remember us. We pray for the day we shall all be together again."

The woman who waited for the girls in their father's new home was not a warm, giving person who was aching to mother her new step-children. She had married for financial security, and if children were part of the bargain, so be it.

From the first day, it was obvious to Ada that theirs was not going to be a happy home. Her father's wife — she could never get used to called her "mother" or even "step-mother" — was impatient with the upheaval that the three returning children created. Then came the issue of religion. Sidney, at age nine, was a devout Catholic. Betty, at ten, prayed assiduously as a Protestant, and Ada, who had no idea what she really was, was vocal about her confusion.

Overwhelmed by this chaos, the step-mother in frustration picked up a hammer and struck the table in front of her. "There will be no religious practice in this house until you are twenty-one," she decreed.

Ada's new life in Amsterdam was limp, unfriendly and full of reminders of all she had lost. Her father's sunken eyes made her wonder how the family would survive his grief. He had lost both his parents and seven of his ten siblings. For reasons beyond her understanding, her father wasn't in contact with those who had survived.

Ada missed her maternal grandmother. From bits and pieces of conversation she put together the sketchy story. Ada's grandparents had been hiding under the boards of their hair salon for nearly a year when the authorities came to search the salon. They must have received specific information that Jews were hiding beneath the floor because they went directly to the spot where Ada's grandparents were and lifted the boards. They were last seen in Sobibor. "She was a real grannie," Ada recalls today with a hint of tears clouding her voice. "She was such a sweet lady. How could anyone want to harm her?"

Adolescence was the hardest period in Ada's life. Each and every time she passed by the piano, her eyed burned from seeing the empty spot where her mother's picture used to stand. She requested time and again that her father put back the photo, but her step-mother would not hear of it, and her father lacked the energy to fight for his daughter's wish. Endless arguments ensued between the young woman and the stubborn step-mother who would not concede the slightest victory. When the step-mother ran out of arguments, she would hit Ada with the wicker rug beater. This humiliating practice stopped only when Ada left her father's house at the age of twenty-one. Everything was a potential source of struggle for the two of them. Every day brought either a new threat or the reiteration of old ones. Ada never stopped longing for the loving and nurturing times she had spent under the wings of the Hamstras. What hurt perhaps the most was her father's inability to stand up for his children. Ada was aching to hear him say to his wife just once: "Let those kids be. It was and is still hard for them."

But her hopes were forever frustrated. Maurits never seemed to notice the war between his wife and his children. He was busy with teaching piano. It was painful and infuriating for Ada to see how much time he spent with other people's children and how happy they made him, whereas for his own he had nothing but silence and tears. Whenever Ada looked at him, she was sure that something was troubling him. "And yet," she says with sadness in her eyes, "I know he loved us. But he loved us with a wounded heart in grief. He could never put himself beyond the loss of my mother. Thus, in reality, when the Germans took my mother, they took my father, too. Isn't it a bizarre twist of fate that I never felt so much an orphan as I did in my father's home?"

In fact, many hidden children shared Ada's fate, among them Aniko Berger. For some, it was easier to adapt to a new life when neither parent returned and the child settled into a loving foster or adoptive family than to live with the grief of a broken father or mother. He or she returned from one or another killing field captive to everything that had been lost. In a very real sense, it was up to the fragile children to heal their parents' wounds. And most of the time, the children rose to the occasion. Aniko, while still in the grip of her own memories of a recent ordeal, had to struggle with an emotionally broken mother. Ada's fate was similar and was exacerbated by her bitterness over having been torn from a happy life in the home of loving foster parents. Both ended up with a choiceless choice: If not I, then who will take care of my mom or my dad? What would happen to me if I didn't look after her or him?

Aniko and Ada found themselves in the predicament of all children who, in their early years, discover their parents' utter dependence on them. When they come to this realization, they do everything to make sure that their parents feel taken care of. Both these hidden children did their best to chase the dark clouds from their parent's soul. Their efforts were rewarded by meagre results — neither received any care in return. But sooner or later most children, including Aniko and Ada, discover that they can survive without their parents and that their parents can survive without them.

In 1957, it all came to a rapid end; Ada left the embattled continent, and with it, her father and his world. At the age of twenty-one, she decided to put an end to her hiding. Some Canadians encouraged her to come to Toronto. They claimed to know a couple of women there who had spent time with her mother in the medical block at Auschwitz. Upon her arrival, these two women came to meet her at Union Station. They did indeed recall Sara; she had been with them as part of Dr Mengele's diabolical experiments.

The news was devastating. Yet it gave Ada some concrete news about her mother's fate. And as the horror of the details began to fade, the irrevocable facts of her mother's demise allowed a healing process to begin.

Ada began to construct her life in earnest. Thanks to her knowledge of English, she found work and was soon married to the president of the establishment. He was Jewish, and Ada was propelled into liberal Judaism, including the learning of Hebrew and the observance of High Holidays. She devoted most of her time to her young son and to their adopted son. Life began to feel normal.

"Even my casual observance makes me feel connected to my murdered family, and they feel a little less dead," explains Ada.

After a crisis in her marriage, Ada found herself alone. As a consequence, all the anger that she had denied herself surged to the surface. For lack of an audience, she gave free rein to her rage, out loud, alone: I should be living in Holland, surrounded by a large and loving family. I should have grown up under my mother's wing. My son should have grandparents, uncles, aunts, cousins. Instead, all he has is a mother who's struggling to change who she is into who she is not because she no longer knows who she is. For goodness' sake, why did I have to have such a desolate life? What is going to become of us?

At the age of sixteen, her son decided to "search for his roots," and he moved to Holland. Ada made no effort to hold him back, but the familiar feelings of abandonment resurfaced.

But she still had her adopted son. Against all professional advice, when the boy manifested signs of mental illness and needed hospitalization, Ada kept him by her side. She and the boy won.

Despite her struggles with the past, Ada has carved for herself a life she considers good. Every morning she has her own radio show in Dutch. It allows her to stay in touch with the culture of her childhood, with people who benefit from the information she makes available to them. During the day, she works as a trustee in bankruptcy, helping people through one of the greatest hardships a person can experience. "I'm not a psychiatrist, but I tell you, I should be one," she says proudly. "They come to see me with disaster in their heart and I show them how they can actually survive it. In matters of survival, I've become some kind of an expert."

For the past three years, Ada has been closing one door after another that used to open on painful memories. In 1988, she participated in a ceremony, initiated by Ed van Thyn, the mayor of Amsterdam, one of the thirty-two children from the crèche taken to the holding place in Brunsum to honour the members of that heroic group. Ada was one of eleven hundred who came to honour all the foster parents and the resistance workers who linked the children to their future rescuers. Among them was Major-General Ted Meines, the NV Groep member who took charge of Ada for three weeks until the van Breugels emerged as her future foster parents. Ada did her best to make sure that not only Meines but also her two foster families were recognized by Yad Vashem, the Israeli war memorial and documentations authority, with the medal of the "Righteous among the Nations."

A couple of years later, Ada took it upon herself, with two Dutch Jewish friends, to raise funds to convert the site of the infamous Westerbork camp into a memorial park: each of the 102,000 Dutch Jews who had been transported from there to their deaths in Nazi camps were to be honoured with a stone. When Ada went to Westerbork in May 1992, she carried with her a cheque for $11,000. "It wasn't just a matter of contributing to the purchase of memorial stones," Ada explains. "Each stone was an opportunity for me, and for all Dutch Jewish survivors, to see their loved ones honoured. We need to bury our dead in the earth and with a stone so that we may also bury the pain in our heart."

Ada went to Westerbork with her sister Betty and two cousins. They participated in the ceremony and had an opportunity to find out finally what had happened to the members of their family who never returned from the darkness. They were able to see the official documentation of every Jew dispatched from Westerbork. Eight pages in the sorrowful book of departures were filled with the names of their family members, among them their mother and grandparents.

Ada finally saw with her own eyes what she had known all along in her soul. Some years prior, she had discovered a letter from the Red Cross, addressed to Maurits Moscoviter, informing him that his wife had been last seen in 1943 in Auschwitz. She found the note in the piano bench where her father hid all his important private papers. They never spoke about it because Maurits wanted to protect his children from the pain of digging up what they had known all along.

But that day in Westerbork, Ada saw it all. Her eyes were burning with dry tears. "Finally I saw it with my own eyes," she says. "Now they are really dead."

That day in Westerbork was the next-to-last day of the war for Ada. Four months later, she returned to Amsterdam to gather with hundreds of other Dutch hidden children. For many it was the first time they ever admitted to anyone, including their children, including themselves, that they belonged there: they were hidden children and they were survivors. Ada did not expect to stumble on any great discovery since she had been exploring her past for many years, but still she needed to be there.

"Crèche children, your pictures are here," she heard the announcement made. She went to see the pictures and she felt tremendously moved. Looking at the pictures, Ada could not believe how little she was and how much that little girl had endured.

There they were, all the crèche children in a book of pictures. Three of them showed Ada and her siblings. Those pictures brought back long-forgotten memories. She did not like to be reminded of those days. Once again, she felt the bitter anguish of waiting with Sidney and Betty to be adopted. For years she had not thought of those days. The pictures forced her back into that dark world. But when all was said and done, Ada was happy to have gone to the gathering and even to have seen the pictures. "I have survived. That is what I learned from those pictures and those people," she asserts.

Pierre, her companion for the past six "wonderfully happy" years, would have preferred it if she had not attended the gathering. He feared she would come back devastated. He was wrong. She returned stronger than ever, enriched not only with the feeling that finally the war was over for her but also with some powerful resolutions. "I have new priorities," Ada explains. "Like a typical hidden child, I have always put everyone before me, even people at my work who answer to me. Now, I want people to start doing things for me. I want them to put me first sometimes."

Ada's journey is now complete. She has learned to get rid of the various false selves and finally can live without masks. She no longer feels the insecurities of the abandoned child that led her to feel confused about just about everything and as if there were something wrong with her, as if she were abnormal. In Amsterdam she learned that most hidden children shared the experiences she had thought were her exclusive burden. Meeting other hidden children almost fifty years after the war finally convinced her that she was normal, that the insecurities she struggled with all her life were common to all hidden children. This realization finally freed her from the need for any kind of hiding. She was free.

She also learned, thanks to the excellent care she had received from her foster families, the value and commitment of reaching out to others. Like many of the hidden children portrayed in this volume, the acts of generosity extended to her as a child at a time when she felt worthless ("at age six you're worth nothing") inspired in her the natural urge to serve others.

P.S. Thanks to Ada's relentless efforts, in 1992, Ted Meines, Ali and Jerrit van Breugel and Anna and Peter Rombout were honoured posthumously by the State of Israel. As for Ada, for her countless acts of commitment and generosity, in March 1993, Her Majesty Beatrice, Queen of the Netherlands beknighted her with the Order of Oranje-Nassau.

5

✧✧✧

Don't Remember, Think!

The Story of
ERVIN STAUB

"My cousin Eva went to the neighbourhood bakery for some bread. She left home without her yellow star. Someone recognized her and identified her as a Jew. Three Nazi thugs followed her insisting on taking her away. Eva ran into our building. Her mother, my aunt Julia, was waiting for her under the doorway. She confronted them yelling at them whatever came to her mind. She must have somehow intimidated the threesome for they retreated, but not without uttering threats about coming back with the police.

"This is a very intense early memory for me. I was six years old."

Young Ervin Staub witnessed this altercation between the three fascist thugs and his aunt Julia from the mezzanine of the dark staircase just above the front gate of their apartment building in St Stephen's Town, a modern district of the bustling Pest side of the Hungarian capital, Budapest. Ervin remained silent and was relieved once the heated exchange subsided. He was scared: for himself and for his cousin, Eva, six years his senior. Ervin loved his three cousins who shared his life, but Eva was his favourite. She was playful with him and told him jokes.

And now she was in serious trouble. She went into the street without displaying the yellow star. Ervin knew that because they were Jews, the law said that they all, including the children, had to wear a yellow star on their chests. And he also knew that it was less and less possible for Jews, even the children, to appear in public. The Staub family, including Ervin and one-year-old Agi, and the Friedmans, Ervin's aunt, uncle and their three children — Eva, fifteen-year-old "Big" Ervin, and twelve-year-old Öcsi — observed the rituals and traditions of Orthodox Judaism. Ervin did not know why but he understood that laws existed against Jews just because they were Jewish.

The five cousins were more like brothers and sisters. The adults spent most of their time and energy on the family business, and the children were cared for mostly by Macs, the maid. Like boys his age anywhere, he and his cousins and other children orchestrated many pranks. One day, they filled a large sack with all sorts of junk and tossed it over the banister on the fourth floor and screamed: "Someone fell, someone fell!" But as the laws restricted their freedom more and more, to their neighbours' displeasure, they played inside the courtyard surrounded by ground-floor apartments.

At night, when the parents huddled around the kitchen table, the younger children were sent to bed in the large living-room. Macs, after her long day of looking after two families, would tell the children stories. When she would doze off, Ervin would wake her and she would continue her story.

"One of my earliest recollections has to do with the coal merchant from across the street," Ervin reports. "He used to sit by the door of his basement store and wait for the Jews to pass by so that he could shower them in scathing invectives. All of us Jewish kids shivered every time we laid eyes on him. When he realized that Jews crossed to the other sidewalk to avoid being abused by him, he would venture out and take his venom to them. One day, he came inside the courtyard of our building to scream threats at the Jews. My fifteen-year-old cousin began to organize the Jewish kids of the building for self-defence.

"'We will protect ourselves,' Big Ervin taught us. 'No one is going to hurt us with impunity.'"

One night, his beloved uncle Lajos came to hug him in bed and say goodbye. First, Ervin felt sad because his uncle was leaving him. He had been sent to a forced labour camp. The boy went to sleep with a heavy heart.

The next morning he woke to the sounds of crying from the other room. He joined the others. In spite of the early hour, everyone was already up. When Uncle Lajos crossed their threshold, adults and children were in tears.

Shortly after this, the authorities came for all the young boys over the age of fourteen. They were to assemble in the courtyard. Big Ervin was about to obey the orders when his mother told him to go inside and stay there. Overwhelmed by the conflict between the authorities and his mother, the boy resisted. Finally she slapped him across the face and shoved him inside the apartment. "The others were marched off, never to be heard from again." says Ervin. "With her usual assertiveness, she saved my cousin's life."

On March 19, 1944, Macs took Ervin and his little sister, Agi, on a stroll along nearby Szent Istvàn Körut (St Stephen Boulevard). Suddenly, a column of soldiers on trucks, motorcycles and armoured vehicles rolled towards them. Macs froze in her tracks, holding Ervin's hand tightly. Nothing else happened, but Macs's terror had conveyed itself to Ervin. He was scared, but there was nothing anyone could do or say.

This was the first of many occasions when Ervin, like so many children all over Nazi-occupied Europe, felt resourceless. There was no use complaining to their parents; they had no answers to help disperse the menace. Most of the time, they seemed preoccupied, too. Much of the time, trying to spare the children from useless worry, they whispered. On occasions when they expressed their anxiety, Ervin sensed that the adults in his family were unable to chase away the clouds of danger; they could not guarantee the safety of his life.

"Can a retreat from pain in early childhood carry the seeds of a life without memories of those tender years?" muses Dr Ervin Staub, now a professor of social psychology at the University of Massachusetts, at Amherst. "Those fears could remain hidden even to the self, until one learns — one way or another — that it's safe to attend to them."

By April 1944, the family's business had to be closed down. Suddenly, the adults were home all the time. Rather than feeling more secure, he was exposed more often to their concerns and anxieties. They made less and less effort to hide from their children how badly off they were. It was clear to Ervin that they were in grave danger.

"Over the years I have been trying to re-experience those feelings, but they kept eluding me. I was cut off from most of my memories, and from reliving the anxiety of that time. Now, as I'm talking about it, I have a touch of anxiety."

His parents' presence allowed Ervin to get to know them better. His aunt dealt with the conflicts and crises, and his uncle played the role of the father in the family. Ervin's own father was a more shadowy person. But he was more playful with the younger children. Ervin's mother was either too busy or preoccupied and would only occasionally approach her children in a physically affectionate way. "The affection and care I was receiving from Macs was, therefore, especially welcome."

The Staubs' home had always been animated by prayer. Even during the worst of times, they stopped to commemorate the Sabbath by lighting a candle and saying a blessing. Uncle Lajos was even more zealous than Ervin's father, and he officiated at these private services until the day he had to report for forced labour. When Ervin's father got his walking papers, Ervin's mother took over the role of the spiritual leader. All the adult members of the family observed the dietary laws of *kashrut* (eating only kosher food), but, at the end of the war, the children were allowed to eat whatever the adults could find to put in front of them.

It was not long before the Jewish population of the city was concentrated into buildings designated as "Jewish houses" and marked by a large yellow star on the front gate. Ervin's building was one of them.

The nightly bombings by the Allied air forces forced most of the city's population down to the cellars. Since the bombing raids occurred mainly during the night, many children were carried down to the cellar. Deep in the sleep of the innocent, many of them didn't awaken until the morning. Ervin was not one of them. Half asleep, he walked with the others into the dark cellar. A vague candle-light made the tired and apprehensive people sitting in their coats over their night-clothes look like silent shadows.

During one of those air raids, a bomb fell right in front of their building. The explosion shook the structure to its foundation. The detonation rattled those in hiding below. After the all-clear was sounded, they went upstairs. The bomb had cut a deep crater in the pavement in front of the Staubs' window reducing their furniture to rubble.

Ervin remembers another time when the men of the Arrow Cross, the Hungarian fascist militia, came to search the premises. "I broke into tears," Ervins recounts.

One of the men asked Ervin why he was crying. When the boy told him that he was scared they would take his family, the man promised him that nothing would happen to them.

As the number of restrictive measures against the Jews increased, Ervin's parents and his aunt spoke all the time of imminent deportations. They decided that the children had to be moved out of the Jewish house.

One morning, amid tears and hurried farewells, Macs ushered Ervin and Agi out of their branded building towards the home of a Christian family. After what seemed to the children an endless march, they arrived in a part of Pest they had never set foot in before.

They entered a cluttered doorway and climbed the steep steps to the fourth floor. They were received by strangers. "I remember nothing about the time I spent with those people," Ervin states in a voice darkened with regret. "Not a face, not a voice, not a piece of furniture. As if the time I spent there had been a time out of my life."

Ervin does not remember how much time passed before Macs returned. She had received word from the family who had taken in Ervin and Agi that some neighbours had seen the children enter the house but no one saw them leave. The family thought it was best to move the children to another hiding place.

This time, it took just a few minutes to reach their destination. The building was nearly a carbon copy of their previous hiding place.

Shortly after this, Ervin's family managed to obtain a sufficient number of the much-sought-after Swedish letters of protection, and Ervin and his sister returned to their home.

The letter of protection was the ingenious invention of Raoul Wallenberg, scion of a Swedish banking family, who went to Budapest with the sole purpose of saving Jews. He issued spurious Swedish documents, which claimed that the carrier enjoyed the protection extended to all Swedish citizens. For some mysterious reason, the Nazis were willing to tolerate these letters for a while. Wallenberg had purchased a number of apartment buildings very close to Ervin's home. Those buildings were designated as "protected houses." When, towards the end of November 1944, the central ghetto was inaugurated, Jews in possession of these letters of protection were allowed to relocate in the protected houses instead of filing into the ghetto.

When they got their order to leave the building, the Staubs loaded a few belongings on a cart Macs had managed to locate. When the time came to abandon their home, they looked back with sadness. None of them said a word.

In spite of the curfew, they set out through the streets under the cloak of darkness. The distance they had to travel was only four city blocks but it was fraught with danger. There could have been an air raid; they could have run into a roving guard unit or, for that matter, anyone with an anti-Semitic penchant. It would be obvious to anyone that they were going into hiding.

At one point, they were stopped by some civilians who had no obvious authority, but in those days anyone with any design on the Jews could act with impunity. After a few minutes of interrogation, the family was allowed to proceed. Shortly after, they reached the protected house without further incident.

"I feel anxious as I think back to this whole period," Ervin says. "Back then the anxiety was always diffused because you were always in danger. But now, some of my feelings of distress have to do with remembering so little. Obviously, it was my life, and all I can come up with is flashes. What is missing? And why can't I conjure up those memories? I am staring into darkness with occasional flashes of light allowing me to unearth bits and pieces of life."

This emotional response to the turbulence of hiding days is a relatively new experience for Ervin Staub. He used to cope with the torments of the war by imposing an intellectual distance. He did his best to keep the topic alive in his research and teaching activities and to look at the facts with academic detachment. By using his intellect to make sense of the betrayal of his youth, he was continuing the hiding for as long as he felt the need.

Life in the protected house was not kind to children. They had one small room to shelter the seven of them, in addition to a sick old lady — the original tenant in the apartment — who was bedridden. They could not leave the building, and there was no courtyard where the children could play.

Once again, Macs proved to be a life-saver. Since she was not about to abandon her "family," she moved into the protected house with them. But being Christian she was able to come and go. She would scour the city for food. Somehow she managed to find flour that she made into dough. She took the dough to the baker in a baby carriage and came back with the bread.

Once she was stopped by the Arrow Cross militia. What was she doing with all that bread? Where did she get it and where was she taking it? they asked. Then they made her stand against the wall with her hands up in the air. At any moment they could have shot her. After hours of this torment, they let her go but they kept the bread. Since she had no bread for all those hungry people, what else could she do but start all over again? That time she returned with a buggy full of fresh bread.

"When I talk about her," Ervin says, "tears come to my eyes. I attribute a lot of the work I have done on helpful, altruistic behaviour to her. She was a concrete presence of goodness in my life. I now know that many domestics helped their former Jewish employers. And many betrayed them. But Macs was not about to leave us to our fate."

One day, to everyone's great joy, Ervin's father Jòzsef showed up at the door. In an act of extreme bravery that stunned his family, he had escaped from his forced labour unit on a stopover in Budapest, en route to Germany. At the protected house where his family was hiding, he enjoyed a second stroke of good fortune: the superintendent of the building, a Christian, took pity on him and allowed him to come in.

Once again, it was Macs who had helped. Unbeknownst to Ervin, she had taken the train to his father's labour camp in the country and given him one of the letters of protection. "According to my mother," Ervin says, "even though those letters were worthless for men, it gave my father the courage to escape.

Whether or not that was the case, he did escape. And he was the only survivor of that group. I was not only happy to have my dad back, I was also very proud of him. He hid with us for the rest of the occupation."

As the war drew to an end, the bombing and shelling became heavier. There came a time at the end of December 1944 and January 1945 when they began to spend much of their time in the cellar to take shelter from the constant barrage of explosives. The residents of the building lived on mattresses that covered the overcrowded cellar. But except for minor altercations caused by forced proximity and anguish, people did not complain about the living conditions.

Ervin was sick for a couple of weeks and had to stay in the cellar, lying on his mattress. To pass time, his father taught him poems, encouraging him to recite them for the benefit of the residents. This connection to his father is one of the rare pleasant memories Ervin recalls from that time.

The authorities made several raids on the building looking for hidden Jews. For those occasions, Ervin's mother devised a plan. Should anyone come snooping around, her husband was to sit in a corner behind a huge armchair. And she would cover the chair with a blanket.

Indeed, one day, after he had recovered from his illness, standing at the window of their room, Ervin noticed a group of Arrow Cross men marching in the street. His intuition told him that they were coming for them. He shouted to alert everyone and ran to the door to see if he was right. By the time he opened the door, the men were inside the building.

There was no time to waste. Ervin's father hid behind the armchair. Then his wife pushed it right on top of him and covered it with the blanket. Within minutes, the search party rang the bell. They checked every possible hiding place, except behind the armchair. They left empty-handed.

The Staubs were safe that time, but next time would not necessarily go as well. Many of the protected houses were raided; the authorities dragged the Jews down to the lower quay and shot them into the Danube. Now and then, someone was taken away from Ervin's building, but there were no mass round-ups. The Staubs' room was searched a couple of times more, but the fugitive was never found.

In the middle of January, Ervin spied men in uniforms. Weapons in hand, they were running from doorway to doorway. The boy realized that they looked different. He called his father to the window. Having been a prisoner of war for eighteen months after World War I in Russia, he immediately identified the men as members of the Red Army coming to rid the city of its German oppressors.

The next day, they were liberated. Everybody wanted to be in the street, to breathe the free air and to stretch their legs numbed by months of huddling in dampness. And they all wanted to touch their liberators. Outside Ervin's hiding place there was a Russian tank and lots of soldiers.

Ervin wanted to join the crowd, so Macs wrapped him in a blanket to protect his frail body from the bite of the January cold, and she carried him outside. When a soldier saw the pale young-ster all bundled up, he reached into his pocket and gave the boy some candy.

Following liberation, chaos dominated the commercial districts of Pest. Ervin's cousins joined the crowds. They went to see what was left of the city and to search for food. Store windows every-where were broken, and the merchandise taken. Ervin was envious of his cousins. He wanted to go with them, but his parents did not let him.

The Staubs walked over to Visegràdi Street to see their old flat. The place had been used as headquarters, first by the Germans, then by the Russians, who had brought their horses into the apart-ment. The bath tub was filled with human and horse feces. There were grooves on the wooden floor from the hooves. And yet no one shed too many tears over the destruction. What they had just survived afforded them a new perspective.

Then they went to see the store on Szent Istvàn Körut. A pile of bricks covered the front. Ervin and the others began to clear them away to gain access to the door, but it proved to be too much for their emaciated bodies.

Soon life began to return to the city still reeling from the blows it had sustained during the winter months. Like many other mer-chants, the Staubs reopened their store. The first time Ervin was allowed to walk home alone on the boulevard, he walked by a group of boys his own age. They began to shout at him, "Dirty

Jew." "I felt helpless and degraded."

Just before the end of January, right next to the Staubs' apartment, two women opened a school in their own home. Ervin was happy to start school. It was a sign that he could return to being a child. He completed the year in that makeshift school. By the time next September rolled around, he was enrolled in a Jewish school two blocks away. There he lived the life of a normal child — learning, playing, fighting. He stayed there until the end of Grade 5 when the Communist authorities closed down all religious schools. He had no choice but to register in a public school.

The children brought to school their parents' anti-Semitism. Although he was not the only Jewish child in his class, he alone sported a cap. Furthermore, his parents arranged with the school that Ervin not have to write on Saturdays. He felt singled out and self-conscious.

After a while, the children got used to each other, and their differences faded into the background. Most of the time it did not matter that many of the Christian children were from working-class families and Ervin was middle-class, by background if not by wealth; it mattered little that he was Jewish and they were not. However, there was a fair bit of ambivalence in their friendship — sometimes they got along well; at other times, they were hostile.

One day, Ervin got into a fight with one of the Christian boys. When it looked as if Ervin was going to beat him, another Christian boy joined in. Now there were two against one.

"A Jewish kid came to my help (although at that time I didn't think of his Jewishness). I was moved by his intervention. It felt terrific to have someone to fight on my side. Now the sides were even. Later, Pali, the boy who came to fight on my side, became my lifelong friend."

Although Pali saved that day for Ervin, in retrospect it is clear that even though the overt hostilities that threatened Jewish children during the war were behind them, these child survivors were far from safe or carefree. Anti-Semitic sentiments often died hard during the post-war period, especially in Soviet-bloc countries. Furthermore, as we learned from Aniko and Ada, there were hardships to face at home when only one of the parents returned from deportation. Ervin's story, on the other hand, shows that even for those children who went into hiding with their parents, the post-war turmoil sometimes brought the abandonment other children faced during the war.

Like many other Jewish youngsters, Ervin's three cousins became involved in the Zionist movement. It linked them not only to a young secular community but also to the new state of Israel. Since the new communist government made it illegal to leave the country, the Zionists formed an underground railroad to help Jewish children escape from Hungary. The cousins spent more time with the Zionists, leaving Ervin to his own resources. With the adults in the household too preoccupied putting their losses behind them and making a living, the absence of his cousins from his daily life was a loss of his own. The three of them left the country. Without intending to do so, they abandoned Ervin.

"I went through an experience of abandonment," Ervin says as he thinks back. "I've never dealt with this feeling of abandonment. It surprises me now."

Was it only a matter of abandonment? Or was it related to some awareness that they were taking charge of their lives while Ervin had no choice but to remain passive?

Ervin greatly admired his mother for her courage and strength in leading the family. And he discovered that he had other reasons for admiring her. She did her best to help people in various ways. If it was her attention they needed, she gave it with good heart. If it was money, her purse was always open. On one occasion a woman desperately needed some money but Mrs Staub did not have any to give. Instead, she gave the woman some gold to sell. For reasons that remain unclear, the woman ended up denouncing her benefactor to the police. (In those days it was illegal to sell gold privately.) Ervin's mother was arrested and sentenced to prison. Having decided that she could not survive life behind bars, she went into hiding, going from family to family. Once again, she was in the hands of brave, benevolent people who put their freedom on the line for her. And once again Ervin was abandoned.

Occasionally, his mother would come by and call from the street for Ervin to come downstairs. On a couple of occasions, she took him to her hiding place. Ervin was happy to spend time with his mother, yet he worried: what if they had been followed? What if someone reported them? These visits brought back the not-too-distant memories of another time when to survive they had to hide from the eyes of the hunter. In order to minimize the risk of being followed on his trips to his mother's hiding place, the boy would run after a fast-moving streetcar and jump on its steps. It felt good to Ervin to take some responsibility for what was going to happen rather than just waiting for his fate.

Without actually articulating it, Ervin and children in his predicament had to revise their notion of a parent's role; in addition to being the source and guarantor of life, the parent was the potential instrument of peril. It was not unusual for such children to remain ambivalent towards their parents and never feel fully attached to them or that it was safe to trust them. (Later in life, when they became parents, they tended to remain somewhat aloof from their children, and stayed that way unless they experienced an emotionally significant event that inspired them to remedy the situation. While Ervin was always very affectionate with his children, initially he also felt a barrier to real intimacy. His own research and writing as a psychologist helped him become aware of this and consciously strive to overcome it.) They seldom experienced the spontaneous self-abandonment of children. Since their parents had abandoned them, someone had to be vigilant to assure their safety and security. In other words, it became clear to many that they could neither rely on nor trust their parents. Often, the children themselves had to assume that responsibility. At the age of fifteen, Ervin quickly learned this fact. The revelation filled him with a paradoxical sense of anguished importance.

In fact, Ervin's precautions were justified; the authorities were following him very closely. One day, on the High Holidays, a stranger stopped by, looking for Ròzsa Staub. Ervin told him that his mother was praying at a synagogue. The man — most likely a detective — took the boy with him to the synagogue in question. They went upstairs to the women's section, and the man asked Ervin to point out his mother. Indeed, she was sitting there, praying. Without flinching, Ervin told the man that his mother was not among the worshippers. With his fast thinking and his courage, he saved his mother from a hefty prison sentence.

By that time, the principal presence in the growing boy's life was his friends. Many orphaned child survivors of the Nazi débâcle filled the void by creating their own family and investing themselves, body and soul, in a relationship with a few select friends. Although both Ervin's parents were alive, and he knew they loved him and cared about his welfare, there was little sharing of feelings and therefore little intimacy in his family. Thus, the group took on the contours of the family.

One of the many losses Ervin had sustained as a consequence of the Nazis' war against Jewish children was his faith. His family's commitment to their religion had not been shaken by their ordeals. On the contrary, as soon as they returned, they founded a synagogue next door to their apartment. Its popularity among the emotionally and physically battered survivors was instantaneous: it was a safe place for confronting one's losses.

Ervin attended services but without fervor. His attendance was more a matter of being a proper son to his parents than of devotion.

Then, while in the sixth grade, he overheard a conversation between a Jewish boy and a Christian friend. The former, keen on appearing more mature than his years, claimed to have had sex with his family's maid. But, no, he was not worried about divine retribution because he did not believe that God existed in the first place. The Christian boy was stunned: how could he say God did not exist?

Ervin admitted to himself that he agreed with the Jewish boy. Yet he continued to go to temple every week — mostly on Friday nights and not on Saturday morning, when he preferred to sleep in. But rather than surrender himself to the sweet mysteries of prayer, he scanned the small temple unable to believe that what he saw around him was authentic religious devotion.

In order to protect his parents from painful disappointment, Ervin tried to keep up appearances. He slipped further and further away from religious observance, but he felt no shame for it. As soon as he was out of sight of his parents, he took off his cap. In later years, he spoke of believing in God with a cynicism that stunned even Pali, a Jew with free-thinking parents. He was concerned about Ervin's blasphemy.

Ervin was not alone among hidden children in confronting God and demanding that He account for the horrible fate of the Jews. Many of them turned away from God. Some, like Ervin, had come to the only tolerable conclusion: an abandoning God is no God at all; therefore, the fate of the Jewish people proves the non-existence of God. Others asserted their atheism as an alternative to the rage they had to contain in their silent exile.

Ervin, the atheist, has discovered a wholly human version of spirituality that links him to people rather than to a supreme being. Other hidden children whose psychological means do not allow any spirituality tend to find themselves profoundly alone. For them, shame takes precedence over human connections. For these people, among them Dr Aniko Berger, the hiding continues in such a profound manner that they are unable to contemplate their stories, let alone go public with them. Aniko is adamantly anti-religious and a self-confirmed atheist. She, like many others, agreed to reveal her account of abandonment and betrayal only from the shelter of a pseudonym. Others categorically refuse to tell their stories. In a very real sense, for most of them, the hiding has led to a severing of all ties to their faith. But Ervin reconnected, perhaps not with his faith, but with other Jews. As his older child was about to enter school he got strongly involved with the Jewish community in his town, chairing its "social concerns" committee and in other ways.

In November 1956, like so many thousands of young people, Ervin and his friend Pali escaped to the West. First they stayed in Vienna, where they undertook university studies. About three years later, Ervin decided to explore the New World. Pali, years later, returned to Budapest.

"It was exciting to start a genuinely new life," Ervin explains. "I succeeded in arranging my admission to university. I was a good student. I worked to cover my expenses. It was great to be an agent of my studies, taking exams, learning and knowing something. And for the first time, I knew not only what I was doing but also why I was doing it. In leaving first Hungary and the language in which I had sustained all the losses of my childhood, and in a larger perspective, Europe, the theatre of all those losses, I began to view myself surrounded by light rather than by the darkness that has been with me ever since my life in the cellar. I finally began to understand what it meant that I had been liberated."

In 1959, Ervin Staub started a new life in Minnesota. He finished his undergraduate work as a Phi Beta Kappa and magna cum laude.

Most importantly, he was accepted to both Harvard and Stanford to undertake advanced studies in psychology.

"Later," Ervin remarks, "well settled in my life in the United States, I tended to tell people that I was Hungarian. It took me years to say, 'I'm from Hungary, but I am Jewish.'"

Upon completing his doctorate in psychology at Stanford University, Ervin Staub was offered a position in the psychology department of Harvard University. During his first academic year at Harvard, in 1966, Ervin met Sylvia. From the very beginning of their relationship, she, an American-born Jew, thought of Ervin, to his great discomfort, as a Holocaust survivor. No matter how far he went from the cellars of his childhood, they managed to reach across the ocean and stretch across his life.

Being labelled a Holocaust survivor was a new experience for Ervin. He had not been in a camp. For most people, Christians and Jews, it was not so clear in those days who was and who was not a Holocaust survivor. But Sylvia cut through the defences of the hidden child and delved right into his pains and losses. Ervin did what comes naturally to most hidden children when light is shed on their well-camouflaged darkness: the more she probed, the further he held the whole issue from himself.

"I was not going to allow myself to be identified as a victim, or as a survivor," Ervin recalls. "If I was ever to discover and embrace my identity as a hidden child, it had to be on my schedule."

Shortly after, having become a U.S. citizen, Ervin went back to Budapest for the first time. He was eager to see his family after all that time. He saw his friends and family, but he was not yet emotionally integrated to his past. "It's not that my heart wasn't open to them," Ervin explains. "I just wasn't conscious of their suffering. I didn't hold my life and theirs in such a way that I could really understand the sadness and the tragedy of their lives."

On that trip, Ervin also discovered the fate of his sister, Agi. "I abandoned her with my old parents and Macs," Ervin remembers, "and no connection to other resources. She was a pretty young woman, and yet, because of her near-sightedness, she looked awkward and unsure of herself. Although she was very young at the time, all the tragedy that followed her later in life had to be at least in part the consequences of her early traumas during the war. I didn't realize how devoted she was to me. Years later, during a psychotic episode of her manic-depressive illness, I learned that she felt abandoned, and of the sadness and anger she had kept bottled up inside herself. My leaving created an even greater void in her life than my cousins' departure had created in mine. Oh, I just was not aware of how much pain we were all lugging around. When I put it all together, much later, I felt guilty about leaving my sister behind. It was not within my parents' psychological options to come with me in 1956. Nor could I have taken thirteen-year-old Agi with me into the unknown. And for me to stay behind would have been tragic. I acted unconsciously at eighteen years of age but now feel great sadness, realizing how difficult life was for the family I left behind."

In September 1967, Ervin and Sylvia were married. He was very happy when Adrian and Daniel were born; Ervin realized how much being a father contributed to making his life complete.

In 1970, Ervin's sister came to the U.S. She stayed half a year. "I kept going back to Hungary," Ervin says quietly, "most of the time for reasons of illness and death. I was there several times while my sister was in and out of hospitals. I went in '73 when she died [she committed suicide], in '74 when my father died, and in '75 when my mother died. The only living connections I had left were Macs and Pali."

Ervin did not forget everything that Macs had meant to him and to his entire family. When his parents died, Ervin made sure that she would continue to live comfortably. Since she had joined the Communist Party, Ervin called up the party secretary to remind him of Macs's devotion and service to the party. As a result of his intervention, they set her up with a suitable living arrangement. Ervin also asked Pali's mother to keep an eye on the aging Macs. When his mother died, Pali looked after Macs as if he had been her son. Ervin felt somewhat relieved to know that he had been instrumental in making sure that this woman, who had devoted so much of her life to him and to others, was not left helpless in her declining days.

"I did very little," he says, "considering what she did for us. She was my second mother and I experienced with her closeness, affection and kindness."

Although Macs risked her life for the Staub family, Ervin's mother had not trusted her. "I know that my mother loved Macs,"

Ervin recalls. "But she experienced too much pain at the hands of Christians to trust even her. What a tragedy." During his entire childhood, Ervin felt stuck between his mother's suspicions and his own affection for Macs. She was a loving presence in his life, and he was not supposed to love her. He had to navigate the murky waters of split loyalties, an experience that may have affected him for the rest of his life. "I rarely experienced being in love with a woman. I had affectionate relationships, caring ones, but to truly love a woman was difficult. Perhaps because the woman who loved me, cared about me and saved my life, and whom I loved, I wasn't allowed to love. I was loyal to her, I cared for her and I tried to defend her to my mother. I told my mother she was wrong, but I couldn't convince her."

Almost every year, Ervin went to see Macs. The last time, in the winter of 1990, she was old and sick, and he was worried about her. Indeed, she died during his visit. After all the times she had held his hand to help him through rough moments, it was a solace for Ervin to hold her hand during her final hour. He felt he had paid a tiny portion of his debt to this woman who during the war meant the difference between life and death.

Macs's commitment to others had a profound effect on Ervin Staub. He needed to understand what would make one person stand up for another while most people remain idle and unmoved. He has dedicated much of his academic career to studying the human potential for helpfulness, generosity, altruism and social conscience. His commitment has been so fervent that his friends have told him in recent years that, in spite of his repudiation of all faiths, they found a religious side to him. "I suppose people consider my belief concerning caring about others and loving all of humanity as spiritual," Ervin Staub explains. "They can be seen as social consciousness, but why should I be socially conscious if not to go beyond myself? I want to, I need to transcend my concerns with myself, my own body and even concerns with my own feelings and needs. Transcendence of the self is spiritual."

"I can't say that my budding spirituality has resolved the pain of my childhood. But when I lecture on this topic, on creative caring and the origins of altruism, people often ask me, 'Where does your optimism come from?' I can't help but think that I must have survived for a purpose and that purpose is to search for alternatives to destruction. Having spent countless hours thinking about this topic, I am heartened by my conclusion that people can be taught to live together and they can be of real service to each other instead of killing and torturing.

"So I'm doing this kind of work to help prevent future Holocausts. My commitment to this work has definitely strengthened me. I came away from those experiences of abandonment and betrayal to do my share of the work. Some Holocaust survivors keep saying that what happened to them should never again happen to Jews. And I am doing my modest part to prevent this kind of thing from ever happening to anyone at all."

In the late seventies he discovered in himself an urge to unearth the roots of evil. The intensity of the compulsion mystified him. But it also had meaning and purpose for him. It seemed to be the missing link, very much a part of his personal journey. Out of that compulsion came a book, *The Roots of Evil*, about the psychological and cultural roots of genocide; about how genocides are perpetrated and what to do to prevent them. In *The Roots of Evil*, Ervin Staub did not deal directly with his own hidden childhood, and yet it has allowed him to do something significant in relation to it. In his own way, he has paid a debt for his survival. The book goes beyond his own story, without negating it. Cambodia and the disappearances in Argentina are not his story, and they are his story. "They are my story," Dr Staub states emphatically. "We all share the same humanness and by writing *The Roots of Evil* I proved to the Nazis that I've shed the shadows of hiding, that I am alive, that they didn't get me." The book was also very meaningful to Ervin because through it, and through his concern about genocide, he became connected to groups of people who had been victims of genocide. This has been another avenue for him to reconnect with Jews and Jewish communities.

Shortly after attending the First International Gathering of Hidden Children in May 1991, Ervin sat in his cozy living-room in Amherst to tell his story. At first his memory was shaky, but the more he abandoned himself to the past, the more readily long-neglected memories began to show up. From one telling to the next, new details became available to him, dragging into the foreground hitherto unasked questions. The process of telling the story time after time has proven to be a remarkably efficient weapon in the war against amnesia. Ervin's struggle with the second loss of much of his childhood, due to the absence of actively available memories, this time allows for a measure of optimism. The more he told, the more he remembered; the less he hid, the more he saw. Telling his story may well be the road that leads to mastery over the silence of memories.

6

The Necessity and the Impossibility of Forgetting

The Story of
RUTH KRON SIGAL

"After liberation, my mother would come to see me where I was hiding, but I was not happy to see her: she was Jewish. It was dangerous for me to recognize her as my mother because that meant I was Jewish, too. And to be Jewish meant death. And yet I was happy to see her, to know that she was alive, to see how beautiful she was, to know that she was my mother. Liberation was a very confusing experience for me, indeed.

"To make life easier, I talked to God a lot, not to the God of Israel, but to the Christian God. I spoke to Him often, mostly about how I had let down my little sister, Tamara."

Those bewildering days are still vivid in Ruth Kron Sigal's memory. The eight-year-old girl on the outskirts of Shavli did not feel any freer with the arrival of the Soviet Red Army than she had under Nazi rule. She had seen what the Germans and the Lithuanians had done to the Jews. Now, day after day, she heard from Ona and Antanas Regauski, her rescuers, that the Russians ripped the tongues out of children's mouths.

Life was not always so confusing for Ruth. For seven years, she had been surrounded by a large family numbering in the dozens. The Kron family lived in a red-brick fourplex, sharing the second floor with Ruth's paternal grandparents. Her father, Meyer Kron, a prominent chemical engineer, head of an important tannery in Shavli, and her mother, Gita Schifman, a trial lawyer, provided for her comfort, security and all the luxuries available to a child in the late 1930s in a provincial Lithuanian town, about four hours from Kaunas. She had a nanny from whom she learned to speak Russian. For three years, she had her mother all to herself. Gita dressed her little girl in furs and lace. She took her to the finest cafés and restaurants in town, treating her little "queen" to cakes and chocolates and everything her heart desired. On holidays, they took her to their grandparents' farm not far from town or to Riga, to the family *dacha* (summer residence). In the winter, Gita and Ruth would skate on the ice just around the corner from their house. Everyone — parents, grandparents, aunts and uncles — doted on their little "queen." Ruth lapped it all up — there was no doubt about it: she felt special.

Then, in 1939, her sister Tamara was born. Ruth felt evicted from heaven. Not only did her mother have less time to devote to her, but two weeks after the baby's birth, Gita contracted a serious illness that led to a thrombosis. Her condition was quite alarming. First they tried to cure her with leeches. Ruth was terrified to see her mother with those horrible creatures on her creamy white skin. Gita had to stay in bed, nearly immobile, for five months. That was the first abandonment in Ruth's young life.

The same year, the Nazi menace became a reality for the Jews. After invading Austria and Czechoslovakia the year before, Hitler had declared war on Poland. German troops crossed the border on September 1. Although it would be another two years before Ruth saw German troops in her town, the aggression against Poland was felt as a direct threat in every Jewish household all over Europe.

Ruth heard the adults speak more and more often about what the Germans were doing and how they should all get out of the country before the Germans' arrival in Shavli. The Krons were fortunate enough to have a large family in the United States who did whatever was necessary to provide them with immigration papers. But they were not permitted to enter the United States: the quotas were filled.

Little by little, there were more signs of troubled times ahead. Everyone was worried about the consequences of the non-aggression pact Hitler and Stalin signed. It allowed Hitler full freedom to do whatever he wanted, with the Soviet Union supplying him with whatever he needed. But the Russians, not trusting the longevity of the pact, kept increasing the number of troops stationed in Lithuania. Ruth grew accustomed to seeing camouflaged tanks and artillery all over town. While the young child went on with the business of her tender years, even she could not fail to notice how tense everyone around her had become.

"Still, our lives continued on their regular tracks, most of the time," recalls Ruth Kron Sigal, director of the University of British Columbia's Women's Resource Centre, Vancouver. "As long as we weren't directly affected, we felt quite safe. Some Jews left everything behind, but most of us stayed. There were still dances, as before, but no one noticed that they were dancing on a sinking ship."

Life continued in this vein until the middle of June 1940. While on a pleasant outing in a café, Ruth and her mother heard on the radio that the Red Army had peacefully crossed Lithuania's border. President Smetona quietly fled the country. In a mockery of an election, 99 percent of the Lithuanian people voted to become a Soviet socialist republic.

When the Red Army occupied Shavli, some of its citizens welcomed them with flowers, but others secretly prayed for the Germans to violate the agreement and liberate them from the Communist occupation.

Then, after a year of relative calm in Shavli, without any warning the Soviets arrested many people — entire families, Jews and non-Jews, rich and poor, professionals and prostitutes. Soviet soldiers yanked them out of their homes without explanation. They were driven to cattle wagons that, in the middle of the night, took them to an unknown destination. This went on for several days, apparently in all the three Baltic states. Although the Krons were not among those arrested, they had their necessities all packed. They were ready.

"The Lithuanians blamed everything on us Jews," Ruth explains. "They accused us of provoking the Russians, even though there were many Jews among the disappeared. Some Lithuanians still believe that the Soviet occupation was the Jews' fault."

A week later, Gita was about to take the girls on a picnic, when she heard on the radio that Germany had attacked the Soviet Union. She woke up Meyer, but he did not believe her and went back to sleep. A little later, a bomb exploded a couple of blocks away. He did not need any further proof. Pandemonium and panic broke out in the streets. Only a few bombs had been dropped, but it was sufficient for the townsfolk to take matters seriously.

Everyone prepared for the impending arrival of the Germans. There were endless lines in front of bakeries and grocery stores. Except for the Communists, few people felt the need to flee from the Germans. Ruth's father, however, had been boycotting German products for use in the tannery ever since Hitler had come to power. So without wasting time, he loaded the horse-drawn wagon he got from Gita's father with all kinds of household goods. Perched in the middle were Grandmother, the nanny, Ruth and Tamara. The poor horse could hardly move with all that load. Gita and Meyer walked behind.

They headed towards Latvia, with the Germans behind them. They had lots of company: in addition to Soviet military vehicles, the road was jammed with private citizens, no longer just the Communists, fleeing the invaders.

"It is amazing how inexperienced we were," wrote Meyer Kron in his unpublished memoirs. "Instead of all of us sitting in the wagon and getting rid of the goods, we couldn't part with these things."

As they moved along the road at a snail's pace, the Krons noticed that the soldiers had disappeared from the main route and now were hiding in the ditches. The Krons turned off into a field towards a barn. Suddenly, they froze in their tracks: the Germans' stuka planes were just ahead. One of them split from the squadron and rushed towards them. They all lay down in the field and covered their heads, except Meyer; he was stunned by the ominous spectacle.

"I saw a plane coming directly toward us," he wrote, "and when I lifted my eyes vertically I saw its bombs dropping directly at us. I was sure that these were the last moments of our lives. It turned out that the bombs flew not vertically, but in a curve and they missed us and dropped on the highway crowded with the fleeing refugees. A lot of people were killed. A terrible panic broke out in the area."

They continued on the country road, but when they learned that Lithuanian partisans wearing white arm bands were killing every Jew they found on the road, the Krons decided to go home.

Only two days after their departure, they returned to Shavli. It was desolate. The only signs of life were the patrols at the intersections. The Krons were stopped by the first patrol they came upon, and because Meyer's documents stated that he was the director of the tannery, they let them pass.

A couple of days later, Dr Wulf Peisachovitz, Gita's first cousin and a prominent physician in town, stopped by the Krons' house; he had just seen the first German motorcycles roll into Shavli. The next morning, when Gita was leaving to take her two children over to Wulf's house, Ruth saw cadavers in the street. The pavement was littered with dead Soviet soldiers. Ruth was shaken by a shiver of awe and closed her eyes. Gita decided not to make the trip.

Some immediate unofficial actions were taken against the Jews, showing the zeal of the Lithuanian population. Any Jew found in the street was taken outside the town to bury the dead. Before the Germans would order them to do so, Lithuanians went to Jewish homes to make arrests. Within a couple of days, they had grabbed several hundred people.

German officers moved into old Mrs Kron's suite across from Meyer's family. "My first memories of the Germans," says Ruth, "were seeing them come into our place and taking our things — the buffet from the living-room, the radio, the piano and other stuff. I was terribly confused. My father tried to reassure me by saying that it was not serious. Besides, they gave us some money in exchange for our belongings. I still did not like what was happening. In the end, the German presence in our house turned out to be an asset: the Lithuanians did not dare to come into a place inhabited by Germans. One night we heard a local raiding party arrest our neighbours. As they were coming up the stairs to our second-floor apartment, I heard a Lithuanian voice: 'Don't go there. He's a good Jew!'"

In the meantime, the authorities proclaimed new laws restricting Jewish freedom of movement. None of them made any sense to Ruth. Why did they have to wear a yellow star on their chest and back? Why did they have to walk in the middle of the street where the horses and the cars went instead of the sidewalk? Why did they have to go shopping when there was nothing left in the stores?

Within a couple of weeks, the Jews of Shavli were herded into two ghettos, both in the so-called bad parts of town. The Krons had to relocate in Traku, one of the two areas reserved for Jews, near the tannery. People were crammed into the ghetto like sardines. Fourteen members of Ruth's family had to share two small rooms.

Every morning the adults left for work outside the ghetto, leaving the children, the old folks and the disabled to their own resources. Ruth and Tamara ran loose in the streets on their own. Tamara was Ruth's responsibility. At times, she did not mind having her little sister with her. At others, she wished she could get lost, for the little girl was under her feet. After all, Ruth was a big girl of seven and Tamara was a pesky four-year-old. But Ruth and the other children soon faced hardships and decisions that usually are the exclusive domain of adults. Some, especially the very young and those who had been used to pampered conditions, were dumbfounded by the magnitude of the task ahead of them. Others, among them Ruth, rose to the occasion, navigating troubled waters with a keen intuition coupled with what they could pick up from their elders and from children with more practical experience. In one sense, Ruth was called upon to function as an adult without being qualified for the job, and in another sense, she remained a child playing with others. Her favourite game was hide and seek because that was the easiest way to lose Tamara.

As we have heard in the previous stories, most of those children who had been evicted from childhood look back today and feel that they have been robbed of the experience of being children. Some were burdened with responsibilities beyond any realistic expectation. Many have grown up with a sense that the well-being of others rests on their shoulders. Others never left one version or another of hiding — often behind silence. After all, was not the most important lesson every Jewish child had to learn those days to be quiet, never complain, never speak out when feeling indignant, never assert themselves? These people, too, feel they lost the spontaneity, omnipotence and assertiveness that is part and parcel of a normal childhood. Ruth had always thought of herself as a special child because of all the love and luxuries her world lavished on her. She had to let go of that sense of specialness in the ghetto.

"We were very much like the kids in *Lord of the Flies*," she says. "But much younger. We had to rely on ourselves. We had our own government, taking charge of what was right or wrong. During an interview on CBC, somebody asked me, 'Where did you get the baby-sitters when the parents left the ghetto?' Can you imagine? First, the question made no sense at all. But then, again, how could a Canadian fathom a reality that coerced us to grow up much before our age would have warranted it?"

One of the hardships the children of Traku, among them Ruth, had to endure was witnessing the kind of violence that was not meant for anyone's eyes. In addition to bombs and bullets dropping out of the sky, the occasional cadaver turned up in the streets. The child's emotional circuits were overloaded. Ruth did not yet have the developmental wherewithal to make sense of death. As a child, she should have had no other concerns than the routines of everyday life. Instead, she witnessed a Jewish woman being raped in the middle of the street by a uniformed man, and was forced to watch the hanging of a man named Mazavetzky, a Jew who had been caught smuggling two packs of cigarettes. "It was my first hanging," Ruth states, indicating that there were others to come.

Her version of childhood included horrors children don't see even in their worst nightmares. Was there anyone for her to speak to about those occurrences? Not really; everyone was busy just surviving. So she kept her thoughts, feelings, questions and anguish to herself — yet another version of hiding, yet another version of abandonment.

By 1943, the Krons had no doubt about the fate awaiting all Jews. Ruth overheard them speak anxious words about their fate; they, too, would be killed, like so many others who had been marched off to nearby woods and shot, or taken to one of those camps in Poland. The Germans also began to pick up the elderly and the disabled.

Meyer did everything to find a hiding place for his family outside the ghetto. It proved to be an impossible task to find a Christian family that would hide the girls. The Germans and the Lithuanian police exercised strict control over the population: anyone found hiding a Jew, adult or child, would face death.

Finally, Meyer came up with two alternatives. In the event of danger, Ruth was to take Tamara to the wood-shed in the back of the garden. He had obtained sleeping pills for the two girls to make sure that they would remain quiet. The other place was the house of Dr Wulf Peisachovitz, Gita's cousin. No one would look for children there because he was a bachelor. Besides, he was in the good graces of Foerster, the commandant of the ghetto: he had saved the German's life at a time when all others had given up on him. The highly regarded doctor was also a member of the Judenrat (the Jewish Council) and had a great deal of mobility and excellent connections. Should any harm threaten the girls, they could count on Peisachovitz's help.

On November 3, 1943, there was a Kinderaktion (round-up of Jewish children) in the ghetto in which the Krons lived. The parents had already reported to work. The elderly and the disabled had been taken. The children were left to their own resources, as usual.

"Everyone was ready to report for work," reports Meyer Kron in his memoirs, "but, for some reason, the gates opened half an hour later than usual. This was the sign that something was happening. . . . During the following hours, the news was spread that the ghetto was surrounded and something was happening there."

In fact, early in the morning, the ghetto had been surrounded and the Ukrainian collaborators started to check every house and remove the children.

"I knew that something unusual was upon us," Ruth says. "The dogs did not stop barking. The street was full of Gestapo men. We could see a whole convoy of trucks making their way through our street. The sound of children crying reached us from every direction. I put all that together and it spelled danger. That was my cue to take Tamara to Dr Peisachovitz's house to hide."

The two girls braved the streets. It was very early in the morning, and, except for Germans, there was nobody around. Ruth was shaking with fear. They reached the doctor's house without incident and went straight to the closet where they were supposed to hide. The house was basically one sparsely furnished room. Its only window faced the jail. A sentry in the tower was watching very closely what was happening in the street, less than a block away.

Tamara and Ruth hid behind the row of hanging clothes. There was not enough room to sit down, so they stood for hours. They knew that in such a small place they had to remain silent, so they spoke not a word. Ruth knew well that if they were discovered, they would be killed. Condemned to silence, she conjured up all kinds of catastrophic fantasies. She came to the conclusion that being Jewish was dangerous. And that being a Jewish child had to be the most dangerous thing in the world. The grown-ups could at least get out of the ghetto and hide in the world outside, but Ruth's world was reduced to the narrow and dark confines of a small closet. She was forced to conclude that children were not worth a great deal if they had to disappear to find some security. She swore to herself that, at the first opportunity, she would stop being Jewish. She also discovered, together with thousands of hidden children everywhere, that life was not a given. One had to fight to hold on to it. But how does a child of seven fight against adults, a whole world of adults, equipped with bombs and tanks and guns?

"Be quiet, children, if you're in there!" That was the voice of Dr Peisachovitz. He had run home to check on his cousin's daughters. He did not actually look for them, but it was good to know that someone remembered them. It broke the silent solitude of the two little girls stuck in the closet for hours.

Shortly after the doctor's visit, the noise from outside died down. The dogs were still barking, but the children were no longer crying and the Germans stopped shouting orders. The girls were exhausted. They agreed that it was time for them to come out and scamper to the other hiding place in the room: under the doctor's bed. They lifted the mattress, as they had been told. Two of the wooden slats that held up the mattress had been removed, leaving just enough space for the two of them to crawl underneath and lie as in a coffin. Once inside, they pulled back the mattress and continued to wait.

Eventually, they dozed off. When Tamara woke up, she started to cry painfully for her mother. Ruth was annoyed and scared at the same time. What was she to do with this screaming child? She realized that Tamara must be very uncomfortable and stiff from lying in that tight spot.

She listened for noises. It was all quiet outside. No more barking, crying or shouting. She did not hear the dull noises of the trucks, either. She listened intently for anything at all. But all was quiet outside. Encouraged by the silence and discouraged by Tamara's desperate crying, Ruth made the most important decision of her young life: it was time for them to venture out and make their way to safety. She did not know what that meant, but she was sure they had to leave the hiding place.

The sentry in the tower above the prison spotted them the second they set foot in the street and began to shout.

"What was I to do?" Ruth still wonders today. "I could not continue in the street. We would have been arrested at once. And going back into Wulf's house was useless since now the Germans knew that we were in there. And since it was scarcely bigger than a doll house, it would take a small search party five minutes to find us."

Nevertheless, she dragged her little sister back in the house and they rushed under the bed, replacing the boards and the mattress in their usual place.

"If somebody comes for us, I'll kiss his hand. That would have to inspire pity in him and let us go. I knew that we were in tremendous danger, that we could die if we were caught. And kissing his hand was my best plan," Ruth says. "I also knew with a dark knowledge in my heart that I had failed my little sister, Tamara. I was supposed to hide her and I just could not do it right."

Within minutes, the soldiers were in the room. It took them but a few seconds to find the girls under the mattress. One of them grabbed Tamara, the other lifted out Ruth. They led them away holding them by the hand. Two formidable-looking dogs sniffed at the two little sisters. Tamara screamed as she was being carried out, and Ruth, ignoring her own panic, thought of one thing: If anything happens to Tamara, it will be my fault. I'll never be able to face my parents. What will happen to me?

The last truck was leaving the ghetto. Ruth put her plan into action as they were being carried towards the truck. She kept trying to kiss the man's hand, but he did not let go of her. On the contrary, he did not seem to like what she was doing. Each time she put her lips on his hand, he would swear at her.

A Ukrainian threw the two sisters on the back of the open army truck. He was brutal; he carried a large club that he swung at the children. Each blow caused an outburst of pain. He struck Ruth, but she could stand the blow, but he badly hurt Tamara. And he broke the leg of a little boy next to them who was howling in his agony.

The army truck took off towards the ghetto gates. At that moment Dr Peisachovitz appeared on the scene, accompanied by another cousin, also a doctor, and some other members of the Judenrat. Commandant Foerster arrived and soon he and Peisachovitz were engrossed in a hot argument. Moments later, Ruth was lifted off the truck without a word. But not little Tamara.

"Commandant Foerster," Wulf said to the German. "These two girls are my illegitimate children. I want you to order that they be left behind. You have told me time and again after I saved your life, that if I needed your help with anything you'd be there for me. Well, now I need you to return my children to me."

"I can help you with the big girl," the commandant replied. "She is old enough to work. But there's nothing I can do for the little one."

With that, the truck began to roll. Tamara stood on it with her arms reaching out towards her big sister, terrified, begging her not to leave her alone.

"I will never forget that scene," Ruth whispers with tears choking her voice. "I shall never forget the sight of my poor little sister with her arms stretched towards me and no one coming to her rescue. That vision has haunted me all my life, and it will never leave me alone. Because that was the end of my four-year-old sister, Tamara."

A ring of adults quickly surrounded the distraught girl so that the guards could not see her as they ushered her to safety.

Very few children managed to escape that Kinderaktion. Ruth was one of them. They smuggled her back into the ghetto and hid her under the couch. As the parents returned from work beyond the ghetto gates, they discovered the tragedy. All the children were gone. Inarticulate howling animated the ghetto street. The sound of a shapeless pain robbed many of their sanity. Others found no way to continue to live with a wound so deep and took their own lives. Gita and Meyer were first speechless in their relief to see Ruth home, then they sank into despair when they learned of Tamara's tragic fate. But they had no time to waste on their grief; they had to act at once. Ruth had to be placed in a safe place. They knew that at any time the Germans might come back to scoop up the few who had managed to escape their dragnet. She had to leave the ghetto at once.

The next morning, as soon as the ghetto gates were open, Ruth was smuggled past the sentry in a circle of Jews reporting to work. Meyer hid her in the belly of a truck full of leather supplies. They took her to the tannery. There Meyer and Gita prepared her a hiding place between piles of sacks and various leather supplies next to the laboratory. It was a dark place smelling of glue.

"There were rats running all over me," Ruth says with revulsion written all over her face. "Dark, stinky rats running and I had no idea what was happening. I was scared out of my mind — and, of course, feeling undone by my failure to protect Tamara. If I had only known where she was and what was happening to her! I don't know what was worse: the rats and being terrified for myself, or the heavy burden of my guilt."

Children caught up in the whirlwind of the war against the Jews, and especially Jewish children, were often in the stranglehold of a gambit from which all exits led to pain and sorrow. Was it really up to seven-year-old Ruth to save her little sister when even the powerful Dr Peisachovitz could not accomplish that? Was it up to Ada to rescue her mother from the grip of the German and Dutch authorities who had caught her in that raid? Was it within Aniko's means to do anything at all to change the mind of the two detectives who came for her parents? It made no difference to these tormented children that they were just that, children. With the egocentrism of all children, they thought that if something bad happened to a loved one, it was their fault. In one way or another, they should have done something. If nothing else, they should have offered themselves as a trade for the apprehended parent or sibling. There were those who convinced themselves that they had caused the bloodshed by some untoward behaviour: Ruth could not forget nor forgive herself for having wanted to get rid of pesky little Tamara during her games with friends of her own age.

"I kept wanting her to get lost," she recalls. "Finally, my wish came true: she did get lost. Who would have thought? Is it not possible that I said it often enough for God to have heard me and granted me my wish? How can I feel anything else but guilty? Am I not responsible in some sense for her fate?"

Just as Ada had thought many a time that she would have gladly taken her mother's place, Ruth would have been only too happy to trade with Tamara. Those internal dealings with one's conscience are not all that common at that age. Conscience begins to emerge in children between the ages of eight and ten. The kind of moral bargains that became the unshakable taskmaster to the Ruths, Adas and Anikos knew no developmental stages. Life on the edge had its own moral schedule. Children grow up at their own pace when they are afforded that luxury in their privileged middle-class environments. When they are confronted with abuse, abandonment, rape, betrayal and the inappropriate death of a loved one, it is their ordeal that dictates the pace: they grow up when they must grow up.

Ruth stayed in the tannery for the three longest days of her life. In the meantime, Meyer was able to locate a man named Jocas whom he had helped when he still had authority in the tannery. This Lithuanian was so grateful to him that he had been smuggling food into the ghetto to help the Krons tolerate the near famine conditions. Now, once again, Meyer turned to Jocas for help. And once again, Jocas came through for him.

Jocas came to the tannery for Ruth in a horse-drawn carriage and he took her to his own house. Although Ruth spent only one night at that place, it left a big impression on her. "I'll never forget Jocas's place," she says. "It was tiny, just one room for him, his wife and their children. When you come to think of how we live in North America, you wonder how people could live in such tiny homes. With that, they gave me a bed, all by myself! With pillows and white sheets! I, who not so long ago was dressed in furs and laces, now was moved to tears at the sight of such luxury. It had been so long since I had slept in a bed, and all by myself, to boot! And yet, in spite of this rare pleasure, I found no joy in my good fortune. For the first time, I was left to sleep in a Christian home, all by myself, without anyone from my family. I tasted the bitterness of abandonment. It made no difference that they had to leave me for my own good. All I could think of was their absence. They actually had left me with these people.

How could I be sure that I would ever see them again? Especially those days when people disappeared from one moment to the next without any warning."

The next morning, it was, once again, Jocas who worked things out with a friend of Gita's, a physician, Dr Jasaitis. By then Gita had made several clandestine trips to the doctor's house to arrange for her daughter. Dr Jasaitis came to fetch Ruth at Jocas's with a carriage that doubled as a hearse: Ruth was to be transported as a dead child. They wrapped her in sheets and carried her to the carriage. From there, the doctor took her to the home of Ona and Antanas Regauski, a young Lithuanian couple who ran a day school in the country about ten kilometres outside Shavli. They had a little girl, Grazhina, two years of age. They had planned to shelter another little girl, a child of friends of the Krons. But the parents were not able to bear the thought of separating from their child, and the poor child fell prey to the Kinderaktion. So Ruth took her place.

"Thanks to another child's misfortune," says Ruth, "those people could take me in and save my life. Not an easy reality with which to grow up and go on living. Not that I feel guilty for surviving instead of that other child. I had really nothing to do with that. I just filled a vacancy. A lot of survivors feel that since the others did not survive, what right do they have to go on living. That kind of thinking spins no wheels for me. If anyone at all should feel guilt, it's people who create situations where children have to even consider such matters. It's the Nazis and their satellites who bear the burden of guilt for the death of the Shapiro girl, not I. And I have felt a lot of sadness for her. But I hold responsible those who made it necessary for us to hide. A child's natural place is not in some dark corner. It is out in the sunshine. Hidden children, indeed, what a paradox!"

Ona and Antanas were simple, good people. The Krons offered to pay them for saving their child's life, but they did not understand what the grateful parents were proposing: to get paid for doing the decent thing, the very things their conscience and their faith demanded of them, to get compensated for doing God's work? They operated a day school in their tiny home right on the road to Shavli. Children near Ruth's age came every day to the house for their education. Since the Krons spoke either Yiddish or

Russian in their home, Ruth's Lithuanian was not good enough to pass for a member of the family. Thus, she had to live in a closet until she learned to speak the language fluently and without an accent. Ona would sit by the closet door and teach Ruth through the closed door.

As if living in a closet for four months, cut off from her family, was not trying enough for a seven-year-old child, Ruth had to cope with the pain and discomfort of diphtheria, a life-threatening illness. Her only hope for shaking it was for her rescuers to lay their hands on some antiserum and have a doctor administer it — fast.

As it happened, Meyer had had the foresight to stock some diphtheria antiserum before they had moved into the ghetto. Diphtheria being known as a killer of children, he thought his daughters had enough enemies without that merciless disease.

With her long straw-blonde hair, which she wore in a bun on top of her head, and her light blue eyes and her fair skin, Gita was the image of the Lithuanian peasant woman, so she took off her yellow stars and paid several secret visits to the Regauskis. That is how they were able to get the antiserum to Ruth. Afraid to call a Lithuanian doctor, they managed to find a Jewish doctor who was hiding nearby. He came to administer the life-saving medication.

To help pass the time of sickness, Gita sent Ruth a beautiful rosary made of different coloured beads. It was the closest thing Ruth had to a toy. But more importantly, Ruth felt that by sending her this rosary, her mother gave her her blessing to become an ardent Catholic. It was a symbol of her new life and of her mother's acceptance of it.

When Ona decided that Ruth's command of Lithuanian was flawless, she devised a plan to bring her out into the open. She told her neighbours about a sister who lived in Kaunas who had taken ill. Since someone had to look after her child, Ona had offered to take her. Under the cloak of darkness, Ona smuggled the child out of her house. She took her to Dr Jasaitis's place where they dyed her hair blonde with camomile flowers. The next morning they went home in a *droshka* (a horse-drawn carriage). Ona introduced her niece, Irute, to all her friends and neighbours. From then on, Ruth's life took on a friendlier face.

She became just one of the kids, and she fit into her environment with remarkable ease.

Since living the precarious life of a Jewish child had been a source of endless anguish and even tragedy for the young child, her hosts' Catholicism came as a breath of relief. She enjoyed the pomp and circumstance of the church; she would not have missed a mass for anything. The human faces of Jesus, the child and his mother, Mary, were a source of joy and peace for her: what a beautiful thing — a mother and her baby were to guarantee her life forever. Judaism had nothing with which to woo her away from the new-found peace and exultation. The glittering world of the church claimed an instant victory over the dark gloom of the ghetto. Ona and Antanas watched the child surrender her soul to the soothing mysteries of their faith without ever encouraging her to become a Catholic. They were not seeking to convert her.

To make life easier, Ruth talked to the Christian God about how she had let down her little sister, Tamara. "I needed to know that I could be forgiven for what I did," Ruth recalls today. "While I received no divine amnesty, it was heart-warming to have this benevolent God, the father of Baby Jesus, with whom I could commune. Today, I no longer find solace in a dialogue with God, any God, mostly because it has never been a real dialogue. I prefer to have no rapport with any God rather than having to contemplate what He allowed to happen. Isn't it easier to live with the absence of a God than with the presence of a baby-killing one? But I still feel a great affinity for the quiet mysticism of the church, with its lights and melodies, its ceremonies that take one away from the harsh realities of everyday life."

Ona and Antanas put in place two escape routes in the event of a surprise threat. At the first sign of trouble, Ona would wrap Ruth into a bundle and Antanas would take her to the priest's house on his bicycle. The priest had several other Jews under his roof. This emergency plan was activated several times. When the danger was over, Antanas would take her home. If it seemed too risky for her to go out, she would have to hide in their attic. But the attic was not a very safe place — she would have to be absolutely still or the floor would creak and betray her presence. "Being quiet was indispensable in hiding," Ruth explains. "Silence had to become second, or even first, nature since my life depended on it. And it did not come easily to me. By nature, I was a vivacious, loud child. But what choice did I have?"

One way or another, all hidden children pay tribute to the choiceless choices they had to confront. One way or another, they all were aware that they had no options. Living without options affected most hidden children: one adopted the God of her rescuers as her champion, another became a model of compliance, a third invested all his hope in a benevolent rescuer, yet another remained a prisoner of his fear and anguish.

Ruth's inner world was shaped from bits of all these experiences. Her sense of guilt about what she considered to be her failure to protect Tamara tainted everything else. The image of her little sister's outstretched arms allowed her little respite. Her dark conscience visited her whenever she allowed herself to be lulled into being just a child. Much of the solace she sought to derive from religion was tainted with uncertainty: was she entitled at all to seek God's attention for herself, or did she have to concentrate all her efforts to ask God to take care of Tamara? Without any word about her sister's well-being, Ruth had no choice but to conclude that no one, not even God, could help. What she had done was so horrendous that nobody could undo it, and Tamara had to pay the price.

In spite of feeling the chill of Ona's house in the winter, Ruth would take off all her clothes and kneel at night in front of the image of Baby Jesus. "I thought," explains Ruth, "that if I did that somehow Tamara would come back."

As Ruth's presence became part of the routine of the neighbourhood, her hosts allowed her to attend to chores outside, like feeding the pigs and the chickens in the barnyard. The first time she went out, she nearly fainted in fright: there were eyes peering at her through the cracks in the walls of the barn, and through the straw at the top of the structure. They seemed to be following her every move.

Ruth ran back into the house to tell Ona what she had just seen. The child then learned that her hosts were sheltering fourteen Jews from Shavli. Many of them were well-known to Ruth. From then on, every time she went to feed the animals, she was tempted to speak to them just to have some contact with people from her parents' world. And every time she saw these silent Jewish eyes, burning with anguish and hope, she thought of her own parents. Where were they now?

Were they all right? Was she ever going to see them again? At those moments, she felt like the loneliest child in the whole world. Except for Tamara. She could not allow herself to feel sad for herself without her sister's face competing for her attention. She had to admit that she had a pretty good life compared to other children. And she was luckier than the people in the barn. She lived with Ona and Antanas in the house, she slept in a real bed, and the Regauskis were good to her. But they could not replace the profound love she had for her mother.

In one sense, however, Ruth was relieved to be where she was. As long as she was living in the skin of a Christian girl, Irute, niece to Ona and Antanas, she did not have to deal with the danger of being Jewish. Slowly, she developed a deep hatred for Jews and cursed the day she was born one. She wished no one any harm. All she wanted was to be left alone as a Christian. And if that meant she was to live far away from her parents, so be it. And yet she still longed for her mother's sweet caress, the loving smile on her beautiful face and their intimate outings.

With the exception of Ona's mother, everyone accepted Ruth as an ordinary little girl. The old lady harboured a dark resentment for this young Jew who could bring disaster upon their heads. She never did anything to harm Ruth, but Ruth had the impression that the old woman scarcely tolerated her.

Around the end of June 1944, rumours reached the Regauskis that the liberating Red Army was approaching. Bombing raids became more frequent. A few days later, the fleeing Germans liquidated the population of the ghetto and shipped everyone off to Auschwitz. The column of condemned Jews filed past the Regauskis' place on their way to the railway station. Ruth stood by the edge of the road with everyone else. The child's heart pounded. Would anyone recognize her? Her parents? Her cousins, aunts and uncles, neighbours? Was she going to have to join their ranks and be marched off, and end up like all the other children in the Kinderaktion? Despite her fear, she was longing to see her parents and to know that they were all right. Instead she saw Wulf and some other cousins. They looked right into her eyes and not one of them flinched: no one recognized her. Or perhaps they were just playing it safe. When the last Jew filed past her, Ruth sank into a deep fear: Where were her parents? They must have been killed in the ghetto! Once again, guilt cut through her: Could she be responsible for their disappearance, too? Just as she used to wish that Tamara would get lost, and she did get lost, so she had been thinking that she did not want to be with her parents again. What if God had taken her thoughts literally and had arranged for them to disappear forever? Was she living out some kind of a curse?

The truth was that the Krons managed to hide outside the ghetto shortly before the Germans liquidated it. Then on July 27, 1944, Stalin announced that Shavli had been liberated. As much as the Krons wanted to be reunited with their child, they had to wait a few more days because in the meantime, a Soviet officer who had been billeted in Meyer's mother's flat during the first Soviet presence in Shavli offered his help. Among other things, he put an army vehicle and a couple of soldiers at the Krons' disposal.

"I knew nothing about being liberated," recalls Ruth, "until the day I saw a Russian soldier driving towards us in a Jeep-type vehicle. Next to him sat a very pretty Russian-looking woman. It was my mother coming to get me. I certainly was not eager to go with either one of them: we were told that Russians cut out people's tongues and blinded them and all sorts of untold atrocities. The Lithuanians around me were much happier to be under German domination than to have to face Soviet occupation. There was another matter, too. I hated the thought of being reminded that I was Jewish. What good was it to me to be Jewish or to live with my Jewish parents? I recalled only hardships and horrors when I thought of Jews. I wanted to have none of that, ever again. I was delighted to know that my parents had survived the war, but I had no intention of leaving my secure life with Ona and Antanas for another bout of nightmares."

"Ruth had been at Ona's for nearly a year," Meyer Kron records in his memoirs. "She had grown and looked at us as strangers. She spoke Lithuanian and become quite a pious Catholic. She never failed to make the sign of the cross. She was not very anxious to go home with us. She felt very much at home with Ona and Antanas. What could we tell Ona? She saved the life of our daughter and she would not take anything for it. We left her a lot of food that we had received from our friendly Russian officer. Then we returned to Shavli."

"After liberation," Ruth continues, "my mother would come to see me at my foster parents' house, but I was not happy to see her: she was Jewish. It was dangerous for me to recognize her as my mother because that meant I was Jewish, too. And to be Jewish meant death. And yet, I was happy to see her, to know that she was alive, to see how beautiful she was. To know that she was my mother. Liberation was a very confusing experience, indeed. It meant having to leave again, it meant fear and, on the other hand, tremendous joy with my mother."

With the maturity that the circumstances of her survival forced upon her, Ruth knew that things would never go back to what they used to be. Their cosy home no longer existed. On their way out the Germans had torched the whole city. They left only a few choice houses standing in the unlikely event that they would reconquer Shavli. The Krons' friend, Kaplan, the handbag man, was one of the lucky few with a home to which to return. When Ruth was ready to go home, it was to be at Kaplan's place.

During the time they spent together, Ruth rediscovered the profound bond between her and her parents. When, three months later, she realized that they were no longer dangerous to her, she was ready to go with them. But she set conditions. She did not want to be Jewish. She was not to attend services of any kind, nor to participate in any ritual. On the contrary, she was to continue going to church. Most of all, she requested that her parents never speak Yiddish in front of her. The Krons acquiesced to all of her demands.

Once she returned to her mother and father, Ruth felt more acutely the absence of her little sister. Her sense of guilt grew proportionately. She spent hours by the window facing the partly ruined Catholic church. She shed many tears for that church, since it was easier to weep for it than for everything else that the Nazis had taken away from her. It stood as a symbol for Ruth herself: like the church, Ruth had suffered losses but had not been destroyed.

On Sundays, feeling ill at ease in a Catholic church, Gita traded roles with their Lithuanian maid: the maid took the young Catholic to mass, the mother looked after the housekeeping

chores. And Ruth caught her parents in violation of the "no
Yiddish speaking" rule at home only once. She made such a fuss
about it that they begged her forgiveness and swore that they would
never do it again. In every possible way, they allowed their daughter to do her own healing without any interference. And they let
her go at her own pace. They were so relieved that at least one of
their children had escaped death at a time when almost all the
Jewish children of Shavli had been murdered. They had no concerns about her "anti-Semitism." They understood that it made
perfectly good sense to a child to protect herself from any possible
repetition of the ordeal. They also understood why, after the
humiliation meted out to Jews by their enemies, this child, who
had never made a deep commitment to the faith of her ancestors,
would want to be anything but a Jew. Thus, rather than attempt-
ing to reconvert her, they spent all their energies on constructing
as normal and as comfortable a life as they could.

In the meantime, life in Lithuania became increasingly unpleasant. By the end of the summer of 1945, Gita and Meyer decided
to find a way out before it was too late. Meyer had learned that the
authorities were building a case against him for being the son of
an exploiter, rather than the son of a worker. It was just a matter
of time before he was in serious trouble.

After careful consideration, the Krons joined a group that
planned to cross the Soviet border illegally. They hoped to leave
in April 1946. "I was to leave the office the first day of Passover,"
Meyer writes, "the holiday celebrating the flight from Egypt."
Instead, on that day, he was arrested by the secret police. After four
days of interrogation, he was allowed to go, but on one condition:
he was to spy on his Jewish friends and report the names of those
who wanted to leave the country.

Meyer, of course, had no intention of collaborating. But now he
had no alternative but to leave the country. If he did not, untold
harm could happen to the three of them. Through connections
that Gita had unearthed, they managed to find some people who
were willing to help them escape in exchange for all their
possessions.

The plans were all in place before Ruth was told the details of
the perilous enterprise. She was gripped by fear and distress. Once
again, her life was being put in jeopardy: more hiding, more lying,

more catastrophic consequences. And once again, she felt she was
being punished for having caused the death of her sister, Tamara.

Then, just as Ruth and her mother were about to embark on this
risky journey, the child came down with scarlet fever. The plan had
to be put into action in any case: Meyer was at great risk since he
did not intend to inform on his friends. In addition, Gita was seven
months' pregnant.

Not wanting to look as if they were going on a voyage, Ruth and
Gita left their home without any luggage and went to a cinema.
At the exit, they met a friend, dressed as a colonel, who slipped
them their travel documents. Another man, whom they had paid
dearly and in advance, took them to Lipovka in his horse-drawn
carriage. There they met their travelling companions. As they were
approaching Lipovka, Gita and Ruth noticed a man coming
towards them on the road.

The man was Meyer. He took his wife and child to meet the
truck with the rest of the group of ten people, including their two
guides. The truck was to take them to the train station, but before
they reached the target, they had to make other arrangements. Just
as the sun began to rise above the horizon, they came to a washed-
out bridge. Fortunately, they found a small boat hidden in the
bushes. It took three trips for all of them to cross the river. Once
they had all landed, they found out that they were in rough terrain.
"My mother was grey in the face and scared to death," Ruth recalls.
"With my scarlet fever, I was not feeling any better. Seeing how
scared my mother was did not exactly reassure me, either."

They finally got to a military detachment where, for good
money, the driver was willing to take them to the train station.

"The next morning," writes Meyer, "when we approached the
border station of Brest, border policemen took up positions at the
door of each car. They led everyone to a field nearby. There we had
to wait until the train to Poland arrived."

After a long day of agony, they received a new set of documents
from their guides. One look at them made everyone even more
anxious: they looked obviously fake. But the guides assured them
that everything was going to work out well — the border guards
were their friends.

They boarded the train. A Soviet soldier guarded the door of
every wagon. The tension was tremendous, but finally they passed

the border line and the Russian soldiers jumped off. There was a search at the borders, but the Krons had no luggage at all. Their sole possession — U.S. currency — was rolled in the belly of salted herrings that they left unwrapped next to them on the bench. The guard did not show any inclination to search the smelly, oily fish.

It took them some time to accept the fact that they were finally out of Lithuania. But the hiding was not yet over. To make it to the West, the Krons had to change identities again, but they finally made it to a British camp for displaced persons in Breslau, Germany.

The scene at that camp did not alleviate Ruth's aversion for Jews and Judaism. The atmosphere in the camp was chaotic and belligerent. The Jews of German background blamed the Polish Jews for their miserable living conditions. Indeed, the German Jews informed the British authorities that some of the refugees were impostors — they pretended to be German, but they were really Polish. This unfortunate squabble resulted in a selection according to place of birth. When it was Meyer's turn to appear before the British officer, he was asked when he was born. "I told them I was born on the seventeenth of March, 1905," writes Meyer. "I found out later that that was the key question. . . . Generally, the western people (those from Germany and westward) would give the day, month and year, while the eastern people (those from Poland eastward) would give only the year." On a subsequent page, however, Meyer did not qualify as a German Jew, whereas Gita did.

Gita and Ruth were told to board a truck. Meyer was told to stay on the other side of the fence. When no one was looking, he jumped over the fence and climbed into the nearest truck. Gita picked up several packages that were on the ground and threw them over him. Soon after, Ruth and Gita were loaded in the same truck.

Ruth felt she was in a dream. Her world was in a constant state of upheaval. It seemed to her that wherever there was trouble, it was linked to their being Jewish. The conclusion she reached while hiding at Ona and Antanas's place seemed still to hold true: it was dangerous to be a Jew. But it appeared to be a lot harder to stop being one than she had hoped it would be. Somehow, to others, it was the most important fact about a person: was she or wasn't she a Jew? Nothing else had any relevance. Being Jewish seemed to define a person. All Ruth knew was that she longed to live in one place, in one house, with one name — her own — and without anyone trying to harm them. She ached to go to school and learn like other children. She wanted to feel special again, not picked on.

For the next two years, Ruth's wish was not to come true. Home was to be one room in the DP camp — formerly a Hitler Youth camp — in the Bavarian village of Feldafing. Most of the residents of Feldafing had to share large halls; Meyer was able to secure their own room for his family.

In August 1946, while at Feldafing, Ruth's brother, Leo, was born. "That was our first great celebration," says Ruth. "After all the losses, finally a new life. And he really did usher in a new life. After all the tragic events of the ghetto, all the hiding, escaping from the Russians, the dangerous journey west, all under the cloak of dark fear, we were free, together, with a roof above our heads, good food and even some hope. I found living in freedom wonderful."

Meyer was appointed principal of one of the famous Organization for Rehabilitation through Training schools. It was a well-paid position. Eventually the Krons got an apartment in Diessen, near Munich. Ruth was eleven years old when she finally was able to start her regular schooling. During the week she studied at a Hebrew school in the city; on the weekend she went home. Despite the pleasant arrangements, Gita and Meyer came to the conclusion that they did not want to live on German soil for the rest of their lives. They all agreed that it was time to get out of Germany. Yet another upheaval was necessary.

When they registered with the authorities for immigration to the United States, they gave their own names but claimed they had been born in Tilsit, Germany, just inside the border, across from Poland. The Americans allowed more Germans than Eastern Europeans to immigrate.

First, they hoped to settle in the United States, but with the creation of Israel, a new alternative became available. Ruth was not thrilled with the prospect of moving to a Jewish state. But then, as they were making their plans to go to Israel, the cold war and the Korean conflict became a cause for concern. The Krons, therefore, thought it would be safer to go to Canada than to Israel or the United States.

After a complex and long waiting period, finally they got the good news: they were granted entry to Canada. "It was wonderful to know that we could leave the European continent where we had had to survive so many hardships," Meyer Kron writes in his memoirs.

At the beginning of March 1951, the Krons sailed to Canada and settled in Montreal. But the dark mystery that shrouded the disappearance of Tamara cast a shadow on their new life. "Until then," Ruth says, "the uncertainty was very hard on me. For one thing, her name was hardly ever mentioned in the family. I believe my father never forgave himself for not removing Tamara and me from the ghetto while it was still possible — just as I never forgave myself for failing to keep her hidden. She was a ghost silently hovering above our lives. Not knowing what had happened to her made me pray for her return. I just could not accept the possibility that she was dead. She was just too young to be dead, she had hardly started to live. It could not be that she would have already been taken away from all the living she had ahead of her. I could not stop thinking of her. My memories were haunting me all the time. Besides, there was no grave. How could we be sure she was gone forever?"

Then, one day, far away from the killing fields, they found out that Tamara had been taken to Auschwitz along with all the children picked up during the Kinderaktion. It was more practical to dispose of them that way than by digging mass graves, shooting them and burying them.

The old wound of Ruth's guilt burst wide open. It would have helped if her parents had been tearing their hair, if they had openly yelled at her. Instead they shrouded the whole tragedy in silence. And behind their silence, Ruth perceived the thin shadow of accusation and blame. Whenever Ruth brought up the subject with her mother, Gita would change the subject, leave the room or just refuse to talk about it. Under those circumstances, how could Ruth bury her sister and, with her, her own self-inflicted guilt?

"Later, when my own daughter was born," says Ruth, "I wanted to call her Tamara, but my mother wouldn't want to hear of it. Still later, when my daughter had her daughter, she didn't bother to ask anyone: she went ahead and named her Tamara. All my mother had to say was 'Fine'. But the fact is that no one ever blamed me for her death. I did it all by myself. If I had only stayed inside for another fifteen minutes, the last truck would have left and Tamara would be still alive."

In recent years, Ruth has pardoned herself. She knows she did nothing wrong and that she could not have done anything differently. But in her soul she still carries the seeds of self-incrimination. "We were pretty street smart, we knew how to survive. And the fact is that I fell for the silence: I let it dupe me."

One way or another, silence looms big in the memories of hidden children. It is rarely seen as an ally. It tends to show up as a messenger bearing an ultimatum: stay quiet or else. Since the "or else" is hardly a choice at all, it usually commits the child to her own abandonment or destruction. Silence therefore offers at best hope, never guarantees: you vanish into silence, and maybe no one will notice your existence. In a world where a law prohibited children up to the age of sixteen from staying alive, that is, indeed, an attractive prospect.

But Ruth's and Tamara's encounter with silence on that final November third showed the other face of silence, the one that tricks and offers a false sense of security, the one that kills the body and strangles the conscience of the survivor. One is reminded of the chess game between the knight and Death in Ingmar Bergman's *The Seventh Seal*: Death appears to a knight searching for the meaning of life. The knight wants more time. Death proposes a wager: Beat me in a chess game, and I'll grant you another lifespan. The knight defeats the undefeatable, but Death takes the knight with him anyway. When the knight reminds his gruesome adversary of the deal, Death answers, "I lied."

As much as Ruth had suffered the pangs of guilt for Tamara's fate, she had never experienced survivor's guilt, not even for taking the hiding place destined for another child. She knew that the guilt belonged to the perpetrator, not to the survivor. "My feelings on surviving are very much tied to my feeling special. I always did — up to the time the war started," says Ruth. "And after the war, once I was allowed to settle into what felt like a secure life, I felt special once again. I had survived the assault on children to which most kids, including my little sister, Tamara, succumbed. And to this day I have always felt special. That's why my husband, Cecil, calls me the Queen. In spite of everything, and keeping in mind all the

alternatives, life has been good to me. I'm convinced that I've survived for a reason."

Many child survivors, and to some extent adult survivors as well,
share Ruth's sense of mission. Many agree with Elie Wiesel, for
whom the survivors are the mailmen of the dead; they survive to
link the martyrs to their progeny. Others, in a similar vein, feel
that it is up to them to guarantee the family its endless continuity, to repopulate Israel. And yet others, like Ruth, spend their lives
searching for that special purpose. Was it to educate others by
telling one's story? Was it to perpetuate a lineage in which one
member may become not just a life-giver but also a life-saver?
Many, like Ruth, don't know the answer, so they try everything,
sometimes at a great cost. No matter — what drives them is that
special purpose, that commitment to contribute to the life and
well-being of others.

They don't know why they survived, but they do know how: one
or several people took a risk and saved them from the child-killers.
They benefited from acts of ultimate kindness. Regardless of the
reason for hiding them, even if it was for vulgar material gains, it
was still an act of bravery and other-centredness. Thus, as they were
growing up, the Ruths, Robs and Adas, and myriad others had a
choice: should they build their future persona on the model of the
killers and bystanders who tacitly authorized the industrial-scale
infanticide, or on the quiet heroes who put the life of another —
a child — ahead of their own personal interest? In their professional activities, a high number of the hidden children work in
other-centred professions, such as health care, education, community service, etc. Thus, it makes perfectly good sense that Ruth
is the director of the Woman's Resource Centre at the University
of British Columbia, at Vancouver, dedicated to the enhancement
of another abused and at times persecuted group of people —
women.

This sense of surviving for a special purpose is very much a
double-edged sword in the life of child survivors, and often their
children. It may lead to such an overpowering feeling of mission
that they end up giving so much to others that they lose sight of
their own needs, dreams and personal journeys. Hidden children
are often told by their families, friends and colleagues that they are
driven to be of service.

"No matter how long I live," says Ruth, "I shall always look for a reason: why me? Why did the one and only child who was taken off that truck in the ghetto have to be me? So feeling special is not always a good feeling. I always thought that there had to be a reason and it was up to me to find it and prove it."

Ruth has struggled with other paradoxes. "To this day," she says, "I don't feel comfortable being Jewish. To be sure, I no longer am a practising Catholic, either, although I still love churches. As always, I'm still dazzled by the beauty of Catholicism. As a child, I loved the ornateness of the church. I'll never forget how beautiful my rosary was. But mostly I liked belonging to something that was safe. Even now when my husband and I travel to Europe, my favourite pastime is to visit churches. And if Cecil were willing to stay up that late, we'd go to midnight mass every Christmas eve. But, in spite of all this, I am definitely a Jew. And what's more I know that I have always been a Jew, even in the ghetto, even while hiding in Wulf Peisachovitz's closet, and even when the truck rolled away with Tamara. I am very Jewish, I continue with our Jewish traditions. We always commemorate the Passover. On Friday nights we light candles. Each of my grandchildren has his own pair of candles. I go to *shul* [temple] two or three times a year, just to hear the language, but I don't pray because I don't believe in God. He either doesn't exist because my sister died, or He exists and let her die, which is worse. On the other hand, He must have existed to save me and He must have done it for a purpose. So who will tell me what am I here for? I go around with these existential questions, and I do my best not to allow myself the time to think about them — I make myself very busy, just not to have to face these merciless questions all the time."

When all is said and done, for Ruth being a Jew is a complex experience. She is always scared of anti-Semitism, and she is not comfortable with her children being Jewish with the resurgence of racism in the world.

Each time one of her three children reached the age of four, Ruth felt petrified that the family curse that had taken Tamara away from them would come back to exact the life of her own child, at the same age. For a year, three times, Ruth lived with Tamara's agony. "The numbers have their own magic, I suppose," she says with a sigh that could signal relief as well as resignation to the inevitable burden of pain and anguish. "What does make a difference now is that I know that I am not a freak; others had gone through similar experiences and have felt the restrictions of the same trap as I have. There is a great deal of power in knowing that you're not a freak." Therein lies the immeasurable value of being connected to other child survivors and of telling one's stories to inform the others while healing the self. The choices seemed limited — to banish one's story to the dark corridors of the unconscious, allowing it to undermine one's waking hours as well as one's dreams, or to keep telling one's story to an audience of one, thereby continuing to hide. To testify publicly — in schools, community centres, synagogues and the media — is a source of powerful and painful enlightenment, as it is to gather with others and exchange stories, thereby creating a community. Most survivors opt for one or several of these approaches. Those who risk sharing their stories with others report instances of fear alternating with instances of healing. But, as with all healing, the process is not without its own pains.

Ruth is learning to tell her story in public. Two years ago, encouraged by Dr Robert Krell, she went to a gathering of child survivors in Oxnard, California, where, in small groups, everyone told his or her story. Then, encouraged by her experience, she agreed to participate in a panel in front of an audience. It was hard. She felt exposed. She thought her life was really nobody's business. Most of all, she felt that in front of all those strangers, she could not stay in hiding. And yet, she did it, and she will do it again and again.

"Yes, I had to do it," she asserts. "When you have to, you have to. It is one of those things that connects with why I was spared. With the revisionists denying the truths of the Holocaust, all of a sudden, we all have a job to do. As much as I hate to do it, it must be done. My philosophy in life has always been that it doesn't matter what it is, just do what must be done. So, even though it doesn't feel good, I know it is something that needs to be done, now. I have never spoken to schoolchildren, but Rob Krell is going to get me involved with speaking in schools. It is my job to make sure that they learn the truth, because once my generation is gone, there will be no one to tell our story. We really are the last generation of survivors. We have been forgotten too long. Like it or not, I will do my share in the fight against oblivion. Not only for Tamara, but for the sake of all children, so they don't inherit my sister's fate."

$$7$$

She Lost Everything
But Her Courage

The Story of
ESTHER MAINEMER

"I have such wonderful memories of my childhood. Every one of them is precious. What would I do without them? I could not go on living if I remembered just the horrors and the losses. How could I live without recalling the sweetness and the riches of life in the Jewish community that Hitler took away from me? If I did not remember that Jews used to sing and dance, learn and teach, love and quarrel, raise their young and bury their dead, I could not think of myself as one who has really survived. I can't allow that the world thinks only of death and despair every time they remember the Jews. They have robbed me of my family, my friends and my first love, I cannot let them rob me of the memories of a good life, too."

Esther Mainemer, née Schumacher, now a spritely, vivacious woman in her sixties, sustained nothing but losses once the forces of destruction — both the Nazis and the Soviets — settled into her young life in her native Bialystok, some two hundred kilometres east of the Polish capital, Warsaw.

The early years of Esther's life were idyllic, in spite of the Schumachers' modest means. Second youngest in a family of seven children, she was always surrounded with love and affection. Her father, Michal, like the tailor in *Fiddler on the Roof,* had started out in life with the gift of a sewing machine from his parents. He worked long hours to provide for his large family. And yet he had always had time for Esther.

They lived in an apartment building sheltering thirty-five families. In the warm summer evenings, children played in the courtyard while their parents sat on the steps.

Enjoying the protective love of her brothers and sisters, Esther never thought that any harm could come to her. She felt particularly close to her older sister Hanna. "She was like a second mother to me," Esther recalls. "She took me around wherever she went. She really took care of me, and I adored her."

One fine summer day, in 1930, Hanna had a date with her boyfriend and took Esther along. During the outing, Hanna revealed to Esther that she would soon leave Bialystok for Canada. And, no, there was no way for her to take Esther along.

First, Esther did not know if she had heard right. When the news sank in with all of its frightening reality, Esther began to run. She ran so fast that Hanna could not catch up with her. Tears soaked her cheeks. In her disarray, she could not reach out to anyone, not even to her parents. She found a spot between the large ceramic stove and the wall in the living-room. Grabbing her little blanket, she climbed into that tight hiding place and covered herself. Exhausted, she fell asleep. Everyone in the family searched for her, but to no avail. When a few hours later she woke up, it was already dark outside.

She stepped out from behind the stove and walked into the kitchen. Her mother let out a sigh of relief and then, for the first time ever, she spanked Esther.

"Why did I do such a thing, to give them so much aggravation and so much fear?" Esther never stops asking herself. In doing so, she joins the ranks of countless orphaned child survivors who find it hard — if not impossible — to forgive themselves for actions that, in ordinary circumstances, would be viewed as commonplace for young children. It is quite understandable that upon hearing some frightening news, a six-year-old would hide and fall asleep in the hiding place. When most adults recall such incidents, they find them touching or amusing, certainly not reprehensible. But when survivors, like Esther, lean back over the span of time and recall an event like her hiding behind the stove, they place that event in the context of the ordeals that their parents endured on the way to their annihilation. As such, they can never remember the "trauma" they had inflicted upon their martyred family without thinking of what those people must have endured on their way to their demise. In fact, many of these formerly hidden children have a hard time recalling any details of their pre-Holocaust life without their losses crowding out the otherwise joyful memories. All the good times, all the loving and nurturing are tainted by the ensuing tragedy.

Child survivors also tend to idealize the times they had had with their families before the Nazi deluge. Thus, they attribute all their childhood sufferings to the destruction of the picture-perfect life they had enjoyed prior to the tragedy.

For Esther, the first real abandonment she sustained was Hanna's emigration to Canada.

It would not be surprising at all if some of the child survivors who were old enough to remember even minute details of their childhood prior to 1939 went through life completely disconnected from their early years. To go on with their day-to-day existence, they had to exile their memories of childhood since they offered testimony about some deep wound sustained at the hand of a loved one.

The other great event in Esther's life that year was her first stay at summer camp. It helped alleviate the anguish of Hanna's pending departure to know that she was the first Schumacher to go to a sleep-away camp. But while she was having a great summer, the family successfully completed all the documents needed for Hanna's emigration to Canada.

The day of Hanna's departure had come. She was not about to leave without saying farewell to her little sister. Her father took the train and then walked ten kilometres to the camp to get her. The camp director gave Esther permission to go home for the day. Hand in hand, and in heavy silence, Esther and Michal made the journey back to Bialystok. After Hanna had left, there was as much grief in their home as if she had passed away. "So here I was saying farewell to my sister," Esther recounts, "thinking that I shall never see her again. Little did I know that one day I should end up in Canada, too."

The summer went fast. In spite of Hanna's departure, Esther enjoyed the camp and all the friends she made. When she returned, she began to write letters to Hanna. Since Rachel, her mother, did not write or read in Yiddish, once a week, after Esther had finished her homework, the two of them sat down for Rachel to dictate a letter to her faraway daughter. When a letter would arrive from Canada, everyone gathered around Esther, who read it out loud. Esther enjoyed those moments of intimacy. They were a source of warmth and security.

Hanna's departure left a gaping hole in Esther's life. But, like most children, she went on with the business of living. She was a bright and creative child. From her earliest years in school, she produced plays in their apartment based on stories her father had read to her. After a long day's work, Michal would sit at the kitchen table to sew costumes out of coloured paper for Esther and her friends. He helped also with the staging of his daughter's plays. And the children who came to watch them perform would bring all kinds of sweets for the actors. Esther also enjoyed singing. She used to dream of becoming a singer but her parents did not have the means to pay for lessons.

On summer holidays, Esther spent much of her time in a nearby forest playing with her friends. Esther knew it was midday when she saw Michal approach with lunch for all the children.

"How wonderful it was to see him come," Esther recollects. "To know that he chose to leave his work to bring us food. All those little things are so precious now. To know that I had a father who treated me with so much love and affection."

Esther remembers her mother with the same warm feelings. Having to look after such a large family did not allow her much leisure or energy to cater to Esther's needs as much as the child would have liked her to do. "I never really had a chance to appreciate her as a mother," Esther says with quiet sadness. "I never had a chance to learn from her how to be a wife or just a woman."

In the summer of 1932, at the age of eight, Esther discovered love. He was the cousin of her best girlfriend. They played together all the time. When winter came, they would run in the snow chasing each other with snowballs.

That same year she also learned that as a Jew, her life was always at risk because Hitler wanted to destroy her. From that time on, the topic of the impending menace was on everyone's lips. Soon, they started preparing to receive Jews escaping from Germany; they started to stockpile blankets, bedding and dishes expecting an influx of refugees.

The general flavour of life, however, did not change much for the young girl as long as she remained within the Jewish community. When she ventured beyond its confines, here and there, she was exposed to slurs and a proliferation of swastikas along Sienkiewicza Street, the main thoroughfare of Bialystok. She viewed them with a vague curiosity, although the stories about Jews killing Christian children to use their blood to make matzoh for Passover confused and hurt her.

The Schumachers' everyday life was deeply anchored in the age-old Jewish traditions, and the child felt grounded in her Jewish identity. Her father attended services every day, twice on the Sabbath and on High Holidays. And of course, they observed strictly the ancient dietary laws of kashruth. "I loved the holidays," says Esther. "For me, they were not about religion. They were about closeness and belonging. I'll never forget the fervent preparation for Passover. All the cleaning and scrubbing, it was all so magical. I still miss the almost mystical warmth of Seder around our family table. I hold the Nazis responsible for all the Seders that they had taken from me."

By the time Esther was ten years old, she had realized that, in spite of having always lived in Poland, she knew nothing about Poles, about their culture or about their language. "I realized that living among Polish people without knowing what they were saying was very hard for me. I just had to learn Polish." After considerable resistance, and with some reluctance, her parents enrolled her in a Catholic school. There, for the first time, she had to learn to deal daily with anti-Semitic insults and derogatory stories about Jews. The first casualty of the transfer were the plays she had been producing for years with the help of other children. In her new environment, she no longer had the co-operation of the other children. And, for the first time, due to her insufficient knowledge of the language, she was having difficulties with her studies. Without the warm camaraderie that linked the children in the Jewish school, Esther felt less secure, less active, less alive — inferior. Eventually, she did develop a warm friendship with two Polish girls. Neither one was Roman Catholic — Kasia was a Protestant, Kristina was Greek Orthodox. In the predominantly Roman Catholic school, they, too, were viewed as outsiders. Except for those two friends, Esther never mingled with her other classmates. She remained in her community.

When the body of a Jewish woman from her street was found in the bushes near where Esther and her friends used to play during the summer, everyone was convinced that she fell victim to Jew-hating thugs. From then on, it became obvious that life would never be the same as before.

On September 1, 1939, what they had been dreading for years finally was upon them: Germany declared war on Poland. Esther was in the street on an errand for Rachel, when she froze in her tracks. The deafening wail of the sirens filled her with panic. It seemed that they were never going to grow quiet. Above her head, the sky was black with planes. Everyone was running for shelter. That night, the people in Esther's building, as in the entire country, learned that Hitler had demanded that Poland relinquish the port city of Gdansk, which used to be called Danzig during the period it had belonged to Germany. Hitler, counting on Poland not to comply, had ordered his armed forces to attack the recalcitrant neighbour to the east.

The alarms were sounded every night. The inhabitants of the building all had to hide in one apartment with the lights out. Sitting in the dark, all Esther heard was what was in store for them when the Germans came into Bialystok. Day in, day out, she heard adults speak of terrifying news from Warsaw: they were taking Jewish men to do hard labour, but they tended not to come back. What happened to them? According to some, the Germans had them dig graves, then threw them into the pits and buried them alive. Imaginations were reaching fever pitch.

"Little did we know that those rumours that my father thought to be hysterical outbursts by excessively anxious people were going to pale in comparison to what was really in store for the Jews," Esther comments. "But at that time, for an impressionable young girl like me, who had always been sheltered from the ugly side of life, those rumours were sufficient to keep me in the clutches of fear all the time. Awake or asleep. And since my mother never let me out of her sight, I concluded that my fears were justified. At the age of fifteen I resigned myself to living a life without tomorrow, without options."

Poland was neither ready nor able to resist the might of the Third Reich for any significant length of time. Two days later, Esther's two brothers were called up for immediate service. The war lasted two short but terrible weeks. For a while, the Schumachers could sigh with relief: their sons came back safe and sound.

Three weeks after the beginning of overt hostilities against Poland, the Wehrmacht made its awesome entry in Bialystok. Esther was helping a relative in her boutique of fine ladies' clothes — the first one in Bialystok. It was located right on Sienkiewicza Street, the main artery through the city. Like all Jewish businesses, it had been ordered to close. But every once in a while, the owner decided to tempt her luck. Those days she welcomed the help from Esther, a pretty young girl with a keen eye for fashion.

Suddenly, the windows began to rattle in the small store. Then they heard an ominous rumbling that seemed to come from the centre of the earth. Esther and her cousin ran outside and found themselves face to face with the slowly advancing column of German soldiers. Esther clutched at her throat. She felt as if those armoured faces had sucked the air out of her lungs.

From then on, Esther never dared to look at the sky for fear its darkness would explode above her head and put an end to the life she had scarcely begun. She feared what one single German soldier might do to her. Soon, she had to confront her worst nightmare; one day, walking down her street, she had an eerie feeling of being followed. She stole a backward glance and, to her dismay, realized there was a German soldier behind her, coming closer and closer.

Without a moment to waste, Esther pushed the gate of her building and practically dove inside. She ran to the stairs and began to ascend as fast as her legs and lungs would carry her. Her feet devoured step after step, floor upon floor. Finally, she reached the fifth and last floor. There was no place she could go on running. When she caught her breath, she dared to steal a furtive look to see if the German soldier was in sight. There was no trace of him.

Slowly, very slowly, she began her descent. When she reached the ground floor, she ventured into the street. There was no sight of the German soldier.

With every passing day, Esther's fear grew less and less tolerable. They had started picking up Jewish men at random, promising that they would return soon, and yet not one of them came back. Is that what was going to happen to her father and brothers? She thought she would die if anything happened to any member of her family.

Nothing happens the way one expects it or one fears it will. Esther's sister Chava had married a fine young man just six months earlier. They were exquisitely happy in their own little apartment not far from the rest of the family. Her new husband had a job as a sales representative for a textile company. Since Bialystok was a textile city, the young man had a secure future. And, best of all, Chava was pregnant with their first child. The young couple felt that they were on their way to a wonderful life. But the Germans had other plans. They gathered all the young men, among them Esther's new brother-in-law. The men were put to work loading ammunition onto trains, when the Russians declared war. Without wasting time, the Russians bombed the railroad yards in Bialystok. Among the first round of casualties was Chava's husband.

"I shall never forget that pain," Esther states scarcely above a whisper. "I feel not only my pain but also my sister's and my parents'. I knew, we all knew, that life could never be the same again for our entire family. But the strange thing about all this is that you think you cannot go on, you will not go on, and then you do go on."

Esther could not hide her fear from her two Christian friends from school. After her brother-in-law's tragic death, Esther asked her friend Kasia Czibulski if she could hide out at their place until the Germans stopped hunting Jews. The Czibulskis agreed to shelter their daughter's Jewish friend. Given her blonde hair, blue eyes and fair complexion, no one would suspect her of being Jewish. The Schumachers also agreed that it would be wise for Esther to hide with a Christian family.

All in all, Esther was relieved to move in with her friend's family, who received her with warmth and understanding. They also thought that some safety measures had to be taken. For one thing,

Esther was to leave their apartment as little as possible. There was no need to speed up the already active rumour mill. Besides, the Poles, feeling scared and bitter about the oppression of their lives by the Germans, blamed the Jews for the Germans' presence. Drawing on ancient prejudices, myth and ignorance, many Poles were no lesser enemies of the Jews than the Nazis. But, in spite of their anguish about the uncertainties of the occupation, her hosts reassured her that she could stay with them for as long as was necessary. They could not stress enough that she stay away from Poles; the number of spies grew larger every day.

"If I had not insisted on learning Polish, it would have been impossible for these people to hide me," Esther explains. "Who would have thought that my stubbornness was going to help save my life? It was definitely the right decision to learn Polish. By the time I moved in with my friend's family, I spoke the language fluently and without a trace of an accent. Somehow, it turned out later, I always had the feeling that I was doing the right thing. It was only years later, when I had to confront one loss after another, that I began to wonder: if I had always done the right thing, why do I feel so guilty."

In spite of the kindness and understanding of the Czibulskis, Esther felt uncomfortable. She was very shy and socially awkward. There was also the matter of these people's Christian habits and rituals. Esther was to learn to be a Catholic. She had to memorize all the prayers. They taught her to make the sign of the cross as if she had been doing that all her life. Every Sunday, Esther was to accompany her hosts to church. It was essential that she be seen going to worship alongside her "relatives." Naturally, she had to memorize all the prayers as fast as possible. It would have been suspicious to the Czibulskis' neighbours and fellow parishioners if their young cousin did not partake in prayers. Each time she sat down with her hosts for a meal, she had to say grace. And each time she felt she was lying. How could she mouth those pious Christian words knowing that she was a Jew? By praying "in Christian," how could she not feel like a traitor to the God of Israel? How could she not betray her beloved family?

She had not yet recovered from the malaise of the prayer, when she had to confront food prepared mostly with pork fat. She, who came from strictly kosher home, had to put the flesh of a pig in her mouth! But since she had to eat, a compromise was in order: she would eat soups and vegetables even though there was bacon fat in them, but she would pass on meat.

Meal time was an ordeal for Esther for yet another reason. The dining table was a place of conversation for the family, yet Esther hardly ever said a word around the table. Even Kasia felt more like a stranger than her good friend.

"Esther is a Jewish name," Mr Czibulski said one night shortly after her arrival in their home. "No one would believe that you're a Christian with that name. From here on we shall call you Elzunia." With that, Esther thought, I have to put my real self in mothballs.

Many a hidden child accepted the fact and daily practice of the identity switch. Most of them were very young or they came from primarily secular families. Later, these children were prone to hitherto unknown emotional conflicts over confused identities or a sense of guilt for having "betrayed" their family, faith and even God. Those of them who during their hiding had at least one kind and nurturing caregiver eventually made peace with the chaos in their soul and emerged with a unique identity. For some it was a Jewish identity. For others it was a cultural and social identity — a gravitating towards Jews rather than Christians when feeling lonely or needy.

As for Esther, fifteen years old when she was asked to assume a Christian persona, the experience was a necessary evil. Living her everyday life as a spurious Christian contributed to her sense of profound alienation and solitude — a budding theme in her life. "Once it was no longer necessary for me to live the Christian lie," explains Esther, "I didn't give it much thought. I had other, more immediate concerns. Each time of hiding had its own demands, each demanding that you attend to the current one; you couldn't get stuck in what worried you at the last place. That doesn't mean that each new burden didn't feel heavier than the previous one, just because your back had already been bent under the weight of everything that came before. The same was true for fear."

Fear was never too far from her. Being in hiding had alleviated her constant worry she would be seized by the Germans. But she had new reasons for being scared. She feared being unmasked as an impostor by someone in the neighbourhood. Her hosts had done an excellent job convincing her that her presence in their midst was a tight-rope act. With the faceless enemy around her on the ground, and the faceless enemy of the nightly bombers in the sky, even though she was in hiding, Esther felt there was no place to hide — yet another instance of the "no-options" predicament of hidden children. Instead of taming fear by turning it into a familiar and therefore less demonic presence, she felt more and more oppressed by it; her previous fears weakened rather than rein-forced her emotional foundations. No sooner did one cause for fear disappear around the corner, than another one, even more foreboding, appeared on her horizon.

Two months after Esther had gone into hiding at the Czibulskis' home, unexpectedly, Hitler and Stalin signed a pact that resulted in the partition of Poland. The people of Bialystok saw the exit of the Wehrmacht and the arrival of the Red Army. For the Christ-ian population, this was bad news, but the Jews were jubilant. They had no illusion that the Russians were friends of the Jews but they did not have a program of wiping out all Jews, either.

Esther returned to her family. Life began to smile on her again. When she was told she could go back to school, she thought things were going to be normal again. She did not mind even the heavy-handed Communist indoctrination to which children were being subjected in the new Soviet-dominated regime.

In the summer of 1940, a broad flow of Jewish refugees from Warsaw, still under Nazi occupation, began to inundate Bialystok. It fell upon the local Jewish population to offer them shelter. The Schumachers welcomed five people in their apartment.

Esther threw her body and soul into the care of their guests. She was moved by their plight, and she also became good friends with two brothers, even though they were considerably older than her. Leon was thirty and Mistislav was twenty-eight. She and Mistislav developed a special affection that bordered on romance.

The biggest hardship was finding enough food for everyone. Leon and his brother belonged to a wealthy family and had the financial resources to afford food at any price. But provisions were hard to come by. Now and then, Michal would return with a piece of meat or some fish. The entire family, even Esther's ten-year-old brother, joined the hunt. "As a young girl I was quite able," recalls Esther with pride, "and I used to run out at every opportunity to bring something. I'd come back with sugar, oil, flour or whatever I could put my hands on. I also did their laundry."

By winter, rumours circulated in the Jewish community of Bialystok that the Germans might come back. The Schumachers and their guests spent many a heated moment in search of a way out. Esther's parents decided it was unlikely that a family of eight, among whom was the pregnant young widow Chava, would pass unnoticed. They therefore decided that escaping from Poland was not for them. Leon, Mistislav and their friends, on the other hand, had agreed that they would find a way to make it to a Baltic port and from there take a ship to South America.

In preparation for their big adventure, Leon sneaked back to Warsaw to rescue as much money and gold as he could carry. They would have to hire guides to lead them to the border and beyond. The Soviet rulers of the land strictly prohibited anyone from leaving the country. Anyone caught was severely punished.

When the young man returned from the capital, he told tales of horrors; they were torturing and killing Jews and having them dig their own graves. He was more convinced than ever: they had to leave or they might not be able to save their lives.

When the two brothers informed the Schumachers of their decision to leave, to everyone's surprise, Leon offered to take Esther with them. Everyone was thrilled with the idea of Esther getting out of the country. The memory of her overwhelming fear during the first German occupation convinced her parents to do anything to prevent its recurrence. Besides, when she reached South America, she could arrange for the rest of the family to go to the United States or Canada, where they had relatives.

Esther was of several minds. She was willing to leave everything behind rather than be a slave to the terror of what the Germans might do to her and her loved ones. On the other hand, the adventure ahead was fraught with danger, too. After all, travelling through the night, at the mercy of strangers, hiding at different farms each night, crossing the border illegally and perhaps running into the guards — each of these held enormous risks. And what about leaving behind her family? If something happened to them, should she not share their fate? But didn't she deserve to have a life? And wasn't she a fifteen-year-old, innocent to the world, simple in her sheltered provincial world, in love for the first time, enchanted with a young man thirteen years her senior, experienced, sophisticated, from a big city?

"In the end," Esther recalls, "something inside me told me to go and save myself. So I asked for and got my parents' blessing. But to this day I can't understand how I did it. And how much my parents must have loved me to let me, a young girl of fifteen, go alone in the world with people that they hardly knew, realizing that they would probably never see me again, dead or alive. Up until this day I can't help asking myself what made me do it. How could I, with no experience, I, who have never been anywhere, set out on a journey among the wolves? How brave I must have been to make that kind of a life-and-death decision! But when all is said and done, it must have been the right one, because, although I paid a hefty price for it, I did survive."

The night before they were to leave, a large crowd of relatives and friends, including Kasia and Kristina, Esther's Christian friends, gathered in the Schumachers' apartment. They all came to wish Esther good luck. There was an endless flow of tears. Esther could not tell whether they were crying because she was leaving them behind or because they were already grieving for her.

The next day, the party of seven — the brothers' friends had joined them — took the train to their first stop, Bielobirsk, a small village about twenty-five kilometres from the city. Since they had to stay out of sight during the day, they travelled by night and hid in a peasant's barn during their first night. "It was not a matter of pure generosity on his part," adds Esther, "because he was handsomely paid for his hospitality. But, when you think of it, those days in Poland, it was indeed an act of friendship for a Pole to open his door to a Jew even for money. So many of them turned us in to the authorities and saw us beaten or killed rather than help us."

The next couple of nights were the hardest. They walked silently behind a guide, also generously rewarded for his services. Since walking along the roads was too dangerous even at night, they went through fields and forests. They stopped to catch their breath for a few minutes, and they continued on their way. Esther had great difficulties keeping up. She was always at the tail end of the line. Mistislav stayed back with her.

At times, Esther's heart was beating in her throat. She was terrified to cut through the dense darkness of the forest. In the distance dogs and wolves howled, lacerating the stillness of the night. Esther's teeth chattered each time the beasts began their eerie concert.

At dawn, with the first rays breaking through the mist, they had to hide once again. The guide had made a deal with another farmer and once again, they spent the day, exhausted, in another barn. Esther was asleep before her head could touch the hay. And the following night and day were just the same: guided march and sleep in yet another barn.

After several days of this routine, they arrived in small town where Leon and Mistislav had relatives. It was an almost forgotten luxury to spend the day in a place made for people, not animals. Their relative found a man to guide them the rest of the way to the border and beyond, out of the reach of the Poles.

Shortly after they had eaten, there was a knock on the door. They froze in their fright. Who could it be? Had they been betrayed? Hesitantly, and in combat readiness, Leon opened the door just enough to see who it was.

Esther had the shock of her life. It was her father, Michal. Unbeknownst to her, before they left, the boys, counting on their good fortune and on the expertise of their excessively well-paid guides, had given the address of their relatives to Schumacher.

Esther got dressed and father and daughter went for a walk. What Schumacher had to tell his daughter was without a doubt the hardest words he had ever uttered: "Your mother is crippled by nightmares about your fate. She can't rid herself of the image of you being killed by soldiers. She can't go on like this. I have come to take you back."

As they walked past the little train station, Esther looked at Michal and for the first time in her life, she said no to him. "No, Papa, I am staying with these people. I love Mistislav and I will go with him wherever he takes me."

"I see." He was silent for a few seconds. "I half expected you would refuse to come back. As a father, I've an instinct for what my children have in their heart. Go, my child, I understand you. Follow your heart. Perhaps it will save your life. Perhaps you will reach that promised land on the other side of the ocean. Go with my blessing."

"It took me twenty years to get over seeing him turn around, with his back hunched in his dark overcoat." Esther's words seem to come from the depths of a tomb. "Then he turned around, to say farewell, one last time. To this day, I can never look at a person and say goodbye for fear that I will see once again that pained glance and that I may drown in that sea of sadness."

When she refused to go with Michal, Esther did not think that she would never lay eyes on her father again or that before she could do something for them, they would all be killed. She had unwavering faith in Leon, in Mistislav and in their plan. She fully expected to come back to help her family out of Poland.

"My father left me in the street," recalls Esther amid tears. "I could not move. I felt like my feet were glued to the ground. Suddenly, all I could see was a black cloud. I was covered in tall darkness. For the first time since we left I felt very alone, frightened and without any hope at all. But that's not all I felt for the first time. I also carried in me the terrible burden of guilt. I let my family down. My mother was fighting for her life against her nightmares about me and I didn't do the one thing that would have put an end to her nightmares. How could I feel anything but guilty? What had they done to me? I used to be a caring, responsible daughter and I've become a selfish brat. I felt the agony of a hopeless split between my desire to go on living and my obligation to my beloved parents. Without a doubt, the guilt that was born in me that night has been the most loyal companion I have ever had. I have lost everyone I have ever loved. I had to give up everything that was ever dear to me, but that guilt stood by me."

Slowly, Esther found herself walking back to their hiding place. The others knew at once that she was suffering; it was written all over her face. They tried to comfort her but without success. She sat in a corner, unable to think or feel anything. She felt so much pain that if somehow a benevolent numbness had not anaesthetized her whole being, the suffering would have ripped her apart.

She had been sitting there for some time when the door opened once again. This time it was Mistislav, who had been out on an errand. Esther looked at the man she loved. The grin on his face made it clear that he had good news for all of them.

"All's in order," he announced. "Everything's in place for our safe passage to the border. We have an excellent and highly reliable guide. We're ready to get going at nightfall. A horse and buggy will take us to our man. We should get there by morning."

The good news and the smile on Mistislav's face helped Esther regain some of her vitality. They said farewell to their hosts, and with their hearts full of hope they set out. They travelled all night. At dawn, they reached the house where the guide was waiting for them. He took them to his barn and gave them something to eat and drink. Then they fell asleep in the hay.

At dusk, the guide came back for them and they were on their way, this time on foot. It was a starless, pitch-black night. The first rays of the frosty winter sun led them to a tiny village. Once again, they spent the day resting, hidden in yet another barn. Before she had surrendered herself to the much-needed sleep of the exhausted, Esther daydreamed about being on an ocean liner on her way to the safety of the New World.

When it got dark, their guide was ready to lead them one day closer to freedom. The next stretch was a particularly hard one to negotiate. There was not a flicker of light. Esther kept stumbling and falling behind from sheer exhaustion. The guide was picking up the pace. He kept whispering, "faster, faster, faster!"

They had been walking for a long time when their guide told them to wait, he had to do something in the neighbourhood. They all welcomed the unanticipated rest. A little while later, he returned and they continued their march. Suddenly, Esther heard a noise. She mentioned it to Mistislav walking just in front of her. They both heard the noise again, but they ignored it, and kept on walking.

Then, without warning, they were blinded by the harsh white beam of powerful flashlights. When they got used to the bright light, they realized that bayonet-toting soldiers had surrounded them. They yelled orders in Russian.

"When they asked our guide where were we headed and he said flat out that we were trying to leave the country, we realized that our very capable, highly over-paid guide was an informer, on Russian payroll." Anger animates Esther's words as she remembers their betrayal. "That's why he had to leave us in the fields, in the middle of the night: he had to inform the soldiers where they should expect us and exactly when."

As far as the Russians were concerned, anyone trying to sneak out of the country in the middle of the night had to be a spy. They were very happy with their catch of seven dangerous enemy agents.

Esther and her companions were placed under arrest. Bayonets poking in their back, they were marched off into the night. After what seemed like an endless walk, they reached the police station where they were to be interrogated, one by one, isolated from the others.

"Where were you going?" the Russian kept asking.

"To America," Esther kept answering.

"Then you must be spies," he declared.

"No, we're running away from the Germans," she replied.

"What have you done that you're so scared of them?"

"Nothing. We're Jewish, that's our crime."

This went on for hours and hours, over and over the same questions to which Esther had no choice but to give the same answers. As their level of fatigue and frustration rose, her interrogators began screaming at her from all directions, shoving her around in a circle, and now and then administering a blow on her frail, young body. Esther was more dead than alive in her pain and panic. When they realized that she was not going to say anything else, several Russians started to beat her.

Then one of them decided to have her searched. They got very excited when they found the addresses of her relatives in the United States and Canada.

"So you are spies after all," he said and that was the end of that.

When the interrogation stopped, it was already daylight. The Russians threw her in a cell with all the others. For three days they stayed there. With each day the number of those arrested for trying to flee the country grew.

Esther's heart was dark with bitterness, fear and loneliness. But the worst of it all was that they were just days away from Passover. How was she to ignore her thoughts about home, with her family, remembering all the Seders spent around the dinner table reliving a tragic moment in Jewish history when Jews survived thanks to the power of hope? What was she to hope for in that prison, far away from all her loved ones?

Then they were herded into the back of open trucks fit for transporting livestock. For two days and two nights they were driven until finally they stopped in front of the municipal prison of Bialystok. Esther was back where she started — in her home town.

She had only one thought: to send word to her parents that she was alive and well in the city jail.

As luck would have it, while she was standing in line waiting to be processed into her prisoner identity, a man from her apartment building walked through the corridor. Esther began to gesticulate frantically, but without words so as not to attract the attention of the guard. "Did he see me? Did he pass the information on to my parents?" Esther wonders. "I shall never know."

In the Bialystok jail, they separated the men and the women. Esther suffered day and night from this forced separation. She was, after all, still an adolescent, cut off from her family and from her first love. And now she did not know if she would ever see him again. Every day, she would crane her neck to reach the window, just in case she had the good fortune to catch a glimpse of him during an eventual transfer. But she never did. Nor did she ever learn what happened to Leon and Mistislav.

In the meantime, the interrogations continued. The same questions over and over again: Where were you going? Why? Who are your contacts? What about those American and Canadian addresses in your pocket? And at the end of each interrogation, her captors came to the same conclusion — she was a spy.

Then one day, after nearly a month of incarceration, Esther was ordered outside. Together with a group of strangers, she was to board a cattle wagon for yet another unknown destination. After a couple of days of travelling without food, water and sanitation facilities, they arrived. No one bothered to tell the prisoners that they were in the Ukraine. From the train, they were immediately marched off to yet another jail.

Esther found out that one jail was much like another. Yet, inside, she felt an ever-widening chasm between her present world delineated by bars and walls and the warm memories of a childhood spent in loving security. One day was exactly like another, making keeping a record of the passing time impossible. It mattered little that, after what seemed to Esther several months, once again she was yanked out of her prison just when it began to feel familiar. The authorities were eager to prevent the prisoners from organizing. So they kept moving them. This time she was transported, under conditions identical to her last ride in cattle wagon, to a prison in Bielorussia, not far from Minsk.

After another several months, she was escorted to the warden's office. There, she was informed that her trial had taken place and that she was found guilty of espionage. Her sentence: five years of hard labour in Siberia. From that moment on, she had no hope of letting her family know that she was going to the other end of the world, to the edge of civilization. And for what? For being a Jew, a hidden child who had chosen to end her hiding.

Esther and her companions were herded into a cattle car, and for two weeks they travelled across the vast expanses of the Soviet Union. The starvation, the cold and the brain-rattling train rides quickly numbed Esther's senses; she felt she had vacated her body, and she watched with indifference what was happening to it. It was hard to remain human under those conditions. And yet, by splitting off her self from her body, Esther was able to hide from her assailants. She had promised herself to be smart and obedient, not to give her captors any reason to abuse her, to torture her. "The moment we arrived in Novosibirsk, in Siberia, I went into deep hiding. No one was to know who I really was and what I thought or felt. That way no one could destroy me. They could kill me but they could not destroy me," Esther says with resolution.

After her two-week Transiberian ordeal, Esther's group faced a seven-kilometre forced march until they reached the barracks in Marinsk. The next day, at six o'clock in the morning, she reported for roll call. After roll call, she had twelve hours of forced labour to endure with hardly any food. Esther was young and healthy, yet it would have been just a matter of time before she collapsed of starvation had she not been lucky enough to be transferred to the kitchen after a couple of months. There she was warm and much better nourished. "The kitchen detail saved me from succumbing not only to starvation but also the cold." The barracks were not heated; a flimsy blanket was her sole shelter from freezing to death. Within days of her arrival, her feet were frost-bitten.

The guards treated the prisoners with a routine savagery that Esther could never have imagined. There was no place to hide. And yet, Esther found the way to hide herself behind a façade of obedience and invisibility. Whatever she was told to do, she did without hesitation and in silence. At times she felt as if she had vanished in the landscape between the dirty snow and the ubiquitous grey sky.

Soon, she discovered the need for another level of hiding. Except for the camp personnel, no men were allowed on the camp's premises. But quite a few women in spite of the malnutrition and the exhaustion needed tenderness, affection and physical love. By means that were unclear to Esther, some of them, as evidenced by the number of pregnancies in the camp, either managed to find male partners, or were raped by the guards. And others reached for the bodies of their fellow inmates in their moments of arousal or despair. Esther had never even heard of women loving women and the word "lesbian" was absent from her vocabulary. When women made advances towards her, they frightened her and she saw no other alternative but to hide from everyone, except for a few friends.

Being Jewish no longer meant a threat to her life, and yet it, too, required that she hide from many Poles who brought with them, to the end of the world, their deep seated hatred for Jews.

One morning, light pierced the darkness. The supervisor announced that prisoners who still had family in Soviet-occupied Poland might write home. Esther wasted no time. The same day, after work, she managed to get some paper and a pencil and she wrote to her parents. "I can still remember that moment," Esther says. "My first two pages were smudged with my tears. But slowly I settled down to write. Mostly, I wanted them to know that I was alive, where I was and that all was well with me. There was no point tormenting them with the raw facts of my existence. Not to mention the possibility that our letters would be censored before sending them on. It would have felt so comforting to share my story with them, but what right did I have to tell them about the suffering that was my daily diet without them being able to do anything other than feel oppressed by my pain and theirs? In a very real sense, I had to hide from them, too. After all the anguish my departure had inflicted on my parents, I thought it was time I take care of them."

She did let them know that she could do with some foodstuffs, especially with some garlic and onions, and some clothes. By that time, she had virtually nothing left. From then on, Esther lived for the day she would get an answer to her letter.

The next month felt like an eternity to Esther. But a letter from home finally did come. She got news from every member of her family. She just kept reading the letter as if she expected that it had some magic power. And, in some sense, it did. It allowed Esther to bridge thousands of miles of absences. "I still have the letter," Esther says. "I kept it over the years, no matter where I went or how many times I had to pick up and move. That letter never left my sight. It has always been my most priceless possession." Every night before she fell asleep, she would read her letter, like religious people read their holy texts. It gave her courage and strength.

A couple of weeks later, Esther received a parcel containing new clothes and some food, including garlic and onions. "Onion and garlic were essential to our survival," explains Esther. "We all started to lose our eyesight because of the massive lack of vitamins. The minute I started to eat garlic, my sight began to improve."

Shortly after Esther's parcel arrived, the Germans returned to Bialystok. They rounded up all the Jews and deported them to various killing centres. Esther never again heard from her family.

Towards the end of 1941, the war was raging in Europe. A number of Poles, mostly people of influence, managed to flee to England. Among them was Wanda Waszilewska, a brave woman committed to helping the Poles withering away in Soviet prison camps in Siberia. She intervened on their behalf and took her plea directly to Stalin. After several rounds of negotiations, the Poles were to be transferred to agricultural centres under more clement conditions.

When she heard the news, Esther felt a chill of panic: since the authorities were fond of separating prisoners, she feared she would be cut off from her lifeline to survival — her friends. She begged to be allowed to stay behind rather than face separation. After having had to say farewell to her big sister Hanna, her parents, her family, her friends back home and Mistislav, she could not cope with another separation. The commandant was stunned. It was the dead of winter in Siberia, and this silly girl did not want to go to a warmer climate. He dispelled her anguish: it would be easier in the new place, and seven of her friends were going on the journey with her.

The eight friends were jubilant. They had no idea where they were going but anywhere would be better than Siberia. Esther felt like she was soaring, not walking towards the exit to prison camp Marinsk.

"I can still see the gate," recalls Esther. "From the barracks to the gate was the longest walk of my life. I had spent over a year in Siberia. I wasn't even sixteen when I had landed in that frozen hell on earth. I was totally cut off from my family, indeed, the whole world. I had been robbed of my youth by having to take responsibility for my survival in that wretched camp. And yet, that morning I felt on top of the world because I had just survived it all, because I was young. I had proven to them that it is not that easy to destroy a child."

They had to wait twenty-four hours in the train station at Novosibirsk. For one last time they endured the chilling winds and the soldiers' harassment. "Come with us and we will give you shelter," they told the young women. After several hours, some of them began to waver, but not Esther. She concentrated on rising above her pain and defeating any temptation to give in to the offers of comfort in exchange for services she did not want to render.

Esther was full of optimism as she boarded the cattle car: she was young, she had survived the worst, and one day, she was convinced, she would be set free. She did not care that they had to sleep, night after night, on the bare floor of the car, or that their only food was *kipitok* (boiled water), six hundred grams of bread and a sardine tin of soup. She survived Siberia for over a year, she could survive this train ride, too.

After four weeks in the cattle car, they arrived in Tashkent, the capital of Usbekistan, from where they travelled down the Amu Darya River on a barge for a distance of five hundred kilometres until they reached their final destination: Urgentsch. They were installed in a *kolkhoz* (state-owned collective farm), where the eight of them were to work in the cotton fields. In Urgentsch, life presented a warmer face to the eight detainees. They had a room for the eight of them, and there were no more roll calls. In a warm climate, it was also easier to secure food.

Life was hard but simple. Esther picked cotton seven days a week. Because of the tropical climate, work started at five o'clock in the morning. If Marinsk was a frozen hell on earth, Urgentsch was hell's kitchen.

Then, in the summer of 1943, Esther fell victim to the most vicious enemy in the tropics: malaria. For two months she languished in the grip of a fever that threatened to burn her alive. Even when she was finally allowed to leave her bed, every two months, the malaria revisited her body. Had it not been for quinine and her essentially strong, young constitution, she would have succumbed to the fever. "I survived the malaria," says Esther, "but it had marked my liver for life. One way or another, my enemies had managed to get under my skin permanently."

During her illness and the ensuing convalescence, Esther learned, once more, the life-sustaining value of friendship. It was the loving care of her friends that nursed her back to life. They catered to her every need and even managed to find a little extra food. "After all that I suffered, I remember with my heart my friends' care and affection for me more than anything else. It kept me warm during the chilling hardships that were to follow me throughout much of my life. They taught me that when you have been deprived of absolutely everything in life, including life and hope, they make the difference between despair and the willingness to go on."

Then the day came in 1944 when Esther was told that she could return to Europe. She endured another journey by cattle car and weeks of *kipitok* and bread, but at the end of it, she was in Zaporozh in the Ukraine. It was then that she learned the war still raged in Europe.

Esther was sent to work in a *kolkhoz* operated exclusively by women; all the men were at war fighting the Nazis. For most people, the routine that waited for her would have been extremely harsh, but after Urgentsch, she found it quite manageable. For a while she worked in the fields, harvesting whatever crop was ready to be picked. Then her good fortune led her to an office job. Thanks to the generosity of some farmers, she supplemented her meagre food ration. While this was far from liberation, Esther appreciated these basic human liberties, such as finding her own way to nourish herself instead of being totally reliant on her captors' whim.

On May 8, 1945, finally, Esther tasted the joy of liberation. People danced and sang, kissed and hugged in the fields. They rushed to be together to toast to the end of the war.

But Esther did not return to Polish soil until 1946 when she was repatriated to the Lower Silesian town of Walbrzych and then to

Gluszyca. "When I was given a room to be shared with one friend only, with a bed covered in real white linen and a pillow with a white case on it, I knew that, for sure, I was free," recalls Esther. "Straw — on the naked floor or in a sack — and corn husks for a bed were the symbols of my slavery."

In Gluszyca, she was given an apartment that belonged to Volksdeutscher (ethnic Germans living abroad). When the law dispossessing them as enemies of Poland was proclaimed, they had to leave the country at once without any of their belongings, many of which had been stolen from Poles. When Esther entered the kitchen of her new home, the soup the Volksdeutscher had put on the stove was still cooking.

Soon after her arrival in Gluszyca, Esther met Leon Mainemer, a recently repatriated Polish Jew, who had undergone many of the same ordeals as Esther. The two young people who had lived without warmth and love for so long wasted no time: they got married shortly.

After the war the newly founded Jewish Congress of Gluszyca made it one of its principal tasks to find out what had happened to the relatives of its members. Little by little, news began to filter down from Warsaw to the smaller centres. "One day," Esther recounts, "I met a man in Gluszyca who said he had a brother in Toronto. I told him about my sister Hanna who lived in Toronto, too. He said, 'Good, I'll tell my brother to find your sister.' In the world with which I was familiar, it didn't amount to much: how was this man's brother going to find a total stranger, just on a name? I knew nothing about telephone books and that in America everyone had a telephone."

Then, in the spring of 1947, the Mainemers got a message from the Jewish Congress: there was a letter waiting for them. It was from Hanna. The man's brother had looked up her name in the Toronto telephone book and told her that Esther was in Gluszyca, married to a man named Mainemer. A year later, Esther and her husband were on their way to Canada. By then, their daughter Chava was born and Esther was pregnant with her second child, Nathan.

It was in the New World that, from different sources, Esther pieced together what happened to her family. Everybody was killed in one camp or another. She learned that a vicious German shot Chava's baby right in front of the mother.

Still numb from the horrible news of her family's fate, Esther, like most survivors, focused on building a new life. "We all lived in denial," she explains. "We had to escape the realities of the past so that we could focus on the present, otherwise all that pain would have strangled us. It was only later, when I already had a home, I was raising my kids, and my husband was making enough to sustain us without worry, that it began to dawn on me: I'm an orphan. It was then that a new round of suffering found me: I was face to face with guilt. There was hardly a moment when I was not tormented by the picture of my last goodbye to my father. How could I have been so cold, so insensitive as to leave them behind? Who would have thought that I'd never see them again? Even though I was running away from Poland because I feared for my life, somehow I just never thought that those things really happened to ordinary people like me."

When the full knowledge of her losses penetrated Esther's daily existence, life took on, once again, a dark texture. She felt increasingly lonely and desolate. Hanna, as before, was a loving sister, but they had grown apart. Not having experienced the ordeals of exile, she had no understanding or affinity for Esther's memories. They had become strangers. Yet another loss.

As a result of sustained hard work, Esther and Leon achieved material comfort, but they never quite found in each other the partner they needed. Esther craved a life of emotional partnership. Leon, a quiet, retiring man, invested all his energy into building a business and providing his family with the warmth of financial security. Esther, a survivor in all aspects of her life, decided that if she was to pursue her most private dreams, she had to do it on her own. Thus, in 1978, Esther and Leon, agreeing to remain friends for ever, ended their marriage. By then their daughter, Chava, had left Canada to make her home in Israel. And Nathan, their son, was completing his doctorate in clinical psychology. Esther was ready to look for personal satisfaction in life.

But the past still held her captive. Whenever her children had been ill as youngsters, she would bargain with her father. "I never asked you anything for myself, but please, father, don't let anything bad happen to my child." Esther realized that this relationship with her dead father was a signal to get help. In counselling, she made the most important discovery: she had survived for a purpose.

Until then, day after day, she tormented herself with her guilt. She should have been there with her parents, her brothers and sisters, to offer them solace in their last hours. If they perished, she should have perished with them. Those thoughts were never far from her. Then came the revelation. If she had died in the camps, there would have been no one to bear witness to her family's demise. They would have disappeared in the silence of history. She was here, therefore, to continue the ancestral name, she was to tell the world what had happened to a once thriving family in Poland. It gave her peace to "tell" her father what she had learned. "Forgive me, father, for not dying with you. I survived for a purpose. I survived as a continuation of your name. Your grandchildren will see to it that it shall live on for generations and beyond. I survived, father, to guarantee the survival of our family."

From then on, Esther felt less need to be in contact with her father's spirit, and she became available for an emotional commitment to a living man, Bill. And for the first time in her adult life, Esther learned the meaning of being special for someone. Bill took care of her as if she was the most important and the most lovable woman in the world.

Despite Esther's reconciliation with the past, the future had losses in store for her. When her son, Nathan, married a Christian, the fact that her grandchildren would not be Jewish eroded the comfort she had taken from continuing the family's Jewish name. Then, in 1990, after a two-year battle, Nathan lost his battle against a tenacious brain tumor. Esther had never felt so betrayed. With the loss of her son, she also lost her unwavering trust in her father. He, too, had abandoned her. She spoke to him for one last time: "I've never asked you for anything, not even during the worst of my ordeals in Siberia, not when I was struggling against the fever of malaria. I have asked you to save my son and you have let him die. What kind of a father are you, anyway?" Esther hasn't spoken to her father since.

Yet, despite her painful past, or maybe because of it, she found the emotional resources to continue. She reminded herself that during her worst hours in exile, it was her connection to friends that saved her. So she sought out a community that made sense to her. She joined Bereaved Families of Ontario. In a group of parents who had lost their children, Esther found solace and hope. She also found that, indeed, her loss was to show the path to a new purpose: to ease the burden of other parents who had lost a child. She devoted such zeal and commitment to bereaved parents that her efforts were acknowledged in a public ceremony. "This is my diploma," Esther says, showing off her plaque, "my Ph.D. I have mastered the art and science of losses and bereavement."

After the deaths of her sister, Hanna, and of her beloved Bill, Esther boarded a jet to another world, one in which she hopes to live up to the mandate of her life: to continue the lineage. Her twelve-year-old granddaughter, Mihal, was to meet her upon her arrival in Tel Aviv.

"I must go on with my life," she explained just before leaving. "Even if I won't be around to see the fruit of my labour. Even though I am not free to spend as much time with my grandchildren as I would like to, they must be reminded that they, too, have a purpose. It is my job to make sure that one day they remember that they are Jewish and that they had a family who had died for just that, being Jewish. I have been asking myself, is all this pain worth it to stay alive? And now I know the answer: for the sake of my three grandchildren as much as for the sake of my parents and their parents, and for the sake of Nathan, it is not only worth it, it is my duty to go on. It is also my purpose."

8
✧✧✧

Bringing the War Home

The Story of
MAYA SCHWARTZ

"The moment we began to hide was a turning point in my life. From that moment on, I would live in sheer terror till the end of the war; fear was always at my side and I couldn't do anything about it, I had no options."

Maya, the only child of Samuel Mendel and Rachel Leah Finkel, was born in Clichy, a working-class neighbourhood on the outskirts of Paris. Her Polish parents had met on a boat en route to Palestine. Samuel, a left-wing radical in his youth, had spent time in jail for agitating on behalf of Sacco and Vanzetti. In spite of Rachel's mother's objections, the two married in Palestine. Based on his readings in French history, Samuel believed that France was the land of opportunity and human rights. So the newly-weds settled in Paris.

Maya's parents worked from sun-up to sundown to make ends meet. Samuel worked in a brewery while until 1938 Rachel had a job in a paper mill. "We were poor," says Maya. "It was always very hard for my parents to make ends meet, partly because they were foreigners. But we did have a modest but normal life. My parents were humble folks, but they made a happy home for me."

All their friends were Polish garment workers who lived in tiny one-room flats. Every Sunday, Maya and her parents would visit them, one after the other. Even though it was their day off, everyone was sewing either on a machine or by hand.

In the summer of 1939, Maya was sent to a summer camp. The seven-year-old had no desire to leave her parents, and on the way to camp, she threw up in the train. From then on, her stay was a continuous nightmare. While the other children had a great time, Maya nursed her sadness. Finally, her father came to visit. "I was not physically or emotionally ready to part with my parents," reflects Maya. "I was just a little girl who needed to have Mom and Dad all the time. Since I was easily scared, I needed to know that I could always climb into Mom or Dad's lap and everything would be all right."

Although there is nothing more ordinary than fear of the unknown, some children face it better than others. Maya had been raised in a sheltered world. Outside her tiny home and the few people with whom her parents maintained friendly relations, all else was a source of threat. Thus, even before the Nazi horrors overtook her life, Maya's reality was studded with frequent bouts of floating anxiety.

All children confronted with the enormity and unpredictabilities of war experience some measure of fear, anguish and perhaps anger. But not all are in the grip of the terror all the time. But when those children for whom the universe pivoted on one point only, their parents, were separated from them, they were prone to moments of anguished premonition. Later, when they fell prey to persecution, theirs became a paradoxical experience of daily life: fear — a disorganizing principle — ended up as the single organizing theme of their everyday existence.

Indeed, when Samuel went to visit his forlorn child in the summer camp, her fears were dispersed immediately. "He took me and a friend out for a stroll. It was like the sun returned to the sky," she says. "And then he left without a word. At the end of the summer, when I went home, I learned that he really came to say goodbye: by then he had enlisted in the armed forces. I was devastated: he didn't say goodbye to me."

Maya's father had fallen victim to the unemployment that riddled the country just before the war and had decided to enlist in the armed forces. His departure marked the end of a normal family life for Maya.

It was at that time that Maya heard the word *war* for the first time. She did not know what it meant, but she understood from her mother's face that it was something terrible. Gone were the songs from her mother's lips; instead, her legs and lips were always trembling. "From that time on," Maya recalls, "our life as a family was disrupted and broken forever. It would never be normal again."

After Samuel's departure, Rachel looked for work. She was now the family's only source of income. She ended up cleaning house for rich Jews and taking home sewing and mending. Maya buried herself in her school work. She was angry with her mother; now that her father was gone, she expected her mother to spend more time with her. Instead, she was always busy. Maya gave Rachel as hard a time as she could. "To this day I feel haunted by how mean I was to my mother," she says. "I just didn't know how to cope with all those scary changes. Then my father came home for a brief visit. When he heard that I'd been mean to my mother, he spanked me. It felt terrible. But when he left, I treated my mother just as before."

Food became scarcer. Maya, like everybody else, stood in the bread line twice a day. When it was time to get some warm clothes for the winter, Rachel took her daughter to the city hall where they were outfitted with used clothing and shoes.

Early in the war, Samuel fell into enemy hands and was sent to a camp for prisoners of war. Not long after that a man covered in coal dust knocked at the door.

"Mama, there's a terrible-looking man at the door," the child screamed.

"Maya, it's me, your papa." He had escaped from the camp and returned to Paris without reporting to his unit.

For a while, there was happiness in the Mendels' flat. Things were almost as before, except, Maya noticed, that her parents did not look as happy.

Life went on without incident until the middle of 1941. One evening, the apartment filled with men. There was a lot of worry in their words: they had all received notices to appear at the

Préfecture de Police. They advised Samuel not to comply since he was a deserter. They wanted him to go into hiding. But he was a stubborn man; he had respect for the law and he was going to obey.

"Don't go to school today," Rachel appealed to her daughter. "I'm worried about your papa." But Maya was as stubborn as her father; she had decided she was going to school, so she went to school.

Samuel, accompanied by Rachel, reported to the police. While Maya was at school, they arrested her father.

A few weeks later, Rachel took Maya to visit Samuel in Beaune-la-Rollande, a concentration camp for Jews near Paris. Maya was shocked to see how sad and gaunt her once husky father had become. "I remember our last visit to Papa," Maya says. "We took several trains, then we walked on one dirt road after another. I was tired and I whined a lot. My mother carried a big package; she'd knitted a sweater and a balaclava for him and we had lots of food that she'd cooked and baked. I remember the barbed wire and the soldiers with guns, everywhere. I wanted to run away as fast as possible, but we had to wait for a whistle to blow. Then we rushed in. When I saw my papa, we just stood there, the three of us, and hugged without a word. But, before I knew it, the whistle blew again and the visit was over. That was the last time I saw my father."

Nine-year-old Maya could not understand why they took her father away from her. What could he have done that was so bad?

"Your papa is a good man," Rachel said to Maya. "He has never hurt anyone and yet he was arrested. And now we are all suffering. Because we're Jewish. You're too young to know what that means but one day you'll grow up and you'll understand."

She was just a little girl, old enough to understand the Fables of La Fontaine, or arithmetic, but not what it meant to be Jewish, or what was so bad about being so. Even though Rachel came from a religious family, faith was not a part of Maya's life. What a child cannot explain to herself scares her. If that child is vulnerable to anxiety about the unexplainable, she is likely to feel disoriented and close to panic.

When the war came to Paris in 1941, many people chose to leave the city rather than wait for the bombs to fall. People with suitcases scurried through the streets as fast as their legs could carry them.

One day, after they had been running through the corridors of the Paris Metro, breathless, Maya had to stop.

"Mama, where are we running?" Maya asked her mother.

"I don't know, ma petite," she answered. "We're just running." Realizing that what they were doing was pointless, they went home.

Rachel sewed a yellow star on Maya's jacket: no matter what, she was never to go outside without it. "I used to be a happy little girl," she says. "I was playful and clownish. Most of all, I was proud of who I was — my parents' child. But with that star on my chest out in the world, I always walked with my head down. I wanted to hide in shame. I did my best to cover it up with my arm. I felt it burn on my chest."

One day, Rachel received a card. When she read it, she began to cry: Samuel had been shipped abroad. Expect to hear from him soon, said the card in German. In fact, they never heard again.

Sadness settled into Maya's heart, and she turned her attention to school. Thus, even though Samuel was not there to share her joys and fears, she slipped into a new version of normal life.

This new version had ever-shrinking boundaries for Parisian Jews in general and for Maya in particular. One decree after another restricted their freedom of movement. They were no longer allowed outside like other people, and they were barred from most public places and events. Maya and Rachel were allowed to shop only at hours when the stores were already plucked clean by non-Jews. With each new decree, Maya felt more scared and more ashamed of being Jewish.

As if she were not living already with endless fear, every time she went out, she shivered with panic. What if she couldn't get home by the curfew? Air raids became a regular feature of daily life in Paris. It was as if the air and sky had formed walls and were closing in on her. "When I think about all the experts who claim that children faced the assault on their lives with resilience and that they did not mind the bombings if they were with their parents and got a lot of reassurance, I get pissed off. We were terrified. When your life is at gunpoint and the bombs are falling towards your head, what do you mean by resilience? With each explosion you die a little, even if you survive it. With each explosion your heart stops beating. Then you sigh with relief that this time it wasn't your turn. And you don't have the energy to rejoice because the next one is more likely to get you than the previous one. With each bomb, you feel more certain that the next one has to be for you. The one thing you can be sure of is that in that downpour of bombs, one has to have your name on it."

When they heard the siren, Rachel and Maya ran to the nearest shelter. Sleeping became a memory. In the flickering gaslight, Maya discerned a baby being nursed in one corner, next to an old woman knitting. In another corner, a man smoked his pipe as if sitting on the terrace of a café. He was trying to read his newspaper — who knows of what date — in the middle of the dark cellar. Children played quietly as if it were high noon and not the middle of the night. But no one made a sound.

The food shortages became so severe that there was hardly any use going to the store for bread: more often than not, the shelves were empty. They treasured every slice of bread; should I eat this now or save it for later when I will be much hungrier? They lived from one slice of bread to the next, thinking that each meal was likely to be the last before they were either taken away or they starved. Each trip to the store enhanced Maya's fears: the empty shelves threatened her with starvation.

One day in March 1942, Rachel returned from cleaning the house of a Jewish woman.

"There're rumours," she said to Maya, "that they are about to pick up the women and the children. We must go into hiding."

But where to hide? They knew only Jews in the neighbourhood. You can't just knock at a stranger's door and ask him to hide you. Finally, for lack of a better alternative, they hid in the closet. "They will knock at the door," Rachel explained to Maya, "and they will call out our name. And we won't breathe a word."

They hid behind the broomstick, the ironing board and a couple of coats. A couple of days later, there was a knock on the door. They heard voices in French and German. Maya and Rachel bit back their screams. They breathed through their teeth, just enough to prevent choking. They stayed in a motionless hug animated by involuntary shivers. Then, there was silence. "In that moment of silence, my mother saved my life," Maya says in a trembling voice that is never far from tears. "She showed me all her love and care:

in spite of her own terror, she thought ahead to save me. My mother gave me life twice."

Rachel knew that the next time they might not be so lucky. She had to find a real hiding place for Maya, at least. They could not stay in that apartment any longer; the next time the authorities came, the concierge would open the door for them.

They stayed with neighbours for a while. But there the same scene would repeat itself. Sooner or later, there would be a knock on the door. Each time, Maya felt like screaming. The terror was beginning to overwhelm her. "On top of worrying what if someone heard us sneeze, pee, fart or quietly weep, I was always terrified of being found out! As if we had done anything wrong, as if we had been criminals! We were good people, I was a good pupil at school. So what was there to find out? And yet we were being hounded."

The only way Rachel could sustain her child was with help from various charitable organizations. But the meagre assistance she eked out from them required that she run from one place to another. Wherever they went they had to wait and wait. Maya often ended up falling asleep in the waiting room. More often than not, they had to get around on foot: Rachel did not have the money for metro or bus. The distances were enormous for the perpetually hungry child. Why is she doing all this? Maya kept asking herself. It was only much later that she understood that it was the only way for Rachel to keep her alive.

Fearing that she could not survive one more knock on the door, Maya told her mother that it was time for her to find a hiding place with Christians. She was only ten years old, but the events she had endured since her father's departure had matured her. Gone were the days of her early tantrums. Now she felt responsible for Rachel, just as her father had told her on the last visit: "Take care of your mama. You're a big girl now."

"You should leave me with Mme Hurtebise for a while, Mama," she said. "I'm too much of a burden for you."

Mme Hurtebise lived in the village of Draveil, not too far from Paris. She was a severe old woman living on her own and Maya had visited her before with her mother.

"Find out if she'll have me for a few weeks or months," Maya said. "In the meantime you'll organize something for yourself and perhaps for me."

The old lady agreed to hide Maya. Rachel packed a few things and accompanied her child to the railroad station. As Maya walked next to her mother, she noticed for the first time how tiny Rachel was. At ten, Maya was already taller than she. Maya was tall and husky, like her father. Next to her Rachel seemed fragile and insignificant. They marched in silence. Occasionally, Maya would steal a glance at her mother: she was beautiful in her red, white and black flowery dress and her high heels. She looked wholesome as a freshly picked flower. At the station Maya and Rachel said goodbye with a kiss on each cheek and a hug, like any French mother and child expecting to see each other soon.

At Madame Hurtebise's house, Maya constantly worried about her mother. Yet, when she received a note from Rachel, she did not answer immediately. Time was not yet a manageable concept for her. The difference between answering in a day or a week was not clear to her. Nobody told her to sit and write to her mother.

"Once I learned that my mother would never return," says Maya, "that brief delay began to weigh on my conscience; since then, my heart has been heavy with that burden. I can imagine her anguish waiting to hear from me. How cruel of me!"

"I couldn't know that it would be forever," Maya says. "I never saw my mother again. Once I learned that she'd been arrested, I blamed myself for abandoning her. I should've stayed with her."

Like Ada and like countless other hidden children, Maya fell into the trap of self-recrimination for something over which she had neither power nor control. These children felt they had to look after their parents. After all, hadn't their fathers, among them Samuel, admonished them to take care of their mothers? Their fathers' absence promoted these young, helpless children to the status of empowered adult-like beings, at least in their own minds — but without, of course, any of the adults' resources. Abandoned and abused children often find themselves victims of this gambit.

Although it is natural that parents die before their children, many of these youngsters would have gladly given their lives in exchange for their mothers'. Worse, they felt that they *should* have given their lives to save their mothers, as if that bargain was within their means. The ensuing guilt poisoned these children's lives, often well into adulthood. From the time they learned of their mothers' tragic fate, all their life experiences were bathed in their guilt. To this day, Maya feels guilty for abandoning Rachel.

Maya's lot in hiding was, indeed, an inventory of horrors. According to the initial arrangement, Mme Hurtebise was to receive a monthly payment for keeping Maya. At first the money came from Rachel. After her arrest, it came from the Oeuvre de Secours aux Enfants. When it was late, Mme Hurtebise would become violent and threaten to turn Maya over to the Gestapo.

Mme Hurtebise also kept a close check on how much the child ate. She even looked in Maya's mouth to make sure she was not stuffing her cheeks. All she gave Maya to eat was one or two slices of bread. When she saw Maya pick up the crumbs from the table, she made her spit them out. And then she would beat her with her bare hand or with a stick she kept nearby just for that purpose. "I remember getting up from the table as hungry as I was when I sat down. Even though we were on a farm, I never had the right to a glass of milk, an apple or a piece of meat. Just to look at something other than what she pushed in front of me earned me a solid beating."

Nearly any occasion presented a good excuse for her to beat Maya. If the child sneezed, she got beaten. If she coughed, she got beaten. When Maya had the flu, she was seized by coughing fits. Mme Hurtebise was beside herself. "One more cough, and I'll make you sleep in the doghouse for the rest of the night!" What was Maya to do? No matter how much she had to cough, she held her breath. She was terrified of having to spend the night in the doghouse.

Shortly after she arrived in Draveil, Maya received the one and only package Rachel was able to send to her daughter. She could hardly contain her excitement: What goodies was she to get? Was there a letter inside? Besides, she wanted to hug that package just because it came from her mother and she knew how hard it had to be for her to send anything at all. She felt special.

But Mme Hurtebise robbed Maya of the pleasure of opening her mother's package. Instead, she opened it herself. When she saw that it contained a loaf of bread, a rotten pear and some melted chocolate, the old woman started to laugh hysterically. Maya sensed trouble. When the woman calmed down a bit, she lashed out at Maya. "Your mother must be really crazy to send you a package like this."

Maya stood there, without a word, waiting for the blows to rain upon her head. She knew the sequence of events. The woman would get angry for something, she would work herself up to a frenzy and she would shower Maya with blows. Many a time she hit Maya until the child lost consciousness.

This time she just grabbed the package and heaved it into the fire. Then, suddenly, she had a second thought. "Even your mother couldn't be that crazy. Perhaps she hid something in that package." she ripped the singed package out of the fireplace and began to rummage in it. Buried in the bread, she found some money, which she triumphantly tucked in her pocket. The rest went back in the fire. Maya never found out if there was a letter for her.

"My mom sent her last money to me," says Maya. "I never again heard from her."

Mme Hurtebise had Maya look after the garden. Being from the city, Maya knew nothing about yard work. It was back-breaking, and no matter what she did, it was always wrong. She longed for the days when all she had to do was run to the store for a loaf of bread or a bottle of milk and attend to her homework. On top of her garden chores, Maya did the dishes, polished the furniture and kept everything tidy. As a reward, Madame hit her for not doing a better job.

There was one thing that pleased Mme Hurtebise. Her vegetable garden always needed manure. To earn a more generous meal, Maya would pick up two bags and run after the horse and the donkey. With her bare hands, she picked up their droppings and spread them on the vegetable beds. The old woman, pleased with the child's devotion and her cleverness, rewarded Maya by taking her to the forest with a hand-drawn cart. Maya was expected to fill the cart with dry branches for the fireplace. It was a horrible task. Maya was terrified of the dark woods. It was cold and damp in there. At any moment she expected to be eaten by a hungry wolf from the pages of a children's book.

Maya attended a country school in the next town to which she walked with another little girl. Maya was happy to have a link to another child, and the teachers, a friendly young couple, were amazed at how quickly Maya learned. She even finished a *certificat d'étude* (a certificate for completing a level in an academic subject).

For Maya and for children living in similar predicaments, concentrating on and excelling in their studies was their lifeline. When Maya was at school or when she had her nose in the books, she was free of Mme Hurtebise and the oppressive nagging of her hunger pangs. She concentrated on arithmetic or history rather than on her own miseries or her longing for her parents. It was also her way to normalize an otherwise untenable experience: as long as she was studying, everything was as it used to be; she was like every other child. It was her way of not allowing the enemy to defeat her or rob her of her humanity. A child who studies and takes pride in it is not a helpless victim.

Indeed, eventually, Maya decided not to take any more abuse from Mme Hurtebise. One day, as she was walking home from school, she passed the Red Cross office and had an idea. She knew that the Red Cross helped people in trouble, and she was in trouble. She went inside and told the man behind the desk that she was an orphan staying with Mme Hurtebise, who beat her. To support her words, she rolled up her sleeves, exposing bruises on both arms. The man was unimpressed: all children had to be beaten, he said, shrugging his shoulders. But Maya wanted to get his attention. So she continued to speak about all the things the old woman had told her about herself. Among other things Maya related, she told her that in her younger years she had beautiful large breasts and all men were crazy for them.

The man grew agitated. He jumped to his feet and told Maya to go home and not to listen to this kind of nonsense. The young girl thought that was the end of that. She was sad that nothing came of her rebellion, but at least she had tried.

A few days later, however, when she was about to leave school, one of her teachers told her to go home and pack her bag. The man from the Red Cross had notified the teachers, and they contacted the underground. Together they engineered a plan to take Maya out of her horrible hiding place. But the girl, instead of rejoicing, was terrified to leave Mme Hurtebise. What if her mother returned? She would not find Maya where she had left her. How would they ever meet again?

But the wheels had already been set in motion and she had to go. After a year of hell in Draveil, she was transferred to a hiding place near Paris, in a town called Montmorency. It was a huge place. Several Jewish children were already hiding there. While her penchant would have been to run around with children, she was admonished to lie low. Nonetheless, she was no longer Mme Hurtebise's indentured servant, and she had no reason to live in constant terror. But she was far from feeling reassured. The place was quite eerie: there was no apparent supervision at all. What if they needed some adult intervention for some emergency? It was not a reassuring situation at all for Maya. But she ate well. In no time, she began to gain back the weight she had lost on Mme Hurtebise's starvation diet.

In Montmorency, feeling somewhat more grounded in the reality of the place, Maya regained some of her courage. The owners of the home overheard her boast one day that her father, the revolutionary, had taught her to revolt if things didn't go her way. "Don't you ever use those words in this house again!" they admonished her in the sternest manner. "If you do, you'll force us to turn you over to the Gestapo."

Maya decided to return to Mme Hurtebise's place. "Why would I want to go back to that witch who beat me and starved me?" Maya wonders. "There can be only one reason: I lived in constant fear that if my mother came for me, she would never find me unless I was where she had left me."

But on the day she was planning to leave the home at Montmorency, someone betrayed her. Once again, she got a dressing down. Maya resigned herself to stay.

Then a few days later, two Jewish social workers came to take Maya and two other girls away. The social workers shuttled between Paris and Grenoble, placing Jewish children with families willing to hide them from the Nazis.

"You're going to a convent," one of them said. "You must not tell anyone that you're Jewish. You're war orphans. There will be other children there already. Just copy them and you'll be fine."

First, they stayed in Paris, with the Sisters of Zion, for a few days. It was obvious to Maya that this shelter was for children from wealthy families — the children were all dressed in fine clothes and the convent looked more like a castle than a retreat. Maya like it there, but before she could settle in, she was on the train again to Grenoble, escorted by the two social workers.

In Grenoble, she stayed first at the Sisters of Zion, then she was moved to another convent where she stayed until liberation. One part of the convent was home to a reform school for juvenile delinquents and the children of criminals and prostitutes. The other was for orphans and children abandoned by their parents. The former were under government supervision and subsidy: they ate better and more. Maya was to join the latter, the orphans. There were three Jews among them. Without government subsidy, the nuns had no interest in them. "The juvenile delinquents had three solid meals a day and we had none. It sure sent us a powerful message about the value they placed on us," says Maya, not without bitterness.

Maya's life in the convent was tough. That region of the Alps was under heavy bombardment. It sheltered the headquarters of the French resistance, as well as an important German military installation. The sky was often black with American, British and Australian bombers trying to liberate the area. Maya lived with sheer terror. If the bombs did not kill her, she thought, starvation would. She used to be hungry all the time at Mme Hurtebise's farm, but starvation in the convent was even worse. There was never anything for breakfast. For lunch they would serve a watery soup made of potato peels. It was so repugnant that, starved as they were, they could not eat it. The only other food was a slice of bread, two boiled potatoes or some noodles or a small bowl of beans, and a teaspoon of jam, twice a day. Children who were sick got double portions. Most days, the sick bay was full with children claiming to be ill just for the supplementary food. Maya was starved emotionally, as well. The nuns never had a kind word for them. They snapped orders at the children and that was all.

Winter set in with a vengeance. The convent was not heated. When the children took off their gloves or their socks, the flesh came with them from the frost-bite. Maya's fingers were blue and so swollen that she could no longer hold a pencil. At night, the children would soak their hands and feet in hot water, but the sores were always there. In that bitter cold, Maya had to go barefoot — she had outgrown her shoes. At first, she cut the toes open but soon she was unable to get into her shoes at all.

Although the nuns provided neither adequate food nor heat for the young wards, they managed to give them a uniform for weekdays and another fancier one for Sundays and religious holidays.

At four o'clock in the morning, Maya and the others were yanked
out of their sleep to line up and march into the chapel. Maya did
not mind this harsh regimen because the chapel was the only
heated place in the convent. Besides, she liked to feast her eyes on
the chapel — its ornateness was a striking contrast to everything
else in her life. She joined the choir — like her mother, she had a
beautiful voice and enjoyed singing. She loved to listen to the
sermons — they transported her to a world far away from the des-
olation of her everyday existence.

"Later, when I was in a Jewish home and I told them about those
days in the convent, they called me a traitor for getting attached to
Catholicism, but for me it was just a matter of enjoying the warmth
and beauty of the chapel. The time spent in the chapel was a reprieve
from the regimented life that we all hated. I was not at all interested
in their religion. It was not a joyful experience to hear the nuns constantly indict us for having killed Christ. 'The Jews deserve to suffer for two thousand years for crucifying our Lord Jesus Christ.'
Nevertheless, I told the nuns that I wished to become one of them.
To their credit, they told me to wait with my decision until I was
older and clearer in my mind. What attracted me to become a nun
was the security from persecution for being a Jew."

During her stay at that convent, Maya discovered a new face of
fear. She often saw people die, nuns and children, and she became
more aware of her own mortality. Next time would have to be her
turn, she thought. Even though the nuns reassured her that death
would be painless and that all children go to heaven, she was still
petrified when she looked at the waxy remains on display.

Every once in a while, the two social workers stopped by to check
on Maya. Those were rare moments of pleasure for her. They took
her out for a stroll, as if she was family. They encouraged her to
hang in there — the end had to be near. When they left, she felt
even worse in the cold world of the nuns.

Then, the day she had been waiting for finally came: the social
workers returned to take Maya and two other girls away. They slept
that night at the Convent of the Sisters of Zion in Grenoble, and
the next morning, the streets were full of American soldiers. Maya
had just been liberated.

Children experienced liberation differently. For some, it was a
time of jubilation. For others it was a sad occasion, ushering in yet

another separation, and the beginning of a new life with strangers — their parents. For Maya, liberation was just another readjustment. Ever since she said goodbye to her mother at the train station, each change was only a matter of details. No one showed the slightest interest in her welfare beyond keeping her body alive. Liberation meant that Maya's life was no longer at risk. She had been living with that fact for so long that without even noticing it she had tamed it. To her, liberation was simply another place and a new set of strangers she had to endure.

Like many other children, Maya was in the grip of an understandable depression occasioned by her loss of trust in the future and in people. Things were not likely to get better for her, so what was there to be happy about? However, this kind of depression served a purpose for Maya and the others — it prevented hope or joy from turning into bitter disappointment. It was informed by two years of living nightmares. For most children who emerged depressed from the war, their depression was clearly reactive: as soon as they experienced care and genuine benevolence, they responded with openness and optimism typical of most children.

Soon after that, the three girls were separated. Maya was sent to live with a farmer who had just returned from a prisoner-of-war camp. The farm was animated with the joy of a family reunion. Maya liked being surrounded with happy people, but she had no reason to celebrate — she was totally cut off from her family. The more her hosts laughed, the more Maya wept. What hope did she have to reconnect with her parents? Her hosts were so busy celebrating that they failed to notice the sad child.

From there, Maya was sent to another farm in La Bourgeade, in the Department of Isère, a village tiny enough to have only one well for all the inhabitants. Mme Marie, her host, who had two little girls of her own, was a kind-hearted woman. Finally, Maya received the caring attention she needed.

The few months Maya spent at Mme Marie's house were happy times. The war was over. The villagers were warm and friendly. There were weddings to which everyone was invited. They were in a constantly festive mood. Everyone told tales of survival, and they celebrated life, rather than mourning losses. Mme Marie and her husband did their best to cheer Maya up. And much of the time she felt like a child once again.

But the seed of her losses was so deeply planted that virtually anything would trigger in her a spontaneous downpour of tears. Sadness and fear formed a domain in her in which she was more at home than anywhere else. Mme Marie made pretty dresses and underwear for her little girls. Seeing those specially crafted pieces of clothing on those two little girls made Maya feel left out. Thinking back over her short life full of tragedies and disappointments, she concluded that being left out seemed to have been her lot in life.

From La Bourgeade, Maya was moved to a Jewish orphanage on the outskirts of Grenoble. After having been persecuted for being Jewish throughout much of her childhood, Maya was finally introduced to the sweeter side of being Jewish. In hiding, she had no way of experiencing the cultural and emotional side of Judaism, nor to learn anything about the history of Jews. Because she was Jewish, she had been robbed of her parents. But the young couple who ran the orphanage made sure that their wards learned lots of Hebrew songs and stories. They celebrated all the holidays in the most festive ways: the place was decorated in multi-colour splendour for all the Jewish festivals. They put on plays by Jewish authors on Jewish themes. But most of all they had an endless string of stories about Palestine, the land of Israel. They encouraged the children to go to the Promised Land as soon as possible.

Maya would have been perfectly happy in that high-spirited environment if it had not been for one disturbing factor. Every now and then, a stranger would show up — a returning father or mother. The effusive scenes of reunion filled everyone's heart with warmth and hope. Perhaps the next time the bell rang, it would be her mother or father coming to take her home.

But Maya did not believe any more in such miracles. Each time she had trusted that things would turn out for the best, she was wrong. So each of these tearful encounters with a returning parent made Maya's heart sadder, more desolate. Therein lay the dilemma she and many others had to face — the impossibility and the necessity to trust the future.

And then one day the couple who had given her more joy than anyone had since she had last seen her mother suddenly disappeared, leaving behind an orphanage full of disappointed children, abandoned once more by trusted adults. The people who replaced them turned out to be monstrous. Gone were the joys of a happy Jewish home, the plentiful tables and the love and affection. The new people were mean and greedy. In fact, somewhat later, they were caught embezzling the assets of the institution and selling the clothing, shoes and other gifts sent to the children from the United States. Maya was not surprised, nor was she unhappy about their arrest. She was indignant and embarrassed that Jews could steal the food out of the mouths of orphans and the clothes off their backs.

In a moment of quiet despair, Maya decided to write a letter to a good friend of her father's, a man of considerable wealth. His name was Mugnon Herstritt. She hoped that he would write back to her; she longed for contact with the world of her parents. To her great surprise, M Herstritt not only answered, but he came to visit her. Secretly, she was praying that this affluent friend of her father would take pity on her and rescue her. He did no such thing. Neither did any of her parents' other friends. "No one was interested in me," Maya says tearfully. "Not one person ever asked me if I would like to live with them. I felt like a leper."

M Herstritt, however, was instrumental in helping Maya return to the Paris area — one of her fondest desires. She landed in another orphanage called Champfleur, in Maison Laffitte, in the capital region. It was a lot easier for M Herstritt and the child to meet now and then. And it was within Maya's reach to explore Paris, to go to the library or to sneak off to a movie.

At Champfleur, Maya met Dorothée Solomonitis, a Greco-Romanian Jew. She was the Swiss cultural attachée in Paris and had spent the war living an easy life in Geneva, where she achieved a doctorate in literature and social sciences. As a token of gratitude for the wonderful life she was afforded in Switzerland during the war, she offered her time to orphans.

Dorothée was a caring person. She was fond of sitting down on the edge of an orphan's bed and listening to her pour out her heart. Hers was always a good shoulder to cry on. One day, however, Maya did not get out of bed — she felt sick. Dorothée happened to come by to visit. Maya was at a low emotional ebb, and immediately the tears began to flow. But on that particular occasion, for some unknown reason Dorothée was indignant. It was not part of her role as a cultural attachée to have to deal with people's personal aches and pains, she said. Her reaction first startled, then confused Maya.

Dorothée's unwillingness to deal with Maya's sadness mirrored the response of the population at large, often including the adult family members of hidden children. No one wanted to hear what those abandoned and betrayed children had to say. That reluctance amounted to yet another abandonment. Rather than delving into the suffering of those harshly wronged youngsters, the adults denied the children's pain. Worse: they denied that the children had a story to tell.

Many took the attitude that since the war was over, it was time to move on. Rather than acknowledging that they did not have the emotional wherewithal to listen to accounts of the atrocities visited upon little children, adults claimed either that children had no memories because they were too young, or that those who survived could not have had it so bad. If the children had endured hardships, they would most likely forget them and land on their feet like cats.

"According to a psychologist," Maya states with indignation, "child survivors prefer to remain silent. That is a bunch of bullshit! First of all, we spoke whenever anyone was there to listen. Second, we always spoke among ourselves. The children were not afraid to call a spade a spade. We all knew what we meant. We didn't have to dance around each other's squeamish sensitivities. So if any adult, psychologist or not, claims that children had nothing to say or that they didn't want to speak, that person is living proof of nothing less than an inability or unwillingness to listen."

While at Champfleur, Maya paid a visit to her old neighbourhood in Clichy. She first looked up the Tailleuls, friends of her parents. M Tailleul was a popular tailor. From him, she learned the fate of her parents. M Tailleul and Maya's father had been together in Beaune-la-Rollande. Although Samuel's courage had allowed him to escape the POW camp, it was insufficient for a second escape attempt. All he could think of was the consequence of getting caught — never seeing his Maya again. He helped Tailleul escape, but he himself stayed. Consequently, he was sent to Auschwitz with about one thousand Jews — all of whom were gassed on arrival. As for Rachel, she made her way to the free zone with Mme Tailleul. The day of their departure, Mme Tailleul had a premonition; she wanted to wait another day. Not wanting to risk delay, Rachel left as planned. She crossed the Maginot line on her own but got caught trying to enter the free zone. She was taken to Auschwitz on a convoy with 850 others. She, too, was gassed on arrival. "I found out in the *Mémorial de la Déportation* [the record of names and fate of all Jews deported from France] by Serge and Béate Klarsfeld that my mother was killed two weeks after my father."

Maya hoped that her parents' old friends would offer to take her in, but they made no offers. Maya was unable to comprehend how all these people could be so indifferent. She began to worry that perhaps there was something about her that did not inspire kindness and generosity. With the self-centredness of children, Maya assumed there was something wrong with her. She did not know that people were so numb from the horrors of their own survival and from the number of tragic accounts they had heard that, to guard their own emotional and social boundaries, they allowed no story, however touching, to move them deeply enough to make a gesture of generosity, such as inviting a shivering child into their life to stay with them.

One day in 1945, two Americans came to visit Maya in her orphanage. They were related to Rachel's sister, Miriam, who had been living in Los Angeles. During a lavish dinner in their luxury hotel, the two visitors, Charles and Benjamin, self-made millionaires, offered to arrange immigration for Maya. Her aunt would love to have her.

Maya was at first cold to the idea. Now that the Nazis were gone, and she had enough to eat, she was quite pleased to be French and living in France. But when her aunt began to write letters to her promising to get her a piano and pay for voice and music lessons, she wavered. Her aunt promised everything she ever wanted. Besides these wonderful promises were proof that genuine care was available to Maya for the first time in years. She was ready to board the first ship to America.

It took two years, however, before she was on board a freighter sailing for New Orleans. From there, she took a train to Los Angeles. She was fifteen years old and ready to start her life all over.

Charles met her at the train station. Immediately, he warned her not to expect anything from him again. Maya was stunned. But when they arrived at her aunt's place, she understood: her aunt and uncle and their baby lived in poverty. There was no room in their tiny one-bedroom apartment for an accordion, let alone a piano. Maya had to sleep on a hide-a-bed in the living-room. Her uncle was a gambler and a drinker. Every time he was drunk, he tried to rape Maya.

Finally she understood what had happened: her aunt expected that Charles, the rich relative, would make regular contributions to Maya's support and she would skim off the top what she needed for herself. Charles, however, had made a one-time donation and that was that.

Her outlook was bleak. She had no money, spoke not a word of English and knew no one. In 1947, Los Angeles was a sleepy burg. There was nothing to do but stay with her aunt and her abusive husband. Once again, Maya fell prey to fear. She saw no hope for herself.

Maya's aunt fed her as little as possible, and Maya felt she had returned to the farm of Mme Hurtebise. Once again, every time she left the table, she was hungry. She had to clean the house before and after school. And it was never good enough. On the weekend, she had to baby-sit her two-year-old cousin. And all this for thirty-five cents a week.

"They hated me," Maya says with anger in her voice. "There was nothing in it for them to have me, so they made sure that they got enough work from me to pay for my keep. As for my uncle, he had his fun trying to have sex with me."

When she could no longer take it, Maya decided to run away and hide out in the Hollywood hills. She confided her plan to someone who took pity on her and introduced her to an affluent Jewish family in west Los Angeles. They were looking for a companion for their eight-year-old daughter. Maya jumped at the opportunity. She had just turned sixteen when she began her new employment as a companion. It turned out, however, that she was expected to do all the chores and take care of the whole family. Once again, Maya found herself in a home where all they were interested in was what they could get from her.

"At times I didn't know whether I should laugh or cry," Maya says with a sardonic smile. "If they hadn't made me suffer so much,

if they hadn't demeaned me so deeply, I'd say that they were a caricature of themselves. But they were indeed the caricature of the
stereotypical ugly Jew. You can't imagine how it hurts me to say
these words. But there is no escaping them. She starved me then
made an enormous scene when I wanted to supplement my food
with a small can of beans from her pantry. She got hysterical
because I ate a piece of chocolate that she and her friends left after
a bridge party. How can I not think that these people were monstrous and ridiculous at the same time?"

Many hidden children who ended up orphaned report similar
tribulations. Their "benefactors" knew that these young people
had no champions — no parents, no protectors to stand behind
them and ask that those who mistreated them account for their
ignominy. They masqueraded as altruists, but in reality they were
the worst kind of exploiters of children. Their betrayal of these vulnerable youngsters often led to a new version of hiding: the children, knowing they had no recourse or better alternative, buried
their turmoils and kept their pain to themselves. Thus for orphans
like Maya the hiding never really stopped. Nor did the fear that
life would never stop tossing pain their way.

And yet, Maya never gave up waiting for the day when things
would be better, when someone would emerge with her best inter-
ests at heart, a truly benevolent witness. Here and there, Maya did
meet people who were touched by her obvious solitude. At John
Marshall High School in Los Angeles, teachers and some parents
were moved to generosity: they brought her boxes of gorgeous
clothes. "It was the first time that I had such pretty clothes. They
really cheered me up," Maya says with a smile. "I don't know what
felt better — looking in the mirror and seeing an attractively
dressed young woman look back at me, or looking in the mirror
and finding a couple of caring faces smiling back at me."

One day, while she was still at John Marshall, a social worker
from France visited the school. Maya ran to her and poured her
heart out. The visitor listened patiently and lovingly. At the end,
she encouraged Maya to excel in her studies and to carve out her
own niche in life; build your own family, your own network.
Provide for yourself what life and people failed to provide for you.

That advice was easy for Maya to follow. The only pleasure she
had in life was her studies. Her teachers were caring and

nurturing people. They became the benevolent witnesses Maya needed to make sense of her life. "I was fortunate to meet these fine people. That is why I chose my profession. I always looked up to my teachers."

Intuitively, Maya pinpointed the reason why so many hidden children are in other-centred professions: education, community service, the helping and healing arts. Those abandoned and betrayed children who had never had the sustained experience of a benevolent witness in their lives, ended up imitating their tormentors. But those to whom someone showed sustained kindness became, in some significant ways, like their rescuers. Robert Krell is unequivocal about how influential his Dutch moeder was on who he became. Thus Maya became like several of her teachers — caring, affectionate and sensitive.

At eighteen, Maya graduated from John Marshall High School. The day after graduation, she married Eugene. Soon, they had a son, Michael, but the marriage was a disaster. Eugene was a violent man who regularly beat his young wife. After four years of abuse, Maya divorced him. "Thirty-six years later," says Maya, "I found out that he was a closet alcoholic. That accounted for his rage."

In 1954, Maya received a bachelor of arts degree in French from the University of California at Berkeley. She did her student teaching in a junior high school in Berkeley with a woman whose husband was the head of a local Nazi party. She herself was a self-avowed anti-Semite. At every opportunity, she humiliated Maya in front of the students with derogatory comments: "Would you mind closing the blinds. . . . Oh, you did that in such a sloppy way, but then again, Jews are a sloppy people. . . . Oh, you've left off an accent mark from this word. Don't you know anything? I thought Jews were supposed to be smart, but you sure are dumb."

When Maya finished her student teaching, her Nazi supervisor gave her a poor evaluation. And when she began hunting for a position as a French teacher, that letter of evaluation haunted her. Finally, after having tasted the most abject poverty with her young son in Los Angeles, she found a teaching position at Westchester High School in south Los Angeles.

One day, five years into her tenure, Maya found swastikas drawn all over her chalkboard and her door. On her desk, there was a letter with a stamp with a picture of Hitler on it. Inside, she found a hate letter suggesting that she should have been killed a long time ago.

First Maya was numb. She was sure this was not happening to her, not again. She took a deep breath and decided to be quite professional about the matter. She had the board erased and began to teach her lesson.

But a few minutes later, she felt nauseous and before she knew it, she fainted. Her students had to walk her out of the classroom. She was sick for several days.

What was she to do? A paralyzing fear inundated her whole being. All she could do was sigh and quiver. She was all too familiar with the unwelcome feeling of powerlessness in face of danger. Should she go into hiding once again? Must she swallow, once again, the unsavoury taste of being humiliated and endangered for being Jewish? Would this persecution ever end? Leaving the school was not a solution. There were no jobs, and her memories of starvation were still fresh. There was no place to run — the enemies without had joined forces with the hidden enemies within.

When she returned to teach, she still had no recollection of the incident until the substitute teacher showed her the letter with the Hitler stamp on it. That refreshed her memory and sent a shiver up her spine. When Maya learned that the only other Jewish teacher in her school had received a similar letter, the two of them took the matter to the principal.

"You're over-reacting, as usual" was his response to the matter. "Can't you take it just for what it is — a joke, a prank."

Maya went to the Anti-Defamation League for advice and possible redress. She filed a complaint.

"It is a known fact," the official at ADL told her, "that your administration is anti-Semitic. But I advise you not to rock the boat, if you want to keep your job." However, he did file a report of the complaint.

Everything quieted down at her school. Maya did her best to forget the unsavoury episode. Then, a couple of years later, around Christmas time someone burned down her classroom. When she spoke to the principal, he accused her of saying something in class to incite the students. "Rather than looking for the culprit, they were interrogating me, looking for a way to hold me responsible for what had happened," Maya recalls indignantly.

The incidents continued. One day her extensive French book and record collection was destroyed. The school deemed it private property and she received no compensation. Another time, all her teaching notes were "accidentally" set on fire. On another occasion, someone had defecated on the table where she usually had lunch.

Like it or not, Maya had to return to a new version of hiding. She no longer knew who was safe. She could not longer negotiate ordinary routines with any kind of predictability. There was no alternative but to withdraw from the line of fire.

When an adult who has been abused and betrayed as a child encounters new instances of cruelty and torment, the old feelings return with exponential intensity. They become more painful because that person endures not only the current trauma, but all previous ones. This is the ultimate torture: "I burn down your room and make it clear that I did it because you're Jewish. I know that in so doing I'm sending you back to all the previous places of hiding so that you can feel hurt again and again. Suffer for these ashes and all the previous ashes in your life, especially the ones scattered all over your childhood. Such is my power over you, such is my disdain for you." This power tends to debilitate those who, like Maya, were never sufficiently reassured that the world was a safe place and that one could indeed run away from one's enemies. Maya's betrayal was so thorough that no safe haven ever emerged for her. The only way out was in the nearly magical hope that one day the persecutors would leave her alone, and her life would become safe and reliable.

To get help with the mounting stress, Maya entered therapy. Finally someone was there to assist her piece together the fragments of the past and the present. She also had remarried, and her new husband shared her struggles.

The conflicts at school did not go away — her students kept launching attacks against her, sometimes in person, sometimes through various kinds of written intimidation and degradation. The response from the administration remained constant: do not overreact. When she sought support from her Jewish colleagues, they turned their backs to her. "If you can't take the heat, get out of the kitchen," they would tell her. They were American-born Jews whose vistas had not been overcast by the clouds of Nazi persecution.

The situation deteriorated to the point that Maya became sick and had to stop teaching after twenty-nine years in the classroom. Her therapist advised her to get a lawyer, and with the lawyer's help, Maya began to fight back. She appeared before a psychiatrist representing the school board. Since he was a mental health professional, she allowed free flow to her emotions and told him her full story. His response was to accuse her of being too emotional and over-sensitive. "These things are like chalk dust," he said. "You just brush them off." Maya was furious. "Don't you dare to deny the validity of my sufferings, nor their depth."

Five years later, she won her battle against a bigoted school administration, a violent student body and general apathy. Her lawyer presented a compelling grievance: owing to the discriminatory and prejudicial treatment meted out to Maya by her principal, her mental and physical health were severely compromised. The persecution she had endured at his hand coerced Maya to relive the nightmares of the Holocaust.

At the end of January 1984, Maya left the classroom forever. Vindicated, she retired with honour. The hiding was over once and for all.

Soon after, Maya read an article in the Los Angeles *Times* about a support group for child survivors led by Drs Sarah Moskovitz and Flo Kunstler. There was no doubt in Maya's mind: she wanted to join their group. Not a day passed that she did not think of those horrible times in hiding. She carried the Holocaust wherever she went.

One of her goals in life was to move beyond the pain and anger of her multiple abandonments and the fear connected to them. Another was to have her parents' names engraved on the *Monument pour les Victimes de la Guerre et de la Déportation*, in her native Clichy. Encouraged by Sarah and Flo, and by her husband, Jay Schwartz, Maya petitioned the French authorities. It took her four years to accomplish it, but in spite of what seemed to be a series of insurmountable obstacles, once again Maya won.

When Sarah Moskovitz and her husband went to Paris, they made the trip to Clichy to take pictures of the monument and of the engraving: Samuel Mendel and Rachel Leah Finkel, perished at Auschwitz.

"I am at peace now," says Maya. "I've fought my battles. Some

I lost, but the important ones I won. I stood up for my rights, I protected my dignity, and I defeated the bigots. My parents did not disappear in the silence of history. Their names will live on forever in Clichy, in this box of photographs, very close to my heart, and in my son, Michael. The Nazis had soiled my childhood, and nothing and nobody will change that. But the last few years have been good and I am looking forward to a lot more years like them. And I'll never experience the terror of persecution again, hallelujah."

9

✧✧✧

Conflicting Loyalties

The Story of
ABRAHAM FOXMAN

The Fucksmans were a family of considerable means. Until the war broke out, Hela — later Helen — and Joseph, lived happily in Warsaw. They had their own home, but the young wife spent much of her time nearby at the home her parents shared with her two brothers and a sister. Theirs was a very tight Orthodox family. Since Hela's father had died very young, his children ran the family's thread factory.

One week before the war broke out, Joseph returned to his family in Baranovichi. Hela, pregnant with their first child, stayed behind with her family. When the Luftwaffe began its massive bombing of Warsaw, Hela's mother insisted that her daughter join her husband in Baranovichi, at that time under Polish rule, about four hundred kilometres east of the beleaguered Polish capital, which was still under Soviet control.

After four weeks of ceaseless bombardments, finally there was a lull, and the expectant mother set out on the journey. It took her weeks to make the short trip. Upon her arrival, she moved in with

Joseph's family. After she gave birth to their son, Henouch Abraham, the young family moved into a place of their own. But the authorities did not allow them to stay, so they moved to the nearby town of Slonim. Joseph worked as a bookkeeper, while Hela stayed home to take care of her baby.

In Slonim, for the first time, Hela and Joseph began to experience real hardships. There were severe shortages of oil for cooking, and often it was a challenge for the young woman to put food on the table. On market-days, when Christian farmers brought milk, cheese and eggs into town, she would leave her son with the neighbours and buy food for the three of them. They had no running water or heating in their tiny room, and the baby was frequently sick.

For the sake of the child, Hela moved to Vilna, where two of her six brothers had been living. Joseph had to stay behind in Slonim. However, as a refugee, Hela was not allowed to settle in the city so she rented a place in the country, about eight kilometres from her work in a bookbindery. Christian neighbours looked after the child while she was at work.

When the boy was eleven months old, Hela retained the services of a Polish woman, Bronislava Kurpi, to look after the baby and the household. Bronislava cared for the child as if he were her own, and the two women lived under the same roof in perfect harmony. Joseph finally managed to find a way to join them, but on his arrival, Bronislava's attitude changed dramatically. She berated her employer at every opportunity, calling him a stupid and stubborn Jew. Hela later learned that the nanny was a lesbian and saw Joseph as the enemy.

The day it was announced that all Jews had to move into the Vilna ghetto, Joseph and Hela were faced with a dilemma. Their Christian neighbours encouraged them to ignore the order and to stay put. Joseph had his doubts: he worried that the neighbours thought they could get a lot of money from them. When the neighbours found out they couldn't, they would kill the family. In the final analysis, he decided, they would be safer in the ghetto. "Later, we found out that those nice Polish neighbours killed the rich Jews who had listened to their advice," says Helen.

But their choice left them with another dilemma: what to do with their son? There seemed to be no alternative but to take him to the ghetto where he would share their fate. Unexpectedly, Bronislava offered to look after the child. At first, the young parents were unwilling to separate from their child, especially under such precarious conditions, but eventually they admitted that Bronislava's offer was the best solution to a potentially bad situation. Besides, they had no worries about the nanny — she had always taken the best possible care of the child. They unpacked the child's belongings and left the woman three cart-loads of their own effects, food and, with the exception of 180 roubles, all their money at hand. Then they loaded a cart with their own things and walked into the larger of the two ghettos in Vilna, humorously referred to as S.S.S.R. — after the initials of the four streets bordering the ghetto: Szavelska, Szpitalna, Straszuna and Rudnicka (the initials also stand for "Union of Socialist Soviet Republics" in Russian).

"I had to turn my back on my twelve-month-old child just as he had learned to take his first few steps on his own," recalls Helen. " 'Whatever money we'll make, we shall give to you,' we promised Bronislava as we were leaving. And we did, and then some."

In the ghetto, there was no room for them to settle. Finally, an acquaintance offered them the counter top in his store on Szpitalna Street — his two-room flat already sheltered twenty-four people.

Living conditions were intolerable. The authorities provided no food for the Jews inside the ghetto. Joseph worked outside but smuggling food into the ghetto was prohibited. Those caught saw their goods confiscated. At the discretion of the guards, they could be beaten or taken away to the nearby Ponary Woods to be killed. To add to Hela and Joseph's hardship, people they had known before pointed their fingers at the couple: look at these shameless people — they had abandoned their child to save their lives.

Once a month, Hela sneaked out of the ghetto to her child. As promised, she gave Bronislava five thousand roubles each time. Whenever Joseph did not make enough to save that amount, the nanny became loud and abusive and demanded her money or else.

They had been in the ghetto for a short time when Joseph and Hela received from the authorities a *lebenschein* (temporary living permit) authorizing them to stay alive for a while. There was only one problem: the permit was for a man, a woman and a child, but their child was not in the ghetto. They set out to look for a child they could claim as their own in the event of a document control. They offered to take one child belonging to a widow with six children, but the widow could not decide which one to choose. Eventually, they found an eighteen-year-old girl who was sufficiently malnourished to pass for a child. When they passed inspection, the guard could not tell the mother from the daughter, but let them go anyway. This was one of the miracles that confirmed Joseph's faith in the God of Israel, in spite of all the cruelty visited upon them. The subterfuge allowed that young girl to stay alive, at least for a while.

"But it gives you an idea about the kind of moral dilemmas parents, including my parents, had to face in those days," says Abe Foxman in his office in Manhattan, where he is the national director of the Anti-Defamation League of B'nai B'rith and one of the most respected and most influential Jewish public figures in North America. "At least my parents did not have to leave me with a complete stranger. They knew her and trusted her, and my mother came to see me once a month. I actually knew my mother as my aunt."

Although Joseph and Hela trusted their son's rescuer, she did not reciprocate the feeling. She demanded that they state in writing that they had given up the child voluntarily. When Joseph complied and Bronislava noticed that Hela's signature was not on the document, she accused them of trying to trick her.

Indeed, Bronislava Kurpi was devoted to the child with the fervour of a young mother. She was attentive, affectionate and very protective. The boy was never allowed to play outside with other children even as he grew older, for fear that he might have to relieve himself and reveal that he was circumcised. When she was displeased with him, she spanked him quite violently. But the boy thought it was all part and parcel of mother love. As soon as he could pronounce it, he called her Momma.

The Polish nanny was a devout Catholic and had the boy baptized at the first opportunity as Henryk Stanislav Kurpi. Indeed, she wanted him to become a priest one day. The boy enjoyed the singing and the glitter of the church and its rituals. "Many hidden children resent having been baptized and converted by their rescuers," says Abe. "Not I. She raised me with faith and ritual. She did it with a good heart and for the benefit of my soul. And by taking me to the church regularly, she exposed herself to being denounced by nasty neighbours who suspected that I might be Jewish. How could I fault her for such an act of spiritual devotion and generosity? Thanks to being exposed to the Catholic practices, I enjoyed, as far back as I can remember, the prayers, the singing and all the rituals of the church. Most importantly, she raised me with faith, allowing my father later to ease me away from that faith and into our faith. It certainly facilitated his task that all he had to do was to substitute, one by one, Jewish rituals and symbols for Christian ones — a talis [prayer shawl] for a crucifix. And, unlike many converted hidden children, I never suffered any latter-day identity confusion or crisis over my early Christian upbringing."

Bronislava, indeed, took risks by sheltering a Jewish boy under her roof. Three times she was betrayed and denounced to the Gestapo for harbouring a Jewish child. Each time she had to go to the police to account for the boy. She never lied: amid profusely flowing tears, she confessed that the boy was Jewish. She told them that she had been working for Jews. One day, while she was out on a stroll with the child, the boy's parents were picked up in raid. They never returned to claim their child. She intended to raise him to be a good Catholic; her intention was to dedicate him to the priesthood. Each time she was set free. In fact, the German officer interrogating her gave her candy for the boy before he sent her home. The child, however, was unaware that his life was threatened by hostile and hateful adults.

In 1941, once again, it came to the attention of the authorities — this time the Lithuanian Gestapo — that Bronislava Kurpi was hiding a Jewish child. That evening, Joseph, exhausted from seventy-two hours of back-breaking labour, found himself face to face with Julian Boyka, a Polish-Lithuanian with a reputation as a ruthless court examiner. Boyka was accompanied by the prosecutor of the Jewish ghetto court and a ghetto policeman. He placed his revolver conspicuously in the middle of the table and warned the Jew Fucksman to utter only the absolute truth or he would shoot him dead on the spot. He wanted to know the truth about "Henyush," the child in Bronislava Kurpi's custody.

As it turned out, Boyka was Bronislava's brother. Not only did he know the child, he was fond of him. Bronislava had tried to cover her tracks by insisting that she had married a Pole who had been mobilized at the very beginning of the war and whom she had not heard from since. But Boyka was a professional — the story seemed suspicious. First he suspected that she was lying to cover up the fact that the boy was born out of wedlock. But when he accidentally discovered that the child was Jewish, it all made sense. Boyka took the news as an affront to him and his entire family. How could his sister, a good Catholic, bring a Jew into their midst, against the law of the land? He felt personally betrayed since he received the boy in his home as if he were his own flesh and blood. And he felt publicly vulnerable given his highly sensitive position as an officer of the court. According to his source, the child belonged to Fucksman.

"Believe me, Fucksman, if it weren't for the fact that I really love that boy, I'd have killed him myself long ago," Joseph quotes Boyka in his memoirs.

Boyka was clear and to the point: the boy was to join his parents in the ghetto within twenty-four hours, or Boyka would shoot him, regardless of his affection for him. If they disobeyed his order, Fucksman, his wife and Bronislava would be shot for the crime of hiding a Jew. Boyka told Joseph to bring the boy to the ghetto police headquarters the next evening. As compensation for the risk he was taking, Boyka wanted two hundred gold roubles and a gold watch. When he was finished, he lit a cigarette and invited Joseph to speak.

Calmly, Joseph confessed that, indeed, he knew the boy, and that everything Boyka said was accurate, except for one thing: he was not the boy's father, but his uncle. His story was quite similar to the one Bronislava told the Gestapo: the child and the nanny were on a visit to the Kolonia Magistraczka, when the mother, Hela's sister, and her husband were arrested and deported. On numerous occasions, Joseph and his wife begged Frau Kurpi to let them have their nephew, but the woman categorically refused — she would release the boy only to his parents. Should they fail to claim him, she intended to raise him as a Catholic. And to add more weight to her words, she had showed Joseph a document bearing the stamp of the Catholic Church — a baptismal certificate for Henryk Stanislav Krupi, son of Bronislava. This would suggest that the child belonged more to her than to the aunt and uncle. Having said that, he made it clear he was eager to have his nephew with him. As for the money, Joseph said, he had never seen that much money in his life, let alone a gold watch.

Rather than being moved by Joseph's storey, Boyka was furious: he wanted the boy in the ghetto and his reward or they would all die by the next evening.

Joseph and Hela sought help from Abraham Dimitrowski, the secretary of the ghetto police commandant, a well-known lawyer from Kovno. He promised to help. Bronislava and the child were to disappear at once. When the Gestapo knocked at her door, it would appear that she had escaped with her son for fear of losing him. The plan put the parents' life at risk, but there was no other way to save the boy. Bringing the boy to the ghetto would mean certain death for the three of them. The plan made sense. The nanny and her ward went into hiding in a summer home eight kilometres from Vilna.

The next evening, Joseph went to the ghetto police station. Accompanied by Dimitrowski, Boyka sat silently while the lawyer conducted the examination. The lawyer reported that he had gone to Frau Kurpi's residence, accompanied by a ghetto policeman, but they found the door locked. According to the neighbour, Frau Kurpi had left town.

Dimitrowski handed Joseph a statement to sign. It affirmed that Hela and Joseph Fucksman were a childless couple, and that they had no knowledge of the Koimorowski child — the name of Hela's fictitious sister — whose parents have been taken away by the Bolsheviks.

After an instant of hesitation, Joseph signed the paper. To his great surprise and relief, still without a word, Boyka pointed to the door. Joseph was free to go. They were all safe, for the time being.

The population of the ghetto was shrinking rapidly. After a couple of years, of the twenty-four people in the flat on Szpitalna Street where Hela and Joseph were staying, only five remained. Hela was becoming increasingly anxious about their fate. Joseph suggested that she ask Bronislava Kurpi for help. Hela was sure that the woman would do nothing for them, but she tried anyway. And she was right: Bronislava was not interested.

They did not have much time to nurse their disappointment. An order was issued that all men in the ghetto had to report to the railroad station to clean the wagons. They also learned that after the cleaning job, they would be taken to Kolga, a nearby concentration camp. Hela was beside herself. Joseph promised to do his best to escape. And if he were successful, he would not come back to the ghetto.

Hela was fast asleep when a knock sounded at her door late next night. It was a messenger letting her know that Joseph had got away. The messenger didn't know it, but Joseph had made it to the factory where he used to work. The person who hid him for the night was the biggest anti-Semite at the plant, someone Joseph always feared.

The next morning, a watchman, a regular drunkard, noticed Joseph hiding in a crate of sawdust. He promised to come back at dusk and take Joseph to a hiding place. When he returned that evening, he took Joseph to a shack not tall enough to stand up in.

In the meantime, Hela decided to escape from the ghetto, as well. Without any idea where to find Joseph, she went to the factory. As she sat on the same crate where her husband had waited a couple of days before, the watchman passed by and recognized her. He later slipped her a note: "At dusk I will come for you and take you to your husband."

While Hela was waiting for dusk, Bronislava passed and saw Hela, dejected and tired, sitting in a corner. "Come home with me," she said. "You look like you could use something to eat." While having some soup and a piece of bread, Hela feasted her eyes on her beautiful son, who did not know who she was. Then at dusk she went with the watchman to join Joseph in his hiding place, but there was no room for her to stay. Another man had taken up the space.

To Hela's great relief, Bronislava allowed her to stay. Every night, Hela would go to her husband with food and would return with his laundry. And every time she ventured out, she risked getting caught because she had no documents of any sort.

"Luckily, no one ever stopped me," Helen Foxman says. "I was blond and blue-eyed and I looked strong — not at all the image most people had of a Jew."

During the day, she spent time with her son. By then he was a toddler over two years of age. He was told that Hela was his aunt. It was heart-warming for Hela to see her son thrive and grow into a bright little boy. She did not mind watching him drop to his knees and pray in Latin or wear his gold crucifix. He was alive, safe, healthy and nourished with the love of not one but two mothers.

"I had a good thing going," recalls Abe. "I have no specific memories of those early times, but when I think back I feel that those were happy times for me. I wish I could recall more, not because it would serve some great historical purpose, but because it is important to me personally to have as complete a private history as possible. It would minimize my sense of having lost something profoundly valuable."

Since the predominant flavour of his shadowy recollection is one of a sense of general well-being, Abe's lack of memories confirms Robert Krell's proposition: we tend to remember only that which insinuates itself by its effervescence — traumas and occasions of extraordinary joy. Since Abe's life seemed to have been marked only by ordinary routine, there was nothing to store for the future.

Hela's situation was not so easy. Her hostess resented Hela's living off her — despite the five thousand roubles a month that she got for the child's upkeep. And she was most indignant about having to feed Hela's good-for-nothing husband. To appease her, Hela retrieved some funds she had hidden earlier.

After several months in the shack, Joseph was allowed to come inside the house and sleep on the bare floor. For that, he paid the watchman ten thousand roubles a month.

Eventually Hela obtained false papers from a Polish friend of Bronislava's. Her new name was Stefania Winczelaitis. The papers allowed her to go to work as a bookbinder and to get a ration card. But each time she was outside, she kept looking behind her, just in case she was being followed.

Hela developed a routine. In the morning, on her way to work, she bought bread. At noon, instead of lunch, she took it to Joseph and then returned to work. This went on for nearly two years. Every few months, Bronislava found the situation exasperating and would throw out both Hela and the child. Then she would take them back right away. More and more often, when the child would ask for his auntie, Bronislava would smack him. Fearing some plot to squeeze her out of the boy's affection, she strictly forbade Hela to touch the child.

Finally, as the war was drawing to an end, the bombardments

started. At the first sign of an air raid, Bronia, Hela and Abe descended to the cellar. Once, a bomb hit Abe's pillow and went right through the floor. "Another miracle, my father used to say," Abe interjects. "He was convinced that all the evil deeds were the work of man, and all the rescues were gifts from God. It was his way of sustaining his unwavering faith at a time when many pointed accusing fingers towards a silent sky. Perhaps God's silence was his way of coping, like hidden children. To protect Himself from all the destruction He witnessed on Earth, God took refuge in silence. My father would likely agree to that."

There were several days of vicious door-to-door combat, during which the retreating and humiliated Germans burned and demolished everything. They killed anyone in the street without asking for documents. Hela could no longer take food to her husband.

Even after liberation, Abe and his two mothers stayed in the basement where they had been hiding for the past weeks.

A few days later, Joseph's street was liberated. He rushed to embrace his wife and son only to find that their place had been wrecked by a bomb. He collapsed — how could it happen that after all they had survived, Hela and his son had been killed in the last days of the war? But soon he found their hiding place and the family was reunited.

When Abe saw his father, he was terrified. Joseph, a total stranger to the boy, was unkempt from days of rushing through the city in ruin and presented a frightening image, indeed. "Pan Pietrowski is coming," the child shrieked. (Pan Pietrowski is a legendary figure who brings sorrow and dry branches to mischief-makers.)

Before acknowledging his son and his wife, Joseph greeted the woman who saved the life of his loved ones. But his gesture did not ingratiate him with Bronislava. She told Joseph and Hela that they could live together, but that she would keep "her" child.

Abe's parents were alarmed but chose to be patient. They decided that all four of them would live together and continue to raise the child as before — jointly. Joseph even found a suitable apartment for his family of four. Everything was going to work out for the best, for all of them. With Joseph's wonderful new job as the director of the factory where he used to work, money was never going to be a problem again.

But Bronislava had other ideas. She made her case in a straightforward, unequivocal manner: the boy is mine, I had him baptized, he bears my name; besides, I have it in writing that you gave him up voluntarily. She used against them the document she had exacted from them when they had their backs to the wall in the ghetto and had no other option but to sign away the right to their only child.

"Her acts were desperate," explains Abe, "but she was not acting out of cruelty. On the contrary, she loved me so much that she just could not give me up, no matter what she had to do. Besides, she had already promised my soul to the Church. She had saved me. How could she go back on her sacred vow? In addition to the immense affection I have for her for all the love and care she showed me at the risk of her own peril, I feel sorrow for her, for my parents, for me. Because none of us deserved to suffer. And what followed played havoc with all our lives. It took me a long time to face it, but I finally did come to feel, to articulate my anger towards my parents. After all, they had yanked me away from a good life. All I knew was that I had an excellent life with the woman I knew as my mother. Then they had to show up and claim to be my parents; the blissful life I had was no more. I got caught between the two sides. I know it wasn't their fault. All this happened because the Nazis took on families with infants as the obstacles to their thousand-year destiny. We were mere extras in a drama played on a larger-than-human scale. But the price of admission we paid with our blood, our peace of mind, with our families, our traditions.

"As for my other 'mom,' I have never felt any anger towards her. She followed her heart. Even when it told her to go beyond reason, even beyond the law when she actually kidnapped me, I've felt only sadness for her. It was such a tragedy. It could have been so different. So much love had turned to hate in her. My father taught me that excess leads to trouble. He was right. She had too much love for me — it ended up destroying what we had and what we could have had. She lost me and I lost her and all the love I could have had. She had a mother who could have continued to be my grandmother. I could have had a family through her. If only things could have been worked out differently. This way all that remains is yet another loss and I feel nothing but sadness for it."

A series of denunciations followed. In the beginning, the four of them lived under the same roof, but after a while, because of the overt hostility, it became untenable. Once Bronislava accused Joseph of stealing from the factory. Joseph was arrested but was set free for lack of evidence. Then she claimed that in order to survive, he had collaborated with the Nazis. Once again that claim landed him in jail. And once again they let him go. The next time, she alleged that Joseph's father was a capitalist who exploited his workers. The same ritual followed. Yet another time, the charge was that he was hiding a large quantity of gold. Thirteen times, she accused him of crimes against the state. The last time, she was told not to bother the police any more with her false accusations. They had no time for playing games.

She had one more plan that almost worked. Kozlov, later unmasked as an international spy, lived in Vilna during that time. Bronislava Kurpi had been his servant for a while. Since he was a powerful local figure in those days, she sought his help. When Hela learned of Bronislava's new ally, she felt a wave of despair and panic. She walked the streets aimlessly, fearing the worst: they had survived the war, but now, more than a year after the end of the overt hostilities, when others were already busy reconstructing their lives, she was still struggling for her child. In her wanderings, she ran into someone she used to know from the ghetto. Hela poured out her heart to the old friend.

"Don't lose hope," she said. "Go see Dr Belt at the hospital. He's a very influential man, and a good man. When he hears your story, I'm sure he'll help you."

Hela did as she was told. Indeed, the doctor listened intently to every word she said. It was his professional opinion that Bronislava Kurpi was a mentally affected person. Even though he and Kozlov were not friends, he promised to help.

But Bronislava did not give up. She took Joseph and Hela to court. She claimed that the child was hers. She had no papers because the boy was born during the war, and he was the fruit of a short-lived marriage — her husband gave his life for the country. The court turned down her claim. In a second trial she admitted that the child was illegitimate, which is why she never had him registered. The case was dismissed again. The third trial, before an appeals court, drew quite a bit of attention, for it was the first of its kind. Abe was the only child to have survived the ghetto. Fifty lawyers came from Moscow to observe the proceedings. Bronislava Kurpi asserted that she had had the boy baptized, and she had the document to prove it. It was paramount for the child to continue living in a devout Catholic environment since she was saving his soul for the Catholic Church.

The judge dismissed her appeal and called the exasperated but happy parents into his chambers. "This woman will never give up," he said. "She will not allow you to live in peace. She may even destroy you. My advice is that you disappear. You are Polish nationals. Return to your country, making sure that she does not know where you are headed."

"Regardless of what I do," says Abe. "I can't conjure up 1946, the year of the trials. By then, I was over five, definitely old enough to remember some specific events. All I know is that, for the first time in my life, I felt devastated: my parents were fighting over me. It must have been quite awful, so I blocked it out completely. I guess it's easier this way."

"Fighting for me" is only one step away from "fighting because of me." Most children feel that their parents' fights are their fault. But Abe had the proof. He lived with their anger and their anguish. Rather than making him feel special, doubly wanted, it made him feel like an object. Children caught in custody battles often report that they feel like furniture.

For a while, Abe continued to be a devout Catholic. His parents had the wisdom not to rip him away from the rituals and symbols of the church. Joseph let his son be both Jewish and Christian, thus, rather than taking away something that was of great value to him, he added something new. Instead of resenting that "she" raised their son as a Catholic, they were grateful that she taught him the value of faith. The rest was just a matter of details. He traded the child's crucifix for a prayer shawl. It did not matter to him that before he used to kneel for his prayers, now he stood, as long as he still had the ritual of prayer. Joseph took his boy to the synagogue while he was still attending mass. The first time was Simchat Torah — a joyous festival celebrating the Torah. There was lots of dancing and singing and happy symbols. They picked up Abe and danced with him and the boy loved the celebration. Naturally, he was glad to return. By the time he was six, Abe went to synagogue exclusively.

"It was an excellent maturation process for me," says Abe. "The way my father did it, I didn't feel any pain for having been weaned from Catholicism. Until then I used to pray in Latin, then I had to pray in Hebrew — but they were both Greek to me."

Before the child could settle into a life with real continuity, the family of three had to run again — not from the Nazis, but from the single-minded Bronislava Kurpi.

After all attempts at reconciliation had failed, Joseph and Hela took the judge's advice to heart: as Polish nationals, they had the right to return to Poland. Under the cloak of secrecy, they relocated in Lodz, hoping that Bronislava would have no way to track them down. They had no belongings, but Hela relished being able to hug her child without having to look over her shoulder to see if the other was around. She was even willing to put up with the obvious anti-Semitism in Lodz. When she walked to the market with Abe, people would point their fingers at them: "Look at the vermin, they are crawling out from under the wall." Hela would feel her son's fingers grip more tightly in her hand. He was scared. And so was she, but she did not let him know. She promised him that it would not happen again, but it did. On their way home, they were taunted by street children. Abe was terrified. It was clear that they could not stay in Lodz for long. To add further weight to that decision, Bronislava turned up.

She had found out that members of the AK Party, a pro-Nazi, Jew-hating Polish extremist organization, were seeking out and killing Jews. She tried to link up with them, and when that failed, she had the boy kidnapped. Before long, however, Abe's parents were successful in finding her and in kidnapping back their own child. This tug of war undermined the child's already shaken sense of security and further confused him about his role in the controversy.

Since Bronislava knew that her "boy" was in Lodz, the three of them had to move on. The sacrifice became increasingly greater. They were in a position to make a substantial amount of money, allowing them to finally build a home and live comfortably, but that could not be a consideration. Hela suggested to Joseph that he stay behind if he so desired but Joseph would not hear of separating from his wife and child again, not even for a day. There was also the matter of Abe's need for a grounded home life. The boy needed to be able to know that when he woke up in the morning, he would be under the roof of the parents who had tucked him in bed the night before.

What followed was a mad dash through Central Europe. The family travelled at night, crossing each border illegally and stopping briefly in Budapest and Vienna. Abe found the adventure exhilarating. He was told never to say a word — he spoke only Russian and Polish, definitely not the languages of choice when one is a displaced person. One word from him during an inspection and the very soldiers who gave him chocolate bars could have sent them to life imprisonment.

"Time and time again," reflects Abe, "silence played a life-and-death role in my childhood. The difference between survival and disaster rested on remaining speechless. Suddenly, I became an important person. Everyone's life depended on me playing dumb. What power for a young child! It was so exciting that I even forgot to think about my other mother."

One way or another, all hidden children pay tribute to the importance silence played at one point or another in their hiding — which, for most, did not stop with liberation. Indeed, that was the only thing Abe could do to contribute to the success of the operation; just about everything else was out of his control. In most cases, hidden children had only two absolutes to respect: silence and, in many cases, invisibility. The former was always within the means of a child; the latter, much of the time. They could control crying, laughing, speaking. That is what saved them. It is extremely important to pay tribute to this version of silence for it proves that children contributed significantly to their survival. They were not just puppets put in a dark corner. Those who chose to remain silent, at the expense of their childhood, enhanced their chance of seeing freedom. Many children were, of course, killed regardless of how quiet or invisible they made themselves.

This benevolent silence is not to be confused with the speechlessness to which child survivors were condemned after the liberation. That one robbed them of the spirit they so carefully safeguarded in hiding. It condemned them to solitary suffering and deprived them of having their ordeal and their losses validated and honoured. It robbed them of their place in history, both public and personal, and it created an obstacle between themselves and the help they needed.

In Austria, the Fucksmans were sent to a series of camps for displaced persons. The first, near Vienna, was the worst. They were lodged in an army base held by the British and were treated with contempt and cruelty. "They treated their dogs better than us," Helen Foxman remembers. "The military police would come in the middle of the night and shine their lights into our eyes just to scare us. Over a hundred of us were crowded into one room. We had to trek through a field of mud to line up for our watery soup."

When General Eisenhower visited the installation, he was stunned by what he saw. He ordered the removal of the inmates at once. Joseph, Hela and Abe were among the first ones to leave.

A couple of years later, in 1950, they entered the United States. As soon as they settled in New York, Abe entered a yeshiva (Jewish school). In the beginning, he felt somewhat like an imposter. He was a baptised Catholic. Did he really have the right to be in a Jewish school with all those Jewish kids? What did they think of him?

For a child who had never been allowed to play with other children for fear that it may cost him his life, nothing was more important than fitting in, being one of the guys. Compared to that, what difference did it make that he would no longer go to church?

His parents also quickly discovered the urgent need to change their name from Fucksman to Foxman. "It was not a happy name to go to school with," Abe recalls.

In the beginning, it was a bit confusing. Abe had never had a chance to learn to become a boy. At ten, his father was fond of saying, Abe was an old man in experience. But he wanted to be a child, he wanted to be a regular guy. Then, once again, he felt confused about his Catholic affinities. As a baptised Catholic attending a yeshiva, he felt like a fake. He was constantly preoccupied with the matter: was he really an authentic Jew in the eyes of his schoolmates?

Abe also felt the shame of not having a family. His classmates belonged to large families who animated their holidays. All the members of Abe's family on both sides had been killed by the Nazis. All he had was his mother and father who did not speak English. That, too, was a bit embarrassing. The older Abe grew, the more confused he became about all these matters.

Things got worse in high school. Adolescents tend to be hard on each other and on themselves: too thin, too fat, too short, too tall, too ugly, too dumb, too smart. Abe had his share of ordinary reasons to be ashamed, and in addition he had a Holocaust-related past and its consequences. For a long time, he did not have friends over to his house because his family was too poor. He could not afford many of the luxuries that surrounded him. And in the background loomed the unchangeable fact: no family.

"Then one day, when you are old and wise enough," explains Abe, "you realize that none of that is your fault. It's not as if you'd done something wrong. Besides, by then you're old enough, hence, you don't feel so terrible. So you conclude that you have nothing to be ashamed of."

The more Abe studied, the more he learned about other people's tragedies and the more he realized that, compared to the majority of child survivors, he was fortunate: most children did not survive; those who did had lost one or both parents. Most children who were hidden had to be separated from their parents for long periods of time. He, on the other hand, had two loving mothers.

There was another thing Abe discovered in his studies, a discovery that living among survivors confirmed. He learned to divide survivors into two groups: those who found no alternative to silence and those who incorporated their experience into everything. The former rejected the Holocaust and continued to hide from it, as if the whole thing had never happened. The latter, the Foxmans among them, lived with it as an active constituent of their existence, a member of the family. Their bookshelves were overloaded with books on the Holocaust. Abe and his parents found it hard to understand how some people would refuse to see a movie or read a book, or look at a picture about the Holocaust. They would say: if I lived through it, I can look at it. It was their version of catharsis.

When Abe brought his future wife home to meet his parents, she was taken aback: "What is it with you people?" she asked. Wherever she cast her glance, there was some documentary evidence of the Holocaust. For Abe, these were the ordinary artefacts of his youth. He did his undergraduate thesis at CCNY on Vilna. He studied anything that dealt with Jewish resistance. He needed to know that the Jews did what was humanly possible, and at times, even what no one would have thought was possible. But however much knowledge he gained, it was still at arm's length. All his experiences were stored in the third person, as if none of them had happened to him. He blocked certain things out, he distanced others, and he cloaked others in euphemisms. Nothing else was within his emotional means. For this reason, he had never had the courage to ask his father questions that would have made sense of his experiences, and his survival. Later, when he realized the terrible loss, and Joseph had already passed away, he knew that he could not afford to lose his mother's account as well. He also knew that he could not interview Helen, so he asked someone else to do the job.

It took Abe many years of flirting with his anger and sadness to conclude that distance is yet another version of silence. Rather than allowing a binding process, it atomizes families and communities into individuals who contemplate their pain speechlessly and privately. "The anger and the sorrow were always there," says Abe. "They were controlled, suppressed and repressed even as emotions. Yes, I was embarrassed to experience and display them. I thought they were too tense. I had no trouble crying. I never was embarrassed by tears. I've always cried at Jewish weddings because to me they represent the Jewish family, not only what it is, but what was lost, all its joys and all the tragedy. But you cannot be angry and sad and build a life. You cannot make love and be angry or sad. You cannot raise children with anger, sorrow or silence. So you sublimate it and you hide it. Besides, I wanted my wife to love me, not to feel sorry for me. I certainly wouldn't show her my anger, so I hid it. My kids, I wanted to protect them, so I didn't show how I really felt to them either. As for sadness, there was really no right way to feel it and show it, for it is un-American to feel sad."

But now Abe's children are grown up. They are strong and they want to know. Abe has allowed himself to feel his own strength. As the national director of ADL, he has ample opportunity to experience anger and sorrow over losses and tragedies. "I used to channel much of my anger into fighting anti-Semites," he says. "That was appropriate for my mandate, and it felt good for me as a child survivor. And it was definitely civilized. But there came a moment when I felt that was not enough. The child inside me had some unfinished or badly finished business. As if by miracle —

my father may have been right about miracles happening when you need them the most — the hidden child phenomenon emerged before me. When the organizers of the Gathering came to my office for support with this Conference on the Hidden Child, my first reaction was: That's just what we need, yet another conference on the Holocaust! Go away, please. But they persisted. They knew that I was one of them. As for me, my initial impulse was to run and hide.

"Now, I knew, of course, that if I allowed myself to be involved, it wouldn't be just another conference. I also knew that I was very tentative in my stance towards looking at my childhood directly face to face, and not through the intermediary of research or public work."

Abe had not yet articulated it but he was faced with a dilemma: the necessity and the impossibility of hiding from his memories. To begin with he was not sure what he remembered, and what he had created out of a need for images and sounds of an elusive early childhood, and what had been bestowed upon him in the stories his parents had told him. Nevertheless, like most hidden children at the Gathering, Abe sensed the need for an encounter between fact and memory: it was time to hang flesh on the skeletal memories of his lost childhood. Yet the Abe Foxmans feel ambivalent about the value of their recollections. How true were the details of their story? How true did they need to be? Did specific things really happen? Did he really go to pray in a church he had been visualizing for many years? Did he have specific feelings towards his two mothers or were they just the sleight-of-hand played by the inadequacy of memory and words? Would he have to sacrifice some of the truth of his internal vision in the struggle for a language that would confirm the veracity of his story?

And then there were the feelings — the muffled anger and sadness. Was it time to allow their edges to become sharp and risk that they would cut into the civility and softness of his private horizons?

In committing his own emotional resources as well as the support of ADL to the Gathering, Abe had decided to end the hiding, all kinds of hiding, including the emotional and the private hiding. "Yes, the truth is very important," he explains, "but it is personally important, not historically. We are not speaking about whether a concentration camp existed at a particular time and place. We are dealing with personal stories. And even if the truth has been handed down to us in a sugar coating, to soften the burden of the lie and the betrayal, it does not make the core of the matter less true. I finally realized that whether something I had been holding true for so many years is so because I recall its details or because I learned it from my parents does not make a difference. What matters is to have a story." After all, it is the story that allowed all the survivors to remain human. It is their memories that confer an identity on their silenced past and their often tentative present.

The litmus test for Abe was his address to the 1,600 hidden children gathered on Memorial Day weekend in New York, in 1991; he was to look at his anger and sorrow right in the face and in public. And this public included his mother, his wife and his two children. For the first time, he was to reveal to them private, emotional truths that would have been too intimidating to utter across the table.

"That speech was the hardest I ever had to prepare," says Abe. "What I realized later is that until then I had spoken about my story as if it had happened to somebody else. And for some strange reason, speaking among hidden children, my words felt not only real but also personal. First, I had a big problem with having my family there, but they insisted. Later, I was relieved to have finally let my true feelings surface, and that they had surfaced there."

After Abe closed his address, a psychiatrist came up to the podium and said: "Thank you for making this happen. Until today I treated others. Starting with tomorrow, I'm going to treat myself."

"Since that day," says Abe, "I've been a lot angrier and a lot sadder because finally I'm confronting the fact that I had repressed both of those feelings."

At first, his anger came from a distance, through the veil of social concerns. He was angry that so many people still suffered from the ravages of the Holocaust, that it is still real for so many of them, that it is not yet history — it is alive. More recently, he has also allowed himself to feel the anger he feels towards his parents for interfering with his peace and security in Bronislava's house. "They screwed up what I had," he now realizes.

After the Gathering, Abe listened to his speech and realized the full impact his childhood ordeal had on his wife and children. In other words, the Holocaust was not over for him, either, nor for his children. "I didn't know when to remain silent and when I could show my anger in front of them," he adds. "I'm glad I did it. I, like many others, had been living a bunkered existence. But we did it at a cost. Those of us who did take the step from behind the wall never regretted it. We spoke out and we have been out since then. For this is a one-way street. Once you're out, there's no way to return to hiding."

Since the Gathering, Abe keeps discovering more people who have not dealt with the abandonment and the loss of their childhood. Many people have told him about their mother, or father, or loved one who has been carrying the same burden privately and is not yet strong enough to put it down. "At those times, a 'sociological anger' comes to the surface in me. I am forced to face the number of people whose lives are still being loused up by what the Nazis did to them fifty years ago! Yes, I am angrier than ever before. I feel it more and it is just fine with me. It is time to face the facts of our betrayal!"

It was to do just that that Abe Foxman returned to the scenes of his childhood to see and to connect with the places where it all had happened. He found that there is nothing left of the past in Vilna. There is no Jewish quarter where there used to be a Jewish quarter. There is no Jewish cemetery. There is nothing a child survivor can stand in front of and say, "I remember."

Abe then went to Baranovichi, where all of his father's large family had perished. He wanted to say Kaddish there. In the cemetery, ninety percent of the graves belonged to Christians and ten percent shelter Jews. He could not find a place to stop and pray. Finally he came upon the grave of a man, and he said Kaddish there.

"I was amazed to discover," says Abe, "that there was no sadness in me. I had only anger on that spot where twenty thousand local Jews perished. So, for the first time in my life, I said Kaddish with anger. But, of course, the mourning came out later."

Having a bit of time at his disposal, Abe went to Kiev to see Babi Yar. His father had gone there in 1945 to see who survived the débâcle. He found no one; they had all been killed. He returned with two jars — one filled with dirt, the other with bones. When Abe was old enough to understand, Joseph asked his son to bury those two jars with him when his time came. He also told Abe that if everything else was covered up at Babi Yar, he should look for a green bridge, for across from it lay the tens of thousand of Jews murdered by the Germans and the Ukrainians.

With the help of a couple of local Jews, who were terrified to have been identified as Jews, Abe found the holy ground of Babi Yar. There, across from the bridge, the Soviet regime had erected a statue to the memory of the valiant Soviet soldiers who gave their lives for their country. There Abe could not say Kaddish. But at least, he was close.

Abe's driver assured him that they were very near the burial grounds. As a child, he remembered, he used to play around the area and would find skulls and bones. He took Abe to an old woman who showed him the place where the Jews were buried.

There, Abe Foxman said Kaddish.

10

Two Against Silence and Solitude

The Story of

AGI STEIN-CARLTON AND ANDRÉ STEIN

"I often wonder what shape our lives would have taken if our parents, indeed our childhoods, had not been yanked away from us," my sister Agi, five years my senior, mused as we sat around my dining-table in Toronto. It was to be her last visit from southern California. A year later, she would surrender her life to a vicious form of leukemia.

We were not in the habit of dissecting our shared past, but on that bright wintry day in my new home in downtown Toronto, she felt too cold to brave the rigours of February.

"This is a good day to sit down with a tape recorder and talk," I suggested.

She shrugged her shoulders and with a timid smile acquiesced. We had defined the occasion as recording her journey through the provinces of darkness. For me, this was a feverish undertaking in the grim context of her illness. It was indeed our last chance to retrieve her testimony from oblivion.

We spent most of the afternoon with the tape recorder sandwiched between our two solitudes. I had known much of what she put forth but only with an outsider's intuition about the layers of tragedies that informed her youth and cast a deep shadow on the rest of her life.

"I've always thought of my life as beginning in January 1957, when I escaped from Hungary, leaving behind all its curses. But, unfortunately, the memories of those curses stayed with me wherever I went.

"The first five years of my life were good. I had Mother and Father (Piroska and Sàndor Stein) all to myself. They were young, and they were poor, but they were generous towards me. I had no friends except the next-door neighbours, the Kleins. Their place also consisted of a kitchen and one room that the parents shared with their daughter, Vera. Like me, she slept on a *chaise longue* at the foot of her parents' bed. There were the Sunday outings to the Liget, a large city park on the edge of the seventh district of Pest, where we lived.

"By the time I was born my parents had lost five children. They were scared of everything. They did not want me to learn to ride a bike, to swim or to climb on the jungle-gym. At times, I prayed for the arrival of a brother or sister just to have them pay less attention to me. At other times, however, I felt superbly safe walking between the two of them, holding their hands. I looked at every child who crossed our path as if to brag 'Look how much I am loved, look how safe I am between my parents.'

"Except for Sundays, I did not see Father much. He worked long hours in a leather goods store on the Teleki Square, steps from where his parents, modest poultry-mongers, used to have their store. Mother worked at home as a seamstress and had time to take walks with me. We would always end up on Andràssy Avenue, the most elegant thoroughfare of the city. I felt rich and important walking past elegant couples, dignified diplomats and beautiful ladies walking their dogs. We would sit in a café and watch the procession of rich people. Over a cocoa, we'd discuss fashion, cooking and other girlish topics. During those moments I felt like the luckiest girl in the world.

"When my brother, André, came along, contrary to my expectations, life became harder for me: they began to baby me as if I, too, were a newborn. Mother was always tired. She was also sick a lot. And so was André. They took him from doctor to doctor.

"Life was harsh for them, and they made it harsher for us. We were model children; much of the time we were just plain meek. Anything else would have been seen as a sign of 'corruption.' Yet Mother would flash regular threats at both of us: 'This is your last warning. Next time, I'll have the police take you away to reform school.' Our crime — speaking above a whisper or arguing over a toy. One day, André must not have been past five, mother took us to the grocery store next door. With her shopping done, we went home. With a great deal of pride André announced that he was going to provide the food for our dinner that evening. With that he opened his fist: it was full of dry lentils that he had sneaked from the open sack standing next to the grocery counter. Mother was livid with anger. She called him a common thief, this incident being the first on a long road to crime that would finish on the gallows. With each word, he looked more and more like one of his stolen lentils. 'You have one chance to escape getting arrested,' she said. 'Go down to the grocery store and return what you stole and beg the grocer for forgiveness.' Petrified, he did just that; the three of us walked to the store but he alone was to enter. This was to be his private punishment. The grocer laughed at him, patted his head and gave him a piece of candy for his honesty and courage. Furious, Mother made him throw out the candy. We were never allowed to accept any treat from anyone, not even from family. That Sunday, they took us to a sombre building with locked gates and bars on every window: 'This is where we'll take you and leave you if the two of you don't smarten up,' Father said. It was the institution for retarded children, the most dreaded place for the children of Budapest.

"How could they think that threats of abandonment were good for children? What had scared them so profoundly that they needed to control us to the point of oppression? It's not as if they did not care for us. I'm convinced they would have sold their souls to the devil just to save ours — and perhaps they did. In spite of all those moments of emotional abandonment, I had never any doubt that they loved us as much as any parent could love a child.

"But even when they wanted to show their love, it often came out as yet another instance of cruelty. Like most Hungarians, including Jews, on December 6 we waited for Santa Claus to bring us either a fistful of dry branches with which the parents were to whack their naughty kids, or a bunch of presents if they were good throughout the year. The gifts were always left between the two panes of our double windows. Every year it was the same degrading ritual: we would wake up and there would be dry branches in the window. We would both be profoundly disappointed and ashamed. Even I, who had gone through it time and again and should have known better, felt the pangs of let-down. The very fact that they chose to indulge their dark sense of humour, or that they had thought that this would teach us anything other than an awareness of our powerlessness, gave me a bad taste in my mouth. When they saw our dark faces, they dragged out the real gifts and they had a good laugh at our expense. We were too happy and too relieved to remember the preamble of this ritual and record it in our minds to be retrieved the following year.

"Nevertheless, when the chips were down, you could not hope for more loving, more responsible parents than ours. At age six, André was hospitalized with scarlet fever. They turned the city upside down to find all kinds of treats. I was immensely jealous and wished leprosy upon myself to seduce their attention away from him. They rushed to the hospital with an orange for him — the first and only one ever to show up in our tiny flat on Elemér Street in the heart of 'Chicago,' a very poor section of Pest, which earned its nickname because of the high incidence of crime. They took the orange to him without thinking of getting one for me."

Agi did not know that the first and only orange of my childhood was stolen from me by anti-Semitic kids on the ward. They kept making fun of me, taunting me for being a Jew with a broken penis. While we were sent for Christmas carolling next door, someone stole my treasure. When I complained, the nurse said, "Jews don't need oranges. They need a kick in the rear end." That's all the others had to hear; at every opportunity they kicked me in the butt, referring to the nurse's comment. "We're just doing what the nurse said you needed."

"The following summer, the summer of 1942, we were taken to the estate of our mother's cousin, a rich veterinarian. It was to be a birthday celebration for our cousins, Tomi and Vera, as well as my eleventh and André's sixth birthday. He and I were in seventh heaven because we had never left the confines of Budapest. They had all kinds of excellent treats in store. Upon arrival, Uncle Alex, our host, bestowed upon each of the four birthday heroes a large box of chocolates. I had never seen anything like it. Mine was a huge round box wrapped in red tinsel, André's was oblong and purple. Before we had a chance to sample our goodies, Father reminded us of the rule: no treats until after dinner. That meant the chocolates had to wait several hours. André hid the box in his bed.

"Later, when we had returned from a tour of the property, he discovered that his chocolates had been stolen! Except for Grandmother, everyone was out in the fields. The only suspect was Teri, a peasant maid who had been in Uncle Alex's service for years. For lack of any other suspects, she was charged with having stolen the chocolates and was summarily fired. As she stormed out, she swore to take vengeance.

"The next day, just as we sat down to a sumptuous feast, two gendarmes showed up and ushered away my two aunts, their husbands and our cousins, Tomi and Vera. Their crime: the husbands were Polish Jews and by then there was a law against Polish Jews being at large in Hungary. Grandmother was sobbing. As she drew her handkerchief out of her pocket, a purple candy wrapper fell to the ground.

"I noticed the purple wrapper. I didn't think anyone else did. Grandmother *was* the culprit. The maid kept her promise: she told the gendarmes about the Polish Jews on the vet's property. Without intending to do so, Grandmother had condemned to death her children and grandchildren."

I saw it, too. But what was I to do? I felt more hatred towards my grandmother than my heart could contain. It took me many years to forgive her. It was, however, a good feeling for me to hate her. It was safe. I invested all my rage into that hatred for Grandmother's greed. When I didn't dare to hate the Nazis, even in private, for fear of conjuring up the enemy, I saw Grandmother as the worst Nazi of them all. I blamed her for everything that happened to our entire family. Now, I know that while my hatred didn't harm her, for she had no inkling about it, it kept me going — I had a precise target at which to shoot my fantasy bullets when the going got rough. She was safe to hate.

"I was angry with Grandmother," Agi continued, "but I felt more pity towards her. She was a miserable creature who must never have had much joy in life.

"After that tragically interrupted birthday party, life never got back into its previous groove. My friends and I were frequently harassed for being Jewish. One day, on the way to school, two boys trampled our assignment books in the mud, telling us that since all Jews would be killed, we didn't need to worry about homework. We showed our wrecked assignments to the teacher. 'You people always have an excuse,' she said. When I told Father about the incident, he ordered me not to make a scene. 'Stay invisible,' he said. 'If they don't see you, they won't find you.'"

A year later, my father told me the same thing. A big bully of a kid in our class always picked on me for being Jewish. One day, after he called me a "dirty Jew" once again, I complained to the teacher. "But you are a Jew, aren't you?" she replied. When I told Father, he said to avoid him. "If he doesn't see you, he won't look for you. Just don't make a scene."

"If he had only known how wrong he was," she continued, "perhaps he would have done something about getting us out of there — out of the country, out of the city, something. Just sitting there, cowering, waiting for them to find us was the worst possible option. But, like most people, he couldn't afford to acknowledge it. Instead, he taught us the survival strategy of hiding. He did such a good job that I believe in many ways I have never stopped hiding."

We learned later that he needed courage just to stay alive. The cowardly thing would have been to give up, to lie down and die, but he fought to the bitter end, the only way he knew how. I believe the greatest gift I got from him was his dogged determination to

survive. He struggled all his life in spite of his losses — five children, his wife, his brothers and their children, his sight, a simple
future. Instead, he died alone, but not defeated. I draw strength
from his example now as I have drawn from that well every time
I felt the burden was too heavy. My father could get up and go on
again, so could I. It took me a long time to see him in this light.
As a child and a young adult, the darkness of my losses and of my
nightmares and the destruction of my dreams had blinded me.

"Soon the fire of hatred glowed ever more vigorously. Even though
our freedom of movement had not yet been restricted, I went out
less and less. Each time I ventured out, neighbourhood thugs, who
seemed to know every Jew, would terrify us. Luckily I was never
physically hurt by any of them, but their vulgar mockery, the occasional rotten apple or egg tossed at us, the vicious threats were sufficient torment for my friends and me to stay in the building as
much as possible. I felt I had to live under self-imposed house arrest
just to protect myself from their hatred.

"We hardly ever saw the relatives. Now and then we got together
with my mother's sister, Sàri, and her husband, Lali. I liked the
two of them the most. They were not only a very handsome couple,
but they always had a smile on their faces. They adored their little
boy, Tibi. I was always envious of the affection they lavished on
him. They kissed him, held him, smiled at him more in one hour
than I had ever experienced in my nearly a dozen years of life. How
could two sisters be so different? I kept wondering. Why couldn't
Mother be like her younger sister? I swore to myself to become like
Sàri.

"But then it all came to an abrupt end: Uncle Lali had to report
for forced labour. Soon after, father had to go, too. But whereas
Father returned after a few weeks, the immense silence had swallowed Lali. After what had happened to her two sisters and their
families in 1942 and her husband's disappearance, Sàri began to
fear for the safety of her boy. She was committed to saving him.

"On March 19, 1944, the sky had caved in on the Jews of
Budapest. The German army marched into our lives with their
heavy boots and their evil designs. At thirteen, I understood that
it was just a matter of time before we could expect serious changes
in our everyday safety and existence. I was frightened. When I

turned to Mother for reassurance, she looked straight ahead as if
to say, I'm helpless, too, I'm afraid, too. 'It will blow over,' she said
without looking into my eyes. We both knew that she was lying.
I tried my luck with Father. 'Just keep a low profile, and everything
will be all right. No one will come looking for a child,' he said. I
didn't know to what extent, but I suspected that he was terribly
wrong. So I turned to Sàri.

" 'What is going to happen to us, Auntie?'

" 'Nothing if I can do anything about it.'

" 'What can you do all by yourself?'

" 'I have a plan, don't worry.' From that day on, I looked to Sàri
for courage.

"Within weeks, we began to feel the weight of the jackboots on
our backs. Life became dangerous at school. Our parents decided
to keep us home. I was never too fond of studying but I loved to
be at school. I felt indignant for being deprived of going to school.
How can you continue to think of yourself as a kid when it's no
longer safe for you to show up at school? Once again, Father had
to go to do forced labour. We all went with him to the South
Station in Buda. I did my best not to cry, but a few tears managed
to escape. He looked so insignificant, so small under his knapsack,
that I just couldn't imagine his being able to withstand the rigours
of forced labour. I wanted to take him in my arms and shout to
those in command: 'Let him be. Don't you see how small he is?
He is just a kid.' I know it makes no sense at all, but I felt guilty
for not being able to help him. I didn't like that feeling of helplessness. I wanted to experience the resolute inner conviction of
our aunt, and not the more realistic helplessness of our parents.

"When I saw his back disappear in the railroad car, I was sure
that I would never see his face again. And I didn't even have a
chance to say farewell to him. How was I to live with that crack in
my life?

"Soon we had to brand ourselves with the yellow star. Another
source of fear, another reason for shame. 'The star of David is the
mark of every Jew,' our next-door neighbour, Mrs Klein, explained
to her daughter and me. 'There is nothing to be ashamed about
stating publicly what you know privately. I proudly wear the star
as a symbol of distinction.' Perhaps that was my problem: I knew
that I was Jewish, but I had no reason for pride. We lived a totally

assimilated existence, without prayer, without ritual. Being Jewish at best was a matter of fact. Having to wear the yellow star made me feel exposed. Now I'm no longer ashamed to admit that it was hard and scary for me to announce to the world that I was a Jew because I was a bad Jew, one who let her God down.

"When I learned that we had to move in with Sàri and Tibi at Grandmother's place in Vörösmarty Street, I rejoiced. I loved the chance to live with Sàri. Grandmother's flat was in one of the designated Jewish houses, with a large yellow star on the front gate. All Christian tenants, with the exception of the super and his assistant, had vacated the thirty-six-unit building in the heart of the heavily Jewish seventh district. There were several children my age, and we spent most of our time either in the attic or in the cellar. We felt the safest and the happiest when we did just what Father had always said: hide from the public eye.

"Mother spent a lot of time trying to find a way for us to leave that fish bowl since no matter how well we hid, it was self-evident that we were Jewish. The Jewish house was a cage in the zoo and we were the monkeys. Outside, the Arrow Cross militia and their sympathizers had grown louder and nastier. They blamed the Jews for centuries of foreign occupation, for economic hardships and for an increasing discord within the population. One day, I heard a speech on the radio by Szàlasi, the leader of the Arrow Cross Party: 'Beware of the Jew, he will infiltrate every Christian home. He will take advantage of their host's unsuspecting kindness and sooner or later, he will take over. Once they have reached their goal, they will go on to the next Christian home. They won't stop until they take over the country. We must rid ourselves of this pest the same way as we get rid of all others: exterminate them.'

"On October 15, the regent of Hungary, Admiral Horthy, declared Hungary's neutrality. We were elated and free. For one day. On October 16, the Arrow Cross Party seized power. Szàlasi became the ruler of the land. He had the power to put into effect his fantasy about the fate of the Jews. The reversal of order was insufferable. I had lost all hope — everything seemed futile. The Germans and the Arrow Cross had assumed full power over the Jews.

"Mother was, once again, in a quandary. To my great relief, she opted for converting to Catholicism. Sàri, who was already beginning to show that she was expecting a baby, stayed away from the church. In her condition it would not have been good for anyone concerned. Her pregnancy would automatically lead to the interrogation of the entire family.

"I was quite confused about Sàri's pregnancy. While I was very naïve and ignorant about sexual matters, I knew that her husband had been gone for more than nine months, so who could be the father of her child? I could not fathom my aunt having an affair. In those days women like her did not have affairs. There was a lot of whispered anger about her condition.

"'You've brought shame on my head,' I heard Grandmother's muffled voice one night. 'Everyone thinks you're a slut.'

"'I'm saving our lives,' she replied.

"'What about me? I don't have the child of an Arrow Cross man in my belly.' Mother entered the discussion.

"'We all do what we can,' Sàri said to her. 'And don't think I didn't die a thousand deaths agonizing over it.'

"'What will you tell your husband when he returns?' Grandmother said in an accusatory voice.

"'"I would not be here today and neither would be your son if I had not sought some protection," that's what I would say to him.'

"'Perhaps he would prefer that. I know I would.' Grandmother was almost shouting.

"'Tell me that when they take the old women like you.'

"'According to you, I'm already a dead woman.' Mother sounded terrified. 'What will happen to my two kids?'

"'I'll take care of them as if they were my own,' Sàri said. 'And perhaps we can hide you. Maybe the church will save you.'

"We went to an improvised church across the street, set up in the cellar. As much as I hated the priest, I loved what he had to offer. His faith sounded so soothing, so safe. I would have believed everything he said about the love of God, the Father and His Divine Son, but I had a hard time with His abandoning His child to be killed. Under our circumstances, that sounded intolerable. Is that what Catholics believe in? Not to come to the rescue of their child when his life is at risk? Not a good lesson for Jewish parents of our times. And what about Mary? Did she do everything to save her Son? And where was the Father? The Holy Ghost mystified me. The whole story reminded me of what might have happened to Sàri: she was pregnant without a visible father for her child, and some way that child was supposed to save us all. I felt a great surge of gratitude towards Mary and Sàri. I wanted Mother to do something mysterious to save us. Perhaps the conversion idea was her way of putting God on our side. I had lost all faith in the God of Israel. It had proven to be either powerless or cruel for abandoning the Jews. The Christian God, on the other hand, was in charge. I would have worked myself up into a religious fervour if it hadn't been for that miserable priest. He made no secret of his contempt for the Jews. He kept threatening us with the Nazis because André kept crossing himself with his left hand. I hated the priest, and I hated my brother for not learning something as simple as telling left from right at the age of eight. I didn't realize how hard it is for a 'leftie' to remember those simple things. When I yelled at him for not making an effort, Mother told me to try to do everything with my left hand for a day. That helped, but I still cursed him for being a leftie. 'You sound no better than the Nazis,' Mother told me. 'You resent your brother for an accident of birth; being born a 'leftie' is no different from being born Jewish.'

"In the end, we were converted. But a lot of good it did us. At the end of November, Mother was deported. By then her youngest sister, Boriska, and her husband had been taken, as well. Their two-year-old daughter, Zsuzsi, moved in with us.

"I can't say it was a surprise that they came for Mother that late November morning. And yet, when all women between the ages of sixteen and sixty were ordered down into the courtyard, I was stunned. It didn't happen the way I thought it would. I believed that Sàri was going to pull the same string that she used to protect herself. Then came another surprise. They gave the women a choice: healthy ones to the left, sick ones to the right. Mother was always sickly, and yet she went to the left. All the younger women reported to the sick side. I was completely baffled by this turn of events. So much so, that in a fit of panic, I decided to join her. She looked as brittle as if she were naked. Somebody had to look after her, so I decided to go with her. But on my way out the hundred-year-old lady from downstairs grabbed me by the arm and yanked me into her apartment without anyone noticing it. I was furious with her. As it happens, she saved my life. And consequently my brother's.

"After that morning, Grandmother was even more angry than usual with Sàri. 'Why should you be spared if your oldest sister isn't?' she kept harassing her own daughter. Sàri had the patience of a saint.

"One day, I lost my temper. 'Would you prefer if she, too, was taken? Where would that leave you and the rest of us?'

"'You just hold your tongue, little brat. I'm your grandmother. You can't speak to me like that.'

"She was right. I should not have spoken to her with such cheek. But I, too, was at the edge of my nerves. I was only thirteen, and yet I was constantly dealing not only with my own fears for my life but also with the fear of the adults. When Grandmother told me that I had no right to speak, I promised myself never to open my mouth again. I would hide behind silence. And I became an expert at hiding. Father would have been proud of me.

"Within a couple of weeks, we had to march into the newly erected ghetto. The procession through the streets was terrible. I wanted to be invisible, but the crowds that lined both sides of Wesselényi Street pierced my protective bubble. Every time I lifted my gaze, I saw spite and hatred in those hard faces. One old woman spat at me. Others made comments about how it was time the Jews were removed from the lap of luxury. 'Christ killers!' another woman screamed as she threw a hard object at an old man in the line. He recoiled in pain as the object hit him in the face. He was about to take a step towards his assailant when he was cut down by a gunshot. We had to step over his dead body. 'Be invisible, be invisible,' I repeated to myself. André's nails dug into my hand as if his life depended on me. And in a real sense, it did. I knew it and I was going to honour that duty while I resented it. I was just a kid, damn it. I should not have had to take responsibility even for my own life, let alone for his, too.

"We marched by huge wooden crates erected on Klauzàl Square in the heart of the Orthodox Jewish area. We were to toss in all our valuables. I was about to pass by the crate when a militia man noticed the little ring I wore on my right hand. He grabbed me and brutally ripped the ring off my finger. I thought he would take my finger with it he was so abrupt. He called me a 'little Jewish whore.' I didn't exactly know what that meant, but I felt ashamed anyway. 'Be invisible, be invisible,' I repeated it as a prayer.

"We were about to leave the square, when I saw Sàri talking to two men. One was a stranger, the other seemed to be our grandfather. I hadn't seen him for months. As much as I liked the eccentric old printer, we hardly ever saw him because Father had some beef with him. Besides, he was in the habit of disappearing periodically. Sàri, I learned much later, hated her father. He used to get drunk and hit Grandmother. When we walked right by them, he looked at me without seeming to recognize me. First I felt a pang of pain. But then I sighed with relief. It works, I thought, I am invisible.

"Later I learned also that the other man was the Arrow Cross man who was the father of Sàri's child. Grandfather knew him because he was the son of the super in their building.

"We were marched off to Dob Street, which used to be the exclusive domain of the ultra-religious. I had always been scared of those sombre men dressed in black and sporting formidable beards. Now, the street was dominated by the procession of scared women, the elderly and children herded by Arrow Cross thugs.

"We ended up in a two-room flat on the corner of Rumbach and Dob streets. There were at least fifty people in our room. I couldn't even sit down. André, Tibi and Zsuzsi were given the table. It was amazing how quiet they all were. Somehow, without anyone telling them to leave behind their childlikeness, they did so.

"I slept leaning against the wall. Sàri sat at my feet. Grandmother was the only complainer. Total strangers told her to shut up or they would throw her out the window. I didn't much believe them because it would have taken at least four of them just to pick her up. That cruel thought brought a smile to my lips. I felt relieved, I could still smile.

"The next morning, Sàri's protector and our grandfather showed up in the apartment. Grandmother wanted to have nothing to do with her husband. I felt disappointed. I was hoping he would join us. I always thought of him as an affectionate man, full of jokes. Sàri went out on the catwalk to talk to them. First I saw her gesticulate frantically at her father. Finally, looking defeated, he threw his hands in the air and left. When she returned to the room, she told us to get going: her friend would lead us to her former apartment on Akàcfa Street, where she used to live with her husband. It fell within the ghetto territory by less than a block.

"'What about Grandfather?' I asked her.

"'He won't be bothering us any more,' she said harshly."

We never saw Grandfather again. I had fond memories of his stories of adventure. Some of them, if not all of them, were tall tales, but it made no difference. I loved to sit on his lap, or go down to the cellar where he had his printing shop. He would give me travel brochures, left-over fliers from the summer fair.

"Life was considerably more comfortable on Akàcfa Street. We had a whole apartment to ourselves. After the first few days in the ghetto, however, we spent hardly any time in the flat: the siege of the city made it too dangerous to stay upstairs. We lived mostly in the cellar. It was dark and damp, but it suited me because there I was literally invisible. But taking advantage of the darkness, the superintendent, a devout Catholic, would come by and feel up the women, including me. No one said a word. He particularly liked Sàri. She had rather ample breasts and a generous rump. I, on the other hand, had nothing. And yet, on occasion, I would feel his hand creep up my body. I was mortified. First I thought it was a rat and I screamed. He became very solicitous and he said he just happened to be close by.

"Hunger became our central concern. We received starvation portions of food: two hundred grams of sawdust bread, one hundred grams of molasses and one or two carrots or turnips per day. Every once in a while, we were given a tiny piece of raw bacon. 'Choke on the pork, you Jewish pigs,' I remember one militia man yell. 'You should choke to death: a pig eating pork is cannibalism.' He was very pleased with his cleverness. When he noticed that he was surrounded by silent Jews, he cocked his gun and demanded that we laugh with him. To give more weight to his seriousness, he fired a shot in the air.

"Then they reopened the bakery on the corner of Wesselényi and Kisfuvaros streets. It meant standing in line for hours every day. Some days they had bread, other days they had nothing. Since it was impossible to know when to wait, there was a steady vigil. Grandmother was too scared to stand in line. Sàri was too pregnant. Tibi was too young. Which left André and me. First, we stood in line together. But when it got too cold, Sàri said we should alternate. It was all right with me to stand alone, but I feared for André's safety.

"One Monday morning, it was his turn to stand in line. It was bitterly cold. I insisted that I should go. But he was stubborn. He left around eight o'clock. When there was no sign of him by the middle of the afternoon, I began to worry. Sàri shared my concern. She mentioned it to the superintendent. He said there had been some nasty business in front of the bakery earlier. We wanted to look for André at once, but the superintendent said it was too dangerous to go out. There was still some shooting out there, and a lot of casualties. He seemed to enjoy scaring us. Sàri begged him to go out to look for André.

"'If he's alive, he's probably hiding,' he said. 'But if he's not back by dusk, I would not make plans for his future.'

"I was more dead than alive during the wait. I kept seeing Mother's face demanding an explanation: 'We never let you go out alone even in peacetime. How could you let an eight-year-old child go out with all the shooting and killing? If anything has happened to him, it'll be your fault.' I had never seen Sàri lose her composure. That day, she was tearing her hair. Even Grandmother sounded scared. 'Why would anyone want to hurt a little boy? It just couldn't happen. When he comes back, I'll really give it to him.' But behind her words I felt terror.

"Then André turned up. I could tell that he must have just seen the face of the devil. He looked like a sleep-walker. His face was covered with what looked like dirt. His clothes were tattered and soiled. My first thought was that he had been in a fight. I rushed to him to hold him in my arms. His body was trembling like a leaf in the wind.

"'What did I tell you?' Grandmother sounded triumphant.

"'Thank God, you're here.' Sàri sounded relieved. 'Come to your aunt for a hug, you naughty boy. You almost made me go into labour I was so scared for you. Come here and tell me all about your day.'

"But he wouldn't go to her. Instead he ran into the darkest corner of the shelter and disappeared before our very eyes. When I put my arms around him, his body felt dead like a slab of ice. His face felt crusty. From the smell on my fingers, I realized with horror that his face was covered with coagulated blood. I wanted to feel his body with my hand and search for an open wound, but he abruptly pushed me away.

" 'What happened to you?' I asked, whispering right into his ear. I swear on Mother's head I won't tell anyone. Just tell me.'

" 'I don't know,' he whispered back. 'I think I had been killed.'

"Little by little I got it out of him. When I did, I wished I hadn't. I was not equipped for that version of madness. Without either one of us fully realizing what it meant, it became obvious that he had been raped. 'For this, I must die,' I thought. I had no other way to cope with that hallucinatory reality.

"He lapsed into a deep sleep in that dark corner. It was the best thing he could have done because Grandmother and Sàri insisted on knowing what had happened. But before he passed out, I swore that I'd never say a word to anyone about what had happened. And I kept my word.

" 'He has been hurt, but he will be all right,' I whispered to Sàri. 'Please, take care of Grandmother. He's scared that she will spank him.' She insisted on finding out the details. I said that he had been beaten up.

"His sleep was punctuated with rapid outbursts of panic and pain. I did not close my eyes the whole night. I was scared to leave him alone. Tears flowed from my eyes incessantly. I was just a young girl, totally in the dark about human ugliness. How could people do something like that to anyone, let alone to a child? In a way, I, too, felt assaulted. From that moment on, with that knowledge cluttering my private world, I felt I had no longer the right to consider myself a child. I craved the darkness as much as he did. I was sure that if I were to stand in the light of people it would show on my face that I had been made the depository of a knowledge that banished me from the rank of ordinary people.

"Still asleep, André began to scream, startling everyone from their dreams. His screams sounded like bursts from a machine-gun. Some people complained. I tried to calm him down, but he would not tolerate me touching him. Each time he felt my body against his, he screamed with such disgust and hatred that I began to feel dirty.

"From that day on, we have hardly ever touched again. A furtive peck on the cheek on birthdays, that's all. If he only knew how much I needed at times for him to hold my hand, or to hug me so that I could feel some of his strength when I needed to be weak and protected at the same time."

A couple of years before my sister passed away, Vicki, my wife, and I met with Agi and her husband, Paul, in Santa Barbara for breakfast. Because of her illness, she was often indignant, irrational and cantankerous. After having caused a scene, she stormed out of the restaurant. I followed her for I knew that she and I had some unfinished business. I caught up with her after a short chase. Abruptly, she turned towards me: her eyes were fuelled by rage and solitude. "You're a cold fish," she said. Her words felt like lashes. "Just like Father." I looked at her, stunned. Where did that come from? "When was the last time you hugged me?" Without thinking, I lashed back: "I'm not a cold fish. It's just that you're not huggable." I could see her soul collapse under the weight of that verdict. I couldn't fathom why I would want to hurt my sister. "It's all your doing," she whispered. "It all comes from that night in the cellar when trying to comfort you after your . . . you know what I mean . . . I kept trying to hug you and you pushed me away each time, as if I were a leper. Ever since then, I hid my desire to hug you, to be a sister to you, not a stranger. You evicted my tenderness not only from your life but also from mine."

It was my turn to collapse. I never knew what happened during my delirium. That day on the sunlit sidewalk in Santa Barbara, I did not have the courage to ask her for details. We parted with a wall of solitude between us. That day in Santa Barbara, I felt we had been forced back into that dark corner in the bottom of our cellar where we had been hiding our respective losses. Agi returned to Los Angeles without her hug. I had discovered that the barbed wire that ran between our two lives had kept us in hiding. I still had time to find the way that led from the torturer to the sunshine. Agi, on the other hand, was never to find the brother she had lost to a faceless, evil man.

I heard the account of what happened in that dark corner of the cellar on that December night in 1944 only on the very last time my sister and I met prior to the disease taking possession of her lucidity. At that time a heavy burden of guilt and sadness afflicted me. Since I thought I had exorcised from my life the imprint of evil, I had been feeling more rooted in the world of the living than in the graveless past. After my sister revealed to me the foundations of the emotional wall between her and me, I felt the heat and the ashen taste of my rage resurface in spite of my commitment to the present.

"For days André refused to come out of that corner," Agi continued. "I brought him clean clothes. He took care in cleansing himself as well as the darkness of his shame had allowed him. I brought him food to that corner. Grandmother kept asking for him, but Sàri held her at bay. Our aunt never asked me again what happened, but she wanted to have 'bulletins' several times a day. André's sleep was so full of horrifying ghosts that I wasn't sure if his sanity had survived. He spoke mostly in grunts and moans. It was too much of a burden for me to live with his silent rage, his wordless plea for another reality."

I remember so little. I recall the pain but not what it felt like. I remember that I thought I was dead when I regained consciousness, and, yet, I prayed to be allowed to live. But when I realized that to be alive meant having to face people and tell them what had happened, I wanted to die. I was not even looking for the words with which to recount such a story — I needed silence to protect me from insanity. The fear of insanity loomed very big. I kept seeing that austere building where Mother took us when we misbehaved — the home for the retarded. So, to protect myself from demons against whom I had no weapons, I banished the memory of that day from my thoughts.

"By New Year's, the sounds of war became louder and more insistent. Explosions alternated with rapid machine-gun fire. We sat in the dark cellar not knowing what to expect or hope for. We were eager to welcome the approaching Russians. We were impatient and anxious to see them arrive. In the meantime, however, a bloodthirsty Arrow Cross thug or a desperate German might have killed all of us just because he felt like it. So we liked the sound of the Red Army shelling German positions, all the while knowing full well that the next explosion could very well be the last one for us.

"Each time we heard a loud burst, we held our breath. Even the

little children remained quiet. Two months of subterranean existence had turned them into experts in survival. We all knew better
than to say anything to the adults and they asked nothing. Sàri's
son, Tibi, was the only one lucky enough to get some unsolicited
attention from Sàri.

"In the third week of January, Sàri went into labour. I was terrified to see her in pain. Her pains were punctuated with loud
moans, which turned into screams. For everyone's sake, the superintendent moved her to the emergency exit, which was separated
from the next building by a layer of bricks.

"Time passed very slowly. Every few minutes, I went to check
on Sàri. 'She seems fine,' I said each time to reassure the others,
but I wasn't all that sure of what was going on. Was it possible to
deliver a healthy child in a cellar? I was ignorant and very scared.

"Hours went by before our aunt's pains turned into inarticulate
howls. As her pains became more acute, I felt close to panic. Tears
bathed my cheeks. I would have loved to scream, but I had no right
to be a nuisance when my aunt was writhing in childbirth, while
above our head one half of the world was killing the other half.

"Suddenly, behind Sàri's constant litany, I detected a rhythmic,
pounding noise. No one knew what to make of it. Except for Sàri's
wailing, total silence dominated our shelter. Then, with a loud
crash, the brick tumbled down. A beam of bright light scanned the
darkness of the shelter.

"A Soviet soldier appeared in the hole between the two buildings. Another one followed him, and yet a third one. They came
to the cellar scrutinizing every shadow for hidden Nazis. They kept
shouting in Russian. Not knowing what they were saying, I felt
too scared to breathe. We all sat frozen to our seats.

"But then, grinning, another soldier appeared with a baby in his
arms. 'Djevoshka, djevoshka, djevoshka (girl),' he kept saying. He
looked as happy as if he had been the father. He was our liberator,
and she, our brand-new cousin, our rescuer.

"A loud cheer followed his appearance. Months of silence and
darkness exploded into jubilation. The arrival of that little girl
inspired in all of us cave-dwellers a brand new taste for life.

"We rushed upstairs into the street. The brightness of the white
January light blinded me first, but it made no difference, I rushed
forth without seeing. I held on to André's hand to make sure he

didn't get lost in the crowd milling around the rubble, the cadavers and the carcass of the horse we had eaten a few weeks ago. Exhausted and emaciated Jews were hugging each other and our liberators.

"I even forgot how hungry I was. Later that evening, a Russian truck drove by and two soldiers distributed bread and bacon. I had tears in my eyes. I was so used to the authorities taking from us that this generosity touched me deeply. They came to beat the Germans. While doing that, it was inevitable that they would liberate us. But they didn't have to distribute food, that was not part of fighting a war. This was purely a matter of heart. Those gruff-looking soldiers gave me more than just food, they rekindled my faith in people.

"That night, for the first time in weeks, we slept in a bed. Now and then cannon bursts still lacerated the night, but I was no longer afraid. We were free. I had full confidence in our liberators.

"The next morning, Istvàn, Sàri's brother-in-law, showed up at our door. No one understood how this strong, vigorous young man had managed to escape the constant searches for hidden Jews. His mother, Mrs Weisz, had been with us for a while. She would have sold her soul to the devil if that had saved her. She had a large suitcase full of goodies that she shared with no one, not even with Tibi, her own grandson. She sat on it day and night. Sometimes I hated her so much that I could have killed her.

"It's so hard not to judge people sometimes. How can I not think of her full suitcase at the same time as I think of her eyes overflowing with sadness? We were kids, abandoned by just about everyone and yet we were called upon by all, including our own conscience, to feel compassion often for the very people who had betrayed us. Why should I feel sorry for Mrs Weisz when her heart was not moved by four starving children? I don't have the answer. All I know is that when I looked at her, my stomach turned upside down and I wanted to alleviate her sorrow.

"I've often felt that we, the children, have had to be better people than our elders. At times, it comes naturally; at others, I feel I'm banging my head against a wall of rage: how dare they expect the victims to learn from their own ordeal? Especially since the perpetrators do their best to deny their responsibility for what they had done to us? How can we be better parents to our parents than they were to us? Where is it written that we must respond to betrayal with love and compassion? It seemed to me that the child survivors had to carry the entire edifice of silence on our backs. We had to be strong enough to carry that burden because we were children and they were not. We had to barter away our childhood for our survival. Nothing will ever undo that fact. And to make sure that it will keep for an eternity, it has come wrapped in guilt and shame.

"I have never said these words to anyone. After all, we had survived. We owe to our dead cousins the respect to shut our mouths about our losses. They would gladly have traded places with us. Sometimes I find this circular trap so awesome that I prefer not to think of anything other than the moment at hand, and damn that cursed childhood. Most of the time, I just go on with my life as if the horrors of our childhood were nothing but a nightmare. At times, I ache for all the dreams I had as a young girl. At those times, I'm consumed with anger and even hate. Then, I think, what happened happened, and let's go on with the living. Is this perhaps another version of hiding? I don't know, but time is so short!"

" 'It's time to go out to look for some food,' Istvàn announced after a short visit. 'And I'm taking this young man with me as my helper.' Before I had a chance to protest, he scooped André up from the floor and he threw him on his back.

" 'Be very careful,' I whispered. 'He's just a little boy.' "

I took over the story where my sister left off.

"We'll have to go beyond the ghetto wall," Istvàn said, once we were in the street. "We won't find a crumb in here."

Even though we had been liberated, my heart began to pound. Nobody told us that we could go out. What if the whole city had not yet been freed and the hunt for Jews still continued?

"I don't have my star any more," I ventured sheepishly.

"You won't need it, little man," he answered with anger in his voice. "Not today, not ever again. Those days are over. We're people like anyone else. You hear? If you walk in the middle of the street it's because you want to, and not because you have to."

As we went past the ghetto wall, my legs turned rubbery. On every corner there were bodies stacked like firewood. Death and destruction dominated the city. For the first time in weeks, I wasn't hungry.

We entered a tobacco store on Dohàny Street. The proprietor was sleeping with his head on the counter. Thinking it was a good opportunity for putting his hand on some tobacco or perhaps even some cigarettes, Istvàn stepped behind the counter.

"Look at this!" he yelled visibly shaken by what he saw.

I looked, then heaved the meagre contents of my stomach: the man's lower body had been separated from his torso by shrapnel and lay in a pool of coagulated blood on the floor. We ran out as fast as our legs could carry us.

The world was still turning around me when we entered the Jewish bath house next door. No sooner had we gone in than we dashed out: instead of water, the large pool was filled with hundreds of naked cadavers dumped in helter-skelter.

"Uncle Istvàn," I begged, "let's go home, or let me just stay outside. I can't take this any more. I'm just a little boy."

"Neither can I, little fellow," he said, "and I'm a man. Although after what we have just seen, I wonder if that's still true."

After combing the city for hours, we finally came upon a treasure: hidden in the cold storage of a small restaurant, we found large jars of white bean and onion salad in vinegar. We carried home our trophies as if we had shot a bear, and we ate one of the two-litre jars in one sitting.

Agi picked up the story. "That wretched bean salad almost killed us. After two months of starvation, it was no longer within the means of our digestive tract to tackle such harsh fare. Except for Sàri, who feared the effects of the salad on her milk, we all spent several days in the grip of abdominal agony.

"It was a miracle that we didn't die. Starvation certainly turns people into idiots. I'm sure that under ordinary circumstances all the adults would have known not to touch that harsh stuff. But I guess there comes a point when hunger reduces the smartest adult to a non-thinking child — all you think of is silencing the nagging stomach. What an absurdity! We survived starvation only to come nose to nose with death thanks to the food we finally ate.

"As soon as we were permitted, we moved back to Grandmother's apartment. It was larger than the place on Akàcfa Street. I was delighted to leave behind that hell that held forever captive all my childhood assumptions about the purity, innocence and special status of children.

"Hunger continued to plague us. The capital had been plucked clean of everything edible. Our aunt had no choice but to leave the baby with Grandmother and comb the countryside for food. She bartered with the peasants. Since public transportation was not yet available, her trips sometimes were several days long. She always came back with a bag of corn flour, potatoes, dry peas, some bacon, sausage, or even a chicken.

"Then, tragedy struck: six weeks after she entered our lives, Judit, our little cousin died. Sàri came home with a big grin on her face, but she fainted when Grandmother showed her the inert child. André and I were convinced that Grandmother killed the baby: we had heard her curse 'the Nazi's bastard' even before the child was born. Many years later, however, I found out that countless newborns couldn't survive on their mother's thin milk. Since those days after liberation were quite chaotic, her birth was not registered, nor was her death, or what caused it. She came, she saved our lives, and she returned beyond the world of people.

"When Sàri regained her voice, she screamed at her mother at the top of her lungs, accusing her of killing the child. She threatened to throw her out. It wasn't enough for her to have caused the death of two grandchildren, two of her own daughters and their husbands, she had to kill another child of her own flesh and blood.

"I tried to calm her down. I feared for Grandmother. But Sàri needed to give free rein to her grief and to the outrage of the past few months. She needed to free herself of the yoke of her guilt and her shame for the decision to conceive the child of a Nazi to save the others.

"'I shall never again speak of this child,' Sàri said upon returning from the funeral. 'She never existed. And that is that. There is some justice in this tragedy. And I beg the Almighty not to punish me.'

"Every night, however, we heard her speak to her dead baby; she sang lullabies to her, and inevitably, she broke down into fits of tears. Sadness settled very deeply in our little home.

"André and I were always hungry — for food and for emotional sustenance. We craved the warmth of a bowl of chicken soup, the sound of a kind word, the strength of an encouraging embrace — a sign that it made a difference in somebody's life that we had survived. There was no one on our mother's side — except for Grandmother and Sàri. Everyone else had disappeared. And we did not know anything about the fate of Father's family.

"We had no idea who had survived and who had perished. All we knew was that the men had been deported to forced labour camps. We eventually found Aunt Szidi, my Uncle Jakob's wife, and Aunt Irén, who was married to my father's youngest brother, Rezsö.

"When we showed up at her door, Szidi was surprised to see us. We looked like two ghosts, she lamented. While she kept talking incessantly, our attention was captivated by the obvious presence of stuffed cabbage in the kitchen. In spite of the aromas wafting to our nostrils, she claimed to have no food in the house.

"André and I glanced at each other. I saw rage in his eyes. When, minutes later, Szidi excused herself to go to the bathroom, we dashed to the kitchen and we stuffed our mouths with cabbage. We didn't even take the time to chew. We had no more than a minute or two at our disposal. When we heard the toilet flush, we wiped our faces with our sleeves, and ran back to the vestibule.

"As expected, when we rang her bell, Aunt Irén received us with open arms and a cup of herbal tea. Our next target was Aunt Lina, Father's oldest sister. Not being able to locate her, we knocked on the door of her eldest daughter, Loli. She and her Christian husband, Tihamér, lived on Kàlvària Square, a notorious spot in the centre of the capital's underworld.

"Tihamér opened the door. He quickly made it clear that we were at best tolerated. We were, however, fed and offered a mattress on the floor of their heated living-room. In return, Loli asked us to make as little noise as possible. Her husband didn't care for children. 'We're experts at being invisible,' I reassured her.

"Our parents' insistence that we speak only when spoken to was an excellent apprenticeship for that version of hiding in public. Indeed, they would have been proud of how self-effacing we were. But the fact that we solicited food from our relatives was a tribute to the eloquence of hunger, whose call was louder than the voice of our parents' teachings. Although we never explicitly asked anyone for food, the sight of us as we stood on the threshold was enough to arouse pity. At the age of eight and a half, André weighted twenty kilos, and at thirteen, I did not weight much more. Our emaciated bodies were another instance of eloquent silence.

"On our first night at Loli's, André woke up and needed to find the toilet. Feeling his way in the dark, he reached his goal and found relief. Exhausted and semi-conscious, he collapsed next to me and we went back to sleep.

"The next morning, however, amid vulgar outbursts and insults, Tihamér threw us out. In typical Stein fashion, Loli stood by silently. When he left, we found out that in his stupor during the night, André had mistaken the kitchen sink for the toilet.

"Dejected and ashamed, we set out for Grandmother's place. What was going to happen to us? Who was going to look after us. I was so caught up in my despair that I did not notice a military truck with a Soviet soldier sitting on its step. When we were about fifty metres from him, he jumped to his feet and began to signal us to come to him. Our feet froze to the pavement. Soviet soldiers had the reputation of molesting young girls. We did not know what to do, but we had no choice.

"Shuffling our feet, we reached him. I was about to close my eyes and wait for the worst when suddenly I noticed tears on his cheeks. He hugged us — the first hug in two months. Then he gave us a thick slice of bacon and a chunk of bread. He hugged us again and sent us on our way.

"We ate as much as we could stuff into ourselves on the way to Grandmother's place. We knew that she would take the rest from us. I hid a hunk of bread under my shirt and André did the same with the bacon. But Grandmother smelled the bacon, and she demanded that we surrender it. After she had eaten our bread and bacon, she informed us that we were to go to an orphanage.

"We didn't want to go to the orphanage. We dreaded the thought of having to face a world of strangers and be at their mercy. But, even more importantly, it was beyond our emotional means to think of ourselves as orphans. Our parents were going to return, we kept repeating to each other and to everyone else. In the end, we had no options. With Sàri combing the countryside in search of food, Grandmother was in charge and she wanted to get rid of us.

"The orphanage in Zuglò, a rich suburb of Pest, was crawling with abandoned and orphaned kids. The atmosphere was nightmarish. We had never seen so many kids in such a small place, all of them vying for a piece of ground upon which to stand. They all had a feverish look in their eyes. An other-worldly restlessness was floating around us. Within seconds, I knew the facts. There were too many children needing food, medical attention, proper care and, above all, lots of love and reassurance.

"A woman sent us to a room on the main floor and told us to stay there until we were told to come out. André tightened his grip around my fingers. I returned the squeeze. I, too, was scared. He might have been hanging onto me for dear life, but without him I would have been lost in a very hostile world. He was tiny and terrified, but he was my little brother. He gave me a purpose, a sense of mission. Besides, hadn't I promised Mother that I would always take care of him?

"We waited patiently. When night fell, I ventured out into the hallway. To my great shock, I overheard three adults making plans to separate the girls from the boys. We had no time to waste. We had to get out before it was too late. I could not bear the thought of us being separated."

When she returned, I remember, my sister's face was white as chalk. Without a word, she grabbed my hand and, crossing her lips with her index finger, she imposed silence.

She led me to a bathroom, lifted me and pushed me up to the window and told me to jump. With my heart in my throat, I jumped. A second later she landed on the frozen ground next to me. Still in complete silence, she dragged me into the street and we ran as fast as we could. We crossed street after street before, out of breath, we stopped. We were safe: she had rescued us.

"We roamed the streets until daylight." Agi resumed her story. "For lack of a better alternative, we went back to Grandmother's. I told her that they didn't have the space for us.

"That night Sàri came back from the country loaded with food. I told her what had happened at the orphanage. She was furious with her mother for trying to get rid of us. 'Nobody will send you away. I promised your mother to take care of you and I'll keep my promise.'

"Two days later, Mother's youngest sister, Boriska, returned from deportation. We were happy to see her, but her return reminded us that we knew nothing about our mother's fate.

"A few nights later, just after the ten o'clock curfew, there was another ring at our door. We jumped out of our bed. All of us crowded into the dark vestibule to see who it was. It was not our mother. Under an enormous knapsack, looking like a skeleton, was our father. We were within a couple of feet of him and yet he didn't seem to recognize us.

"'Piroska, where are you, my wife?' he asked in a loud shrill voice, as if he had thought that his words couldn't be heard. 'Come to me. I've come back from hell just for this moment.'

"When he found out that Mother was not yet home, he staggered under his big burden. How could that be? The superintendent said that she'd just returned. Apparently, the superintendent confused Mother with Boriska. Sàri and I peeled the knapsack off his back and helped him to a kitchen stool. He still had not asked for us. Finally, after having collapsed, he looked up.

"'Where are my kids? They are alive, thank God. Where are they? I can't seem them. I'm almost completely blind. It was a comrade who helped me all the way to the front gate.'

"That's why he didn't reach out to us even though we were under his nose, I thought. With the selfish logic of needy children, I felt relieved. It was more tolerable to me that Father came back blind than the thought of him not reaching for me. Later, in the lap of sad adult wisdom, I punished myself plenty for that selfish thought.

"After an awkward hug, he buried his head in his palms and he wept. 'All these months I put up with beatings, hunger, hard labour, the cruelty of the guards, everything, because I knew that one day, I would return and life would become simple and happy again. I kept hearing Piroska's quiet voice: "Everything will be fine, everything will be fine." But not without her, I can't do it without her.'

"Suddenly, he turned and reached out for us. He held us without a word. I could feel that he had no flesh left on his arm, only his bones came back. But I didn't care. He was there, holding me. He had never held me like that and I felt the layers of pain that had wrapped my entire being begin to loosen, thanks to his embrace. I felt a wave of gratitude inundate my whole being. I would have loved to shower him with a torrent of kisses. But I knew he would not have liked that. I realized that night that he needed us to take care of him as much as, if not more than, we needed his care.

"From that day on, Father remained in the grip of a sombre lethargy. It took us years to extract a skeletal version of his story. He had been taken to do forced labour in the copper mines of Bor, Yugoslavia. When the Germans evacuated the camp, they killed hundreds of prisoners in a nearby forest. Father escaped with three comrades. They came upon Serbian partisans who, upon learning that the four were Jews, went on an orgy of violence, leaving two of father's comrades dead, the third one severely wounded and father with a debilitating eye injury.

"None of his torments would have made any difference if he had had his wife to tend to his wounds. He never asked us how we survived, how we were, how we spent our days. All he wanted to know was that we were staying out of trouble. And we most certainly did stay out of the kind of trouble that preoccupied him — we didn't steal, we didn't get into street fights, we stayed away from strangers. What he did not realize was that his emotional indifference created untold trouble for us, then and later.

"We were quite happy to make allowances for him, but not forever. As we saw life beginning to emerge from the rubble, we grew aware of alternative ways of returning to grief and pain. In the meantime, Uncle Zoli, Boriska's husband returned also. They moved back to their original apartment. I would visit them every day. They were always laughing and singing. They were happy to be alive and together.

"Sàri's husband didn't return, nor did any of the other members of our family on either side, including our mother. Every family around us was riddled with losses. And except for our father, every family seemed to give some evidence of blood beginning to flow in the survivors' veins. Everyone seemed to be more committed to paying tribute to what had survived than to their grief — except our father, whose soul seemed to have drowned in an ocean of darkness.

"In the summer of 1946, after several bouts of surgery, Father regained enough of his sight to take a job as a salesman in a leather store. Before his operations, I had to be his eyes. It meant that I could not return to high school. It also meant that, while other kids returned to their childhood, I had to share Father's dark world of silence. And when he didn't need me, I had to assume the responsibilities of cooking and cleaning. Bitterness welled in me. I had hardly a moment to spend with people my age. And I never had a *fillér* (cent) to my name. There came a time when I began to rebel. I stole things from the apartment and sold them to a junk dealer around the corner. I went as far as stealing one of Father's jackets and later an armchair from the living-room. I got myself a dress and some treats that I shared with André. I occasionally sneaked out to a movie with Erzsi, the girl next door. I would not call that resuming my childhood, but I certainly began to take care of my own needs, too.

"My inability to return to school was a source of deep shame for me. I knew it was not my fault, and still I felt like an outcast, someone condemned to ignorance. Later, just about everyone I knew went to university. And I hadn't even finished Grade 8! I hid my lack of education behind a lie and I claimed to be a high-school graduate. I spent every free moment reading everything, from the classics to contemporaries. I went to concerts, plays, lectures; in the end, I have achieved a far better, more rounded education than if I had graduated from high school, but that did not alleviate my shame. I felt like a failure and a fraud. And all that because Father needed my eyes. I have always resented him for that, and yet, I would have gladly given him my eyes if that would have rescued him from drowning in his blind sorrow.

"He made rare sorties from behind his wall of silence. Whenever he did open his mouth, it was always in response to some grievance he had against us. On those occasions he always ended up lamenting the loss of his wife — our mother. Regardless of the context, it always ended with a bitter outburst that sounded like a blend of grief and guilt.

"'I should have died and your mother should have come back,' he said. 'What am I to do with the two of you? I can't even take care of me. I should have died, and your mother should have come back. The two of you don't care whether I'm here or not, anyway.'

"I hated to hear him say those awful words. Perhaps because at times I thought them, too. And whenever I did, I felt just as he must have felt: grief-stricken and guilty for my grief. But the more I listened to him utter the curse upon his head the more angry I felt with him. He never saw how happy we were to see him back. I felt as if to come back to us was not good enough for him, that Mother and we were a package. I often teetered on the edge of an outburst: 'You sound as if you don't only wish Mother had come back instead of you,' I wanted to spit in his face, 'but also that the two of us, your children, are not sufficient reason to go on living. I feel that you want us to disappear so you can freely die of your broken heart. If that's so, go ahead. This way you are no good to us, anyway!'

"Even though I never said anything of the sort to him, I felt it burn in my chest. The moment came when I truly hated him. But he didn't know it. He was too tuned out to feel the fire of my rage towards him.

"Little by little, a new wall of silence, perhaps higher than all the previous ones, settled between us. His side was built of his guilt at having survived, and my side was erected out of my profound outrage that he abandoned us every time he was displeased with something we did or said."

I reminded Agi that we retaliated. Was it revenge or self-protection? Perhaps a mixture of both. We spent less and less time around him. Whenever possible, we went to friends' homes where we were welcome. When he realized what we were doing, he got very concerned. After all, who knew what kind of people our friends' parents were. In reality, it is largely from those families that I learned how to be a parent, what children need and what they should not have to cope with. I also learned from those simple, often very poor people the immeasurable value of children and how carefully we must take care of them to prepare them for the best possible life, including how to look after themselves when there is no one else around to do that. If it hadn't been for my friends' parents I'm not sure I would have ever wanted to have children. I certainly did not want to impart to my children the version of childhood that ended up being mine.

By the time I was fourteen, between all the things I had picked up from our parents that I swore I'd never do to my kids and the things I learned from these wonderful people that I committed to memory, I knew that I wanted to have lots of children. Our family used to be large. With us it skipped a generation, but the next one will be the foundation of another large family. They will have each other and their offspring to create their own community based on affinity and support. Besides, I thought, if there is no family left behind me for me, I will create my own family around me. I had declared war on solitude.

"I came to the same conclusions," my sister said to me. "But I was cursed with a sterile womb, so I had to bask in the light of your children. Thank God, at least one of us was able to bring new life to our rather macabre family. Your children's laughter gave me the courage to trust the future beyond our own existence. I needed to know that our lineage will continue to thrive. What am I saying — 'continue'? I believe they will be the first to be fully alive, the way children have been meant to be."

This is where my sister's tape ends. We never had the opportunity to continue. When I next saw her, she was in a hospital bed in Los Angeles. There was a strange glow in her eyes and a warmth to her touch that I had never experienced before. She reminded me of my daughters at age four. After a couple of days by her bedside, I realized that it was the first time that I had seen and felt my sister as a pure child. The disease had stripped away all the veils of inhibition. She had no concern for what was right or wrong, whether she was modest or brazen. Just like a small child, she stopped monitoring herself. She reached for my hand. Her grip was silky warm, trusting and yet compelling with the authenticity of a child who knows she would get what she wanted.

"You don't know how good it feels to have a brother," she said, looking straight into my eyes. I drowned in that moist glimmer behind which I detected already an ominous dark shadow. I had to turn my gaze away for tears clouded my eyes, and I didn't want to upset her.

"It's all right, you can cry with me. I kind of like to see your tears. It reminds me of the old days when I was the only one to wipe them away."

We were exactly like two kids — oblivious to time and the

suffering it imposes on the living. We were able to lose ourselves in that distant past, but this time we were the way we should have been — self-abandoned, not abandoned.

On April 13, 1985, she died. She had succeeded in staving off the inevitable for five years longer than the doctors had predicted. Allowing herself to feel and speak her anger and hate when she needed to had contributed to her survival.

Except the price of this moment of rediscovered youth was her life, and that cursed wisdom was never out of my mind. When all is said and done, however, we had four days into which we managed to gather the flowers of two childhoods without worrying about the ephemeral temperament of spring.

What follows, then, is my recollection of an unfolding childhood to which I have no benevolent witness now that Agi has been gone for eight years. It has been lonely, and yet, I don't believe I had spent with my sister more intimate time and warmer words than during these years. Writing this story has compelled me to listen to our tape-recorded memories in that somewhat timid, somewhat mocking voice of hers, spiced with her undeniable Hungarian accent. There are many times when solitude compels me to stay still, but after having made this visit with her, I shall never again be alone with my solitude.

I spent my days in a day-care centre run by a group of Jewish people with access to American funds. It was in that dirt-covered courtyard that I discovered the joyful experience of communal living, camaraderie and human warmth. We received three good and copious home-cooked meals a day, served with affection and good cheer. It was there that I learned to laugh and dance. For the first time ever, I was in the company of joyous Jews. We spent every Friday afternoon in a happy state of frenzy and excitement as everyone chipped in to make the place spotlessly clean and cheerfully decorated for the Sabbath. Dr Glück, a dentist, led our Saturday services. We prayed little, we ate heartily, we sang Jewish folk songs, but most of all, we listened to stories told to us by our guardians. Some of them were very much like our own stories. It was a relief to learn that I did not have a monopoly on ordeals or losses; they went with the territory of being a Jewish child at a time when that was the greatest crime of all. It was there that I learned that, indeed, I was not a freak — I was just Jewish.

My uncle Zoli, Boriska's husband, introduced Father to a cousin of his; she was single and wanted to get married. It made no difference to her whom she married, as long as she could stave off the yoke of solitude and the stigma of being an old maid. She had no objection to a man who had no eyes and two children desperately needing to be loved. Lili and Father married in the summer of 1946. A couple of weeks before the wedding, Grandmother moved in with Sàri on Akàcfa Street. As was the case with most of these hastily arranged marriages between survivors, there was little or no feelings flowing from either direction. At best, one could hope for gratitude, stability and friendship.

I had mixed feelings about our future step-mother. I liked the thought of a woman coming to take care of me, loving me, freeing me from keeping Father company when I would have much rather been with other kids. But our step-mother was a very damaged woman, sexually abused at Mauthausen. She had nothing in her heart but pain and rage. First she made life impossible for Agi. Agi finally had no escape but to rush into marriage at seventeen. Then she made my life untenable by starving me and inciting Father against me. On December 21, 1953, she attacked me with a butcher's knife.

It was a harrowing experience. But it turned out to be a liberating one also. The silence of years of betrayal burst to the surface when I saw her bloodshot eyes while she was rushing at me with the intent to kill me. I disarmed her with one blow and slapped her in the face. For the first time in my life, I felt my own power. I was no longer a victim of adult violence. That wretched woman took the brunt of my rage for all the injuries others had caused in my young life. For the first time, I acted in self-defence and in indignation. It was definitely a turning point in my life. That left-handed slap was a loud assertive statement: No more! I will take no more abuse from adults. I will defend myself and I will retaliate. Father divorced Lili six weeks later.

It was the beginning of a new era for me. I did largely what I wanted to do, regardless of what was expected of me. To a great extent, I stopped being a victim and I became a person.

My teachers at the Imre Madàch *gimnàzium* (high school) had contributed a great deal to my emergence from darkness. They were benevolent witnesses to the struggles we had to wage against the forces of lacerated childhoods. Of the twenty-two of us, only one boy was lucky enough to see both his parents return from deportation. We were not only a bright and lively bunch, we were also angry and cruel. We acted out our frustrations on our teachers in the form of vicious pranks. They tolerated our misdeeds while showing us more constructive ways to give vent to our anger. They taught us the value of looking for poetry in the rubble, the power of humour against adversity, but most of all, no matter how insufferable we were, they suffered us: they showed us that no matter what we threw their way, they would not abandon us. Indeed, they became the active witnesses to our daily combats with the absurdities of life under Stalinism as well as with our memories of a recent season in hell. Thanks to these quiet heroes — not one of them Jewish — I completed my adolescence enriched with the meaning of community, trust, commitment and responsibility.

Agi, too, found her active witnesses when she joined the Habonim Zionist organization. They taught her that she was a person of value, that she was worthy to be one of them and that she could fight for what she wanted. Those Zionist leaders, although they were not much older than my sister, treated her with kindness, good cheer and affection, in short, like loving parents. If she hadn't met them, life would have been a lot sadder for her.

Agi's marriage was at best rocky. No one had ever shown her how to be a young woman, let alone a wife. In a fundamental way, she remained a child who had been too often abandoned for her to trust anyone. But in spite of its obvious limitations, my sister's marriage afforded her a measure of security: blonde and blue-eyed, sheltered by her husband's non-Jewish sounding name, she breathed more freely than ever before.

In the wake of the 1956 Hungarian uprising, Agi and her husband escaped to the West. They settled in California. Agi lived a paradoxical life, surrounding herself with a circle of Hungarian Christians before whom she paraded herself as one of them — she who comes from afar writes her own history. As long as she could hide her Jewish birth, she felt at ease. Agi and her husband enjoyed a few good years before, at the threshold of affluence and general security, he left Agi for her best friend.

Years of hardship and solitude followed. Finally my sister married Laci, a Hungarian who had been living in Australia. He was a man of culture, means and affection. That relationship ended in tragedy. Afflicted with a very painful back condition and burdened with business bankruptcy, Laci committed suicide during a visit to Hungary.

Once again, Agi was alone in the vastness of southern California, where she worked as a buyer for a fashionable department store. She was surrounded with a circle of loving friends and associates. And yet, inside, she longed for the soothing comfort of affection and security — both of them eluding her most of her life. In spite of her elegant beauty and undeniable European charm and flair for presenting herself in the most alluring fashion, she remained profoundly alone. Those men who wanted to enter her life either were thrill-seeking misogynist seducers or they wanted to build a family. She turned away the former without blinking an eye, and she wept as she saw the latter turn their backs to her: her womb was infertile, yet another curse by fate.

Eventually she attracted the attention of a man who showered her with the attention she had always craved. He was well-educated, financially comfortable and handsome. And he was not Hungarian. With Tony in her life, Agi began to liberate herself from the Hungarian burden. She came as close to finding what she had been wanting from life as her sterility permitted when she was diagnosed with a vicious version of leukemia, the kind that affords no more than one year after detection.

"No human being ever had the better of me," she said with determination. "I'm not about to let an army of microscopic enemies succeed where people have failed." She held the illness at bay for five years before she surrendered to the superior power of her cancer. She passed away in 1985, a few months short of her fifty-fourth birthday.

Her death left an enormous chasm in my life. Eight years later, I still find Sunday mornings disorienting. Our weekly telephone conversations guaranteed a place for our respective childhoods in a world where there was little room for our versions of solitude and survival. We knew things about each other that we never shared with anyone else for fear of exposure and shame but also as a token of the uniqueness of our relationship. We fought a lot every Sunday morning, but we would have never missed those calls as long as we both were on the continent. No one around us understood — and how could they? — that our fighting words were really aimed at what we had lost and survived, not at each other. It was the safest way to vent our young anger and to stay young and vigorous at a time when our bodies were no longer either young or vigorous. When she died, she took to the grave not only the end of her story, but also the account of my own ordeal. Now I cannot be sure if what I wish never to have happened really happened.

My aunt Sàri and her second husband, Lajos, escaped Hungary to Austria with Tibi and their three-year-old son, Tomi. They spent fifteen anxiety-filled months in a refugee camp waiting for permission to enter Canada or the United States. Finally, Australia came forth with an invitation for the foursome. Although they had not intended to go that far, they jumped at the opportunity to get out of the camp and give a new beginning to their interrupted lives. Today, my aunt, on the eve of paying tribute to eight decades of a life rich in struggle and victories, lives a quiet, fulfilled existence in a pleasant suburb of Melbourne. Her three sons, Tibi — now Ted — Tomi and her youngest, Rob, have all founded their own families. She is proud of her three boys, all of them successful professionals, all of them devoted to their children, their wives and their mother. Every Monday, the large family gathers in Sàri's house as much to celebrate the beginning of a new week as to pay their respect to a distant past when their mother defeated the might of the Third Reich. Now and then, Ted, the only witness to those dark days, sits down with his aging mother to coax out of her yet another piece of the mysterious past that has not released its grip on him. For him, the struggle continues and as long it does, and as long as her days last, his mother, Sàri, will keep him company.

As for me, I, too, left Hungary in 1956. I discovered the taste of freedom in Paris. With its endless resources, a whole new universe opened for me. I benefited from generosity hitherto unknown to me — I received free university education, room and board, free vacations on the Riviera, and above all, I emerged as a young man whose potential was limited only by his own talents and ambitions.

But the dark cloud of anti-Semitism followed me all the way to my most intimate life. I fell in love with a young woman from

Perpignan whose grand bourgeois family did not tolerate a Jew and an exile in their midst. To continue our relationship, I had to go underground: we shared a romantic mansard in the tip of the Ile St Louis where I figured — as far as the family knew from the distance of a thousand kilometres — as Béatrice Richard. Exiled from my identity to the core of my being, including even my gender, alienation undermined the perfection of my new life in Paris as well as the sturdiness of my liaison. With the dust of defeat in my soul, but with the smile of hope in my eyes, I continued my journey: I joined my sister in California.

I entered the doctoral program at the University of California. There yet another world opened its doors to me. I remained a stranger in that world for quite a while: I was surrounded with self-assertive young Jews, mostly from southern California. They wore their identity with the same natural ease as they wore their skin. First it was frightening to be among them. Little by little, however, I dared to tell my story. It turned out to be a mistake: they felt at home in their Jewishness, not in mine. They wanted to know nothing that interfered with the perfection of a sunset. So I returned my story to its protective case the way one does with a sword that frightens with its latent violence rather than dazzles with its glitter.

Nonetheless, I learned from my friends a way to feel strong and Jewish. So, when in 1965 I became eligible for U.S. citizenship, and my sister offered me a sizeable sum of money to change my name to any non-Jewish-sounding name, I refused without hesitation: yes, I was still in hiding as far as my past was concerned, but my present and future were already free of shame and fear. Most of the time.

I did marry a Christian woman in a Catholic church, for the "sake of her family." It suited everyone's needs, except mine: by agreeing to take care of the others, I failed to see that I tacitly stated that there was something unsavoury about being Jewish. For a while, I relapsed into hiding, with its inevitable evil consequences: shame, fear, guilt and badly camouflaged rage. But the "new world Jew" I became asserted its anger over the masquerade. So I undermined my marriage by withdrawing my affection and my loyalty from my wife. My first child was baptized in a Catholic church, but not the second.

Shortly before defending my doctoral dissertation, I began to suffer panic and anxiety attacks; I became a full-fledged hypochondriac. In spite of my robust health, I convinced myself that I did not have it in me to withstand the struggles life had in store for me. I became a familiar face in many an emergency room. It took me years to discover the connection between my surrendering my personal power and my past as a hidden and abandoned child. It took me even longer to learn that I was not alone with my lack of trust in my ability to sustain myself in my struggles with everyday life. Like many other child survivors who had to face professional and private autonomy on leaving the protective cocoon of the university, I experienced, once again, abandonment and solitude. Once again, I had to face the all-pervasive question: how will I make it on my own? I was not ready. A doctorate gave me a licence to practise my profession, but it did not address the issue of personal confidence and competency. To make matters worse, ten days after I received my degree, my director and protector died unexpectedly. The anxiety attack blossomed into paralyzing panic: they all die around me, I have no one to lean on, to show me the way. I really can't go on. But I had to go on and I did, limping, through successive mazes where fear and determination intersected.

My two-year internship in Toronto, Ontario, after which I was to inherit the research and teaching position of my late director, turned into an indefinite exile. It would have remained an exile had I not been able to build the edifice of my life upon elements of good fortune.

With the taste of ashes in my mouth, I said farewell to my wife. It was less a statement against her than a stance I felt compelled to take towards the Jew I needed to be. Luck and a good measure of audacity brought me together with Vicki, a young woman from New York. She exploded into my life with a kind of taken-for-granted Jewishness that characterizes Jews from New York. It was not a matter of doing, but a matter of being. Together with her visceral personal charms and intellect, her ground-level Judaism left no doubt in my mind: three days after the first sparks in our eyes, I proposed to her.

The road from that October day in 1973 to today has been arduous and full of surprise curves for both of us. In 1979, during a training session at the Gestalt Institute of Toronto, I found myself face to face with the tortured boy I had banished from my awareness for nearly four decades. He demanded attention to his pain and to his grievances for abandonment and betrayal. Neither I nor Vicki, by then my wife and the mother of our first child, Adrian, had known of his existence. Our lives were never to be the same again. He asserted himself into every aspect of my existence — professional, social, family and, to be sure, emotional. For years to come, his rage was to overwhelm my precarious and, at times, spurious inner peace. His wounds began to criss-cross our living-room, at times invading the tenderness of our bedroom. He demanded that I take at least as good care of him as if he were my own child, even if that threatened the emotional balance of my children. He compelled me to line my library with a never-ending collection of works documenting the Infamy — he refused to give a name to our destruction. There came a time when there were more symbols of Nazism in our home than at German Head-quarters in Warsaw. I converted my therapeutic practice into a haven for survivors; I introduced his world to my university classes.

With all that, I failed to satiate his need for acknowledgement, entitlement and redress. It proved to be a task beyond human limits. A current crisis that threatened to explode the entire edifice of my life thrust me back into his world. It afforded me the clarity of vision I needed for dealing with the matter at hand as well as to show the eight-year-old boy I was his proper place in my life. I emerged from both undertakings with a persona that no longer had fatal links to the darkness. Next to the mournful personae of the victim, the survivor and their tormentor, I discovered the presence of goodness in the rescuers. Their very existence — even if they were absent from my life — guaranteed not only the survival of a few thousand but also the possibility of a sturdy future for all, never losing from sight our dark legacy.

In 1949, when I turned thirteen, I refused to proclaim to the world that I was ready to become a Jewish man. It was too shameful and too frightening a proposition. In 1982, just before my first trip to Israel, I took that all-important step: I would not have been able to set foot on that sacred soil without announcing my oneness and my affinity with my people.

The shame had been banished, the fear conquered, the rage no longer spun any wheels. But the solitude and the anger still keep me company. Neither will bring back what I had lost. But within the world of my solitude, I commune with all those who had lost their voices atop the ashes. Thus, I cherish my solitude rather than forsaking it; it connects me to a community that no longer is. And my anger, which connects me to all that was lost, now propels me to achieve what is still possible. The anger is also the fire in the now quiet voice of the eight-year-old who led me from numbness through darkness to a life of love and laughter, to service and responsibility, to a mission that is no longer limited to the role of being the mailman of the dead — a profoundly self-effacing activity I gladly claimed to be my exclusive mandate as a survivor. That mission now includes the commitment to another version of life as well — one in which only the gains figure, and not the losses. A life in which there is no need for children to hide.

Today, a father of four daughters and a son, I am frequently bewildered and exhilarated by the impossibility and the urgency of keeping the young boy I was and my children in contact — close enough that they feel the connection and far enough to protect them from the flames of the anger that still animates my memories. How do I communicate to them the paradoxical experience of being a hidden child? How do I paint the portrait of the little boy waiting for his mother to return while knowing with a visceral knowledge that defies words that she was never to reappear in my life?

Yesterday, I saw a film about a mother who had been taken to Ravensbrück. Her daughter, my age at the time of our liberation in 1945, went every day to the train station with her grandfather carrying a large portrait of the mother in the hope that someone might have some information about her. And every evening, after the arrival of the last train of the day, the child went home a bit more depleted. Her eyes, burdened with betrayal and mistrust for the world of adults, stared at me. I felt the eloquence of that vacant stare in my eyes. I had lived with its enigma for most of my life. It stayed alive in the stubborn query of the child I was at the age of eight: "How do I discover trust again?" I have spent much of my life in the stronghold of a dilemma: how do I make a commitment to a life lived in the moment, every moment, without the buttress of trusting the world around me? How do I dare to trust again a world that landed me in the belly of a mountain of corpses, a world that robbed me of my mother, that coerced a cursed knowledge into my existence hidden from the innocent boy I was?

In search of a palatable answer, I continued to live at various depths of hiding. When the burden of grief and anger grew too heavy, I flew into my head, betraying my own feelings of despair. When the fantasy became too dark, I burst into an anger that threatened to consume me. One way or another, I spent more time in the company of the dead than the living.

Then, one day, I stumbled onto a viable wisdom: I will never learn to trust the world around me as long as I don't let go of those who had betrayed me as a child. A period of grief followed, during which I learned to let go of the shadows so that they, too, could rest in peace. New faces began to emerge, faces that had been around me all the time, and yet to me they were new. They did not assert themselves with authority or insistence — they were just there: they, too, were hidden child survivors.

We began to learn to guarantee the authenticity of each other's stories when memories intrude on the reality of the day with hallucinatory details. Child survivors do not need many words to authenticate their experiences — we all have our own demons but they are close relatives. Having discovered myself in child survivors like Rob, Yaffa, Ervin and the others opened for me the gates of trust.

"When you come to think of it," Rob Krell told me as we were driving along the Pacific on our way to a conference in Seattle, "we're very fortunate people. We keep company with the best — the Elie Wiesels and the Yaffa Eliachs. We child survivors are a very special bunch." Rob's words removed a heavy weight from my soul. He made me realize that I, too, belonged somewhere, here and now. And that this affiliation was, indeed, a privilege rather than a stigma. It was no longer the resignation of having been selected but the joyful relief that I belong to a group of people who had been betrayed and abused, just as I was, and yet, out of their wound they grew powerful lives. And I was one of them. It was that sentence Rob had uttered on the Washington State freeway that removed the veil from my eyes — and what emerged before my eyes, for the first time in so many years, was the robust figure of trust. I was, indeed, on a new road.

And yet, I am still in a quandary when I watch a movie like one I saw last night. "There are two realities I still have to keep at a distance from myself," I told Vicki at the end of the film. "One, that there are children who have to endure the pain and disorientation of waiting for a parent to return when they know that she was not likely to do so, and two, that I was one of those children."

After I pronounced those words, I felt more sad than angry. That was a heartening discovery. I still feel the loss, but I have learned to keep it far enough from my chest that it can no longer rob me of my breath. Now, it is a lot easier to speak to my children about what they and I had lost in the night: I am no longer compelled to drag them into dark places to keep me company: they can contemplate their father's childhood from the sunny side of the street where they belong.

Epilogue

✧✧ All children who lived through the Holocaust and survived were hidden children. Those who were visible could not survive; a law prohibited Jewish children under the age of sixteen from staying alive. Thus we hid in many places: in the bottom of dark ghetto cellars, in the forest with animals, among corpses in death camps and a few — a precious few — by the hearth of true Christians. We all knew that every breath was on loan to us and that it could be revoked without notice by those who hid us. We were quick to learn never to complain about ailments. There would be no relief anyway: gone were the healers and often the parents who might offer comforting words and hands. At the tender age of five or six, we became shrewd, wise and suspicious: in short, skilful at surviving.

We also learned not to trust — anything or anyone, Jew or Christian. Once the world had betrayed us, even the friendliest face could become twisted into an evil grimace. We taught ourselves to forget games and joy. We learned to live without a childhood. We became old before we were young.

Some of us were forced to our knees under the awesome burden of two faiths — one that used to be sweet and reassuring, the other imposed on us by selfish Christians bartering allegiance to their God in exchange for an unlit corner away from the killing fields. When these hidden children looked into the mirror, the face that stared back at them no longer answered to the name they had learned at the beginning of their journey.

We went to sleep at night to be visited by ghosts, corpses and chaos. The death-ridden landscape of our nightmares absconded with our sense of immortality, the birthright of every child. Suddenly, or little by little, the children concluded that somehow life had passed us by, and like shrivelled old folks, we had to be prepared to die at any moment.

And yet, in spite of all the odds, we survived.

Liberation, the long-sought day that sustained us in hiding, dawned. But for many, it was not a bright sunny day. They quickly learned that liberation was not to lavish upon them the gift of spring. In the shadow of the ruins, waiting for comfort and rebirth, they found that it was still not their turn to be heard. For them, the barbed wire continued to stretch across the living-room. Hostility and anger took on new faces, too many new faces, for their overtaxed vulnerabilities. Those who survived in Eastern Europe were the least safe: the Nazis were not the only enemies of Jewish children. It was imperative to be vigilant at all times against the spectre of betrayal (a burden that many have never learned to put to rest).

Some of us survived in hiding, but our rescuers, wanting to hold onto us or to save our souls, didn't tell us that our parents had survived as well. Some children knew the truth and were too scared to speak out. And there were those who, in order to prevail over the enemy, turned on their faith, thereby distancing the danger: they opted for Jesus Christ, the protector and redeemer of Christians. Since the God of Christians — unlike the God of Israel — protected them in their need, they wanted to be Christians.

Once again we had to surrender to the grief of further separations. We had to stare into the vacant spaces where once a family used to thrive. We despaired when confronting the lack of a grave at which to mourn the loss of a vanished mother, father or both. The returning adults had lost their ability to hear the silent pain of their children. They, too, had become orphans. Their eyes and ears were captivated by the impossibility and the necessity of living beyond the pit. Relieved to see their children alive, they mistook survival for a vacation in the country. And how could they know otherwise? Most of them had marched out of their children's sight without daring to steal a last look for fear of drowning in the stunned horror of those they had to leave behind. How could they know what their children endured? Often the person who returned was not the person who had left. And the child they left behind didn't or couldn't recognize in them the parent they craved.

When the reconstruction began, children who had lost the habit of doing child-like things returned to school with an awkward enthusiasm. Those who had been hidden remained in some version of hiding. Those who returned from hostile exile envied the comforts and safety they fantasized for those who had been sheltered by Christians. And the Christian children were often hostile to the survivors, for that's what they learned from their elders. We Jewish children were different from them — we had no parents, no family, and often behind the attempts to play freely, we knew that we had become counterfeit children.

Most of us went about living in spite of people's indifference. We had no way of knowing who would understand and we realized that no one cared how we had survived the war against children. Since we had survived to tell the tale, it could not have been so bad. Therefore, it was assumed that our tales were not worth hearing. Once again, silence seemed the best alternative. The language that we had grown up with failed to serve us well, so we learned instead to speak in euphemisms. And once again we did the impossible: we learned how to play at being like others, while we pledged our secret stories of losses and survival to silence. This silence allowed us to cast a veil over our memories, our dreams, our hopes. And our pain.

In the process, hidden children discovered a new companion — shame. In spite of all the suffering, it was still not possible to be Jewish again. For many of us, our Jewish identity had turned into a tragic flaw. As the list of the martyred children and their elders grew into millions, shame and guilt coerced questions onto our silent lips: Why me? Why not them? Why was I hidden? Did I usurp a place that should have belonged to another? Many concluded that it was a burden, indeed, a stigma, to be Jewish. After all, if the whole world conspired to annihilate Jewish children, we had to be guilty of something! We had to be tainted.

We were told that we were the lucky ones. And yet we often

remembered only the separations, departures and uninterrupted processions of fear. Some of us returned to a world that had changed beyond recognition. We thus had to juggle two debts — one to the Christian rescuer's world, the other to the memory of those who didn't come back. We knew that survival meant responsibility towards the disappeared. We knew that it was our duty to become the mailmen of the dead — it was up to us to make sure that they were not forgotten. We knew that it also meant continuing to be Jewish. One way or another, sooner or later, most of us faced the dilemma: we knew we had to be loyal to the God of Israel, but after what we had suffered for being Jewish, how could we remain loyal to the faith of our dead? The older children were able to draw on the memory of a well-grounded Judaic home, the younger ones lived with a confusion beyond their means. What kind of life was still available for them that they could live just for their own sake? Only the one within. So the hiding continued in earnest.

For many of us, yet another version of separation emerged on our horizon: leaving the world of the childhood we had lost. New shores held out possibilities of oblivion and hope. Some were taken to Israel, silently expecting to be received with open arms. Their disappointment was bitter. Israelis had no patience nor compassion for what they perceived to be the consequence of weakness and cowardice. The children had no alternative but to keep their stories hidden. They lost their old identity and were quick to forge a new one around the vault that contained their shattered hidden selves.

Others settled in the New World. Once again, our stories were not solicited nor honoured when offered. Our hosts, frequently acting from a need to deny that stories like ours happened to good people — like themselves — or that atrocities were perpetrated upon children by ordinary folks — like themselves — told us that our memories were counterfeit. And they created hallucinatory realities for us.

Most of us remained quiet. And quietly we went on achieving. Rather than clinging to our losses, we searched for what was still possible. We raised families, built honourable careers, created financial security and joined communities — in short, we learned to look normal. We achieved a great deal, but we remained silently restless. Phantoms were still haunting us in the dark of the night or in solitude. Inside us there lived an invisible community that kept us company on those occasions. They bore the nomadic names of the people we were born to be, of the people we had become under our names in hiding as well as the names of the people whose identity we had assumed in order to suit our new lives in our adoptive lands. To be sure, our identities suffered from the multiple dislocation we sustained on our roller-coaster existence. When those inner voices make themselves heard inside us, our legs still become wobbly and our eyes are veiled by the fog of silenced memory. But we made accommodations to cut the monster down to a size that we could wrestle to the ground so that we could live like "normal" people.

Normal people! We became obsessed with what the life of normal people felt like. We idealized those without destruction in their soul. Their lives had to be perfect, we thought. Some of us even tamed our memories to contain the rage at all cost. After all, how to live a "normal" life with inappropriate memories? We made new commitments. We chose life partners. Some of us chose a spouse born in the New World to escape the horrors of the past, some even purposefully picked a mate outside the faith. Others, on the contrary, linked their lives to another survivor, to validate the authenticity of their memories, often in silence, for the other had been there too and knew it all. With Auschwitz in their souls, words were superfluous.

But as long as the child inside us remained hidden, it could not grow up. Many of us felt trapped by that hidden child. The past keeps these people captive. They tend to feel an unwavering loyalty to the Jewish State without ever having the desire to live there. For them, Israel is primarily a link to the past regardless of what they think of Israel as a country. In short, many have continued to struggle in silence with the disempowering silence for lack of an alternative. But by compartmentalizing our bad memories, we have managed to mark some victories. We feel at home in many places but no place is really home. Evicted from our childhood and unable to grow deep emotional roots in our adoptive lands, we have been shuttling between two exiles.

Encouraged by our victories, strengthened by the example of many elder survivors who have dared to testify, inspired by our own ability to rise above adversity and fuelled by the anger of having been forgotten, we finally chose to gather and speak out. Finally we came out of hiding. We waited nearly half a century. Why? Perhaps because, as part and parcel of our survival, we learned that sheltering was a preferred mode of living. Our rescuers sheltered us, we sheltered ourselves and then we went on sheltering our children. It took us almost fifty years to leave shame more or less behind us. It took us all that time to accept that even though we are different, and our parents are different, we don't have to be ashamed of showing our scars. It took us all this time to prove to ourselves and to others that we are not freaks, that we are not alone and that it is no longer possible to hide.

The First International Gathering of Hidden Children was for us the beginning of a childhood that had been lost. We finally reached into the black vault and set free that small child, hidden so many years ago, and bathed him or her in the light of day. And since most children who lost their lives died in silence, we must speak also for them. We have therefore elected to be silent no more.

We have started by naming names. Our own and those of our rescuers, our quiet heroes. They gave us life — a new version of becoming a mother or a father. Then we began to inventory our losses so that we could master them. The list was open-ended. Our journey of mastery has been long. But today, we are strong. Our stories are being heard. The more people who honour them, the less we need to shelter them from the anguish of self-doubt. We have exposed our wounds to the healing power of light. Telling our stories has validated our losses and our grief. Now we can go on with the business of living. We have not become "normal" people. We are who we are and, for most of us, that is just fine.